Stoic Six Pack 3

The Epicureans

Epicurus

Cicero

William Temple

Robert Drew Hicks

Lucretius

Stoic Six Pack 3- The Epicureans by Epicurus, Cicero, Lucretius, William Temple and Robert Drew Hicks.

Letters and *Principal Doctrines* by Epicurus. From *Lives and Opinions of Eminent Philosophers* by Diogenes Laërtius. Translated by Charles Duke Yonge, 1853.

De Finibus Bonorum et Malorum by Cicero. Translated by Harris Rackham, 1914.

Upon The Gardens of Epicurus by William Temple. First published in 1908.

Stoics vs Epicureans by Robert Drew Hicks. From *Stoic and Epicurean* by Robert Drew Hicks. First published in 1910.

On The Nature of Things by Titus Lucretius Carus. Trans. William E. Leonard, 1916.

Printed in the United States of America. First printing, 2015. Enhanced Media Publishing. Copyright © 2015 Enhanced Media. All rights reserved.

ISBN-10: 1514178095
ISBN-13: 978-1514178096

CONTENTS

The Letters of Epicurus   4

Principal Doctrines of Epicurus   29

De Finibus Bonorum et Malorum by Cicero   35

Upon The Gardens of Epicurus by William Temple   55

Stoics vs Epicureans by Robert Drew Hicks   83

On The Nature of Things by Lucretius   100

LETTERS
By
Epicurus

LETTER TO HERODOTUS

Epicurus to Herodotus, greetings:

For those who are unable to study carefully all my physical writings or to go into the longer treatises at all, I have myself prepared an epitome of the whole system, Herodotus, to preserve in the memory enough of the principal doctrines, to the end that on every occasion they may be able to aid themselves on the most important points, so far as they take up the study of Physics. Those who have made some advance in the survey of the entire system ought to fix in their minds under the principal headings an elementary outline of the whole treatment of the subject. For a comprehensive view is often required, the details but seldom.

To the former, then—the main heads—we must continually return, and must memorize them so far as to get a valid conception of the facts, as well as the means of discovering all the details exactly when once the general outlines are rightly understood and remembered; since it is the privilege of the mature student to make a ready use of his conceptions by referring every one of them to elementary facts and simple terms. For it is impossible to gather up the results of continuous diligent study of the entirety of things, unless we can embrace in short formulas and hold in mind all that might have been accurately expressed even to the minutest detail.

Hence, since such a course is of service to all who take up natural science, I, who devote to the subject my continuous energy and reap the calm enjoyment of a life like this, have prepared for you just such an epitome and manual of the doctrines as a whole.

In the first place, Herodotus, you must understand what it is that words denote, in order that by reference to this we may be in a position to test opinions, inquiries, or problems, so that our proofs may not run on untested ad infinitum, nor the terms we use be empty of meaning. For the primary signification of every term employed must be clearly seen, and ought to need no proving; this being necessary, if we are to have something to which the point at issue or the problem or the opinion before us can be referred.

Next, we must by all means stick to our sensations, that is, simply to the present impressions whether of the mind or of any criterion whatever, and similarly to our actual feelings, in order that we may have the means of determining that which needs confirmation and that which is obscure.

When this is clearly understood, it is time to consider generally things which are obscure. To begin with, nothing comes into being out of what is non-existent. For in that case anything would have arisen out of anything, standing as it would in no need of its proper germs. And if that which disappears had been destroyed and become non-existent, everything would have perished, that into which the things were dissolved being non-existent. Moreover, the sum total of things was always such as it is now, and such it will ever remain. For there is nothing into which it can change. For outside the sum of things there is nothing which could enter into it and bring about the change.

Further, the whole of being consists of bodies and space. For the existence of bodies is everywhere attested by sense itself, and it is upon sensation that reason must rely when it attempts to infer the unknown from the known. And if there were no space (which we call also void and place and intangible nature), bodies would have nothing in which to be and through which to move, as they are plainly seen to move. Beyond bodies and space there is nothing which by mental apprehension or on its analogy we can conceive to exist. When we speak of bodies and space, both are regarded as wholes or separate things, not as the properties or accidents of separate things.

Again, of bodies some are composite, others the elements of which these composite bodies are made. These elements are indivisible and unchangeable, and necessarily so, if things are not all to be destroyed and pass into non-existence, but are to be strong enough to endure when the composite bodies are broken up, because they possess, a solid nature and are incapable of being anywhere or anyhow dissolved. It follows that the first beginnings must be indivisible, corporeal entities.

Again, the sum of things is infinite. For what is finite has an extremity, and the extremity of anything is discerned only by comparison with something else. Now the sum of things is not discerned by comparison with anything else: hence it has no extremity, it has no limit; and, since it has no limit, it must be unlimited or infinite.

Moreover, the sum of things is unlimited both by reason of the multitude of the atoms and the extent of the void. For if the void were infinite and bodies finite, the bodies would not have stayed anywhere but would have been dispersed in their course through the infinite void, not having any supports or counter-checks to send them back on their upward rebound. Again, if the void were finite, the infinity of bodies would not have anywhere to be.

Furthermore, the atoms, which have no void in them—out of which composite bodies arise and into which they are dissolved—vary indefinitely in their shapes; for so many varieties of things as we see could never have arisen out of a recurrence of a definite number of the same shapes. The like atoms of each shape are absolutely infinite; but the variety of shapes, though indefinitely large, is not absolutely infinite.

The atoms are in continual motion through all eternity. Some of them rebound to a considerable distance from each other, while others merely oscillate in one place when they chance to have got entangled or to be enclosed by a mass of other atoms shaped for entangling.

This is because each atom is separated from the rest by void, which is incapable of offering any resistance to the rebound; while it is the solidity of the atom which makes it rebound after a collision, however short the distance to which it rebounds, when it finds itself imprisoned in a mass of entangling atoms. Of all this there is no beginning, since both atoms and void exist from everlasting.

The repetition at such length of all that we are now recalling to mind furnishes an adequate outline for our conception of the nature of things.

Moreover, there is an infinite number of worlds, some like this world, others unlike it. For the atoms being infinite in number, as has just been proved, are borne ever further in their course. For the atoms out of which a world might arise, or by which a world might be formed, have not all been expended on one world or a finite number of worlds, whether like or unlike this one. Hence there will be nothing to hinder an infinity of worlds.

Again, there are outlines or films, which are of the same shape as solid bodies, but of a thinness far exceeding that of any object that we see. For it is not impossible that there should be found in the surrounding air combinations of this kind, materials adapted for expressing the hollowness and thinness of surfaces, and effluxes preserving the same relative position and motion which they had in the solid objects from which they come. To these films we give the name of "images" or "idols." Furthermore, so long as nothing comes in the way to offer resistance, motion through the void accomplishes any imaginable distance in an inconceivably short time. For resistance encountered is the equivalent of slowness, its absence the equivalent of speed.

Not that, if we consider the minute times perceptible by reason alone, the moving body itself arrives at more than one place simultaneously (for this too is inconceivable), although in time perceptible to sense it does arrive simultaneously, however different the point of departure from that conceived by us. For if it changed its direction, that would be equivalent to its meeting with resistance, even if up to that point we allow nothing to impede the rate of its flight. This is an elementary fact which in itself is well worth bearing in mind. In the next place the exceeding thinness of the images is contradicted by none of the facts under our observation. Hence also their velocities are enormous, since they always find a void passage to fit them. Besides, their incessant effluence meets with no resistance or very little, although many atoms, not to say an unlimited number, do at once encounter resistance.

Besides this, remember that the production of the images is as quick as thought. For particles are continually streaming off from the surface of bodies, though no diminution of the bodies is observed, because other particles take their place. And those given off for a long time retain the position and arrangement which their atoms had when they formed part of the solid bodies, although occasionally they are thrown into confusion, Sometimes such films are formed very rapidly in the air, because they need not have any solid content; and there are other modes in which they may be formed. For there is nothing in all this which is contradicted by sensation, if we in some sort look at the clear evidence of sense, to which we should also refer the continuity of particles in the objects external to ourselves.

We must also consider that it is by the entrance of something coming from external objects that we see their shapes and think of them. For external things would not stamp on us their own nature of color and form through the medium of the air which is between them and use or by means of rays of light or currents of any sort going from us to them, so well as by the entrance into our eyes or minds, to whichever their size is suitable, of certain films coming from the things themselves, these films or outlines being of the same color and shape as the external things themselves. They move with rapid motion; and this again explains why they present the appearance of the single continuous object, and retain the mutual interconnection which they had in the object, when they impinge upon the sense, such impact being due to the oscillation of the atoms in the interior of the solid object from which they come. And whatever presentation we derive by direct contact, whether it be with the mind or with the sense-organs, be it shape that is presented or other properties, this shape as presented is the shape of the solid thing, and it is due either to a close coherence of the image as a whole or to a mere remnant of its parts. Falsehood and error always depend upon the intrusion of opinion when a fact awaits confirmation or the absence of contradiction, which fact is afterwards frequently not confirmed or even contradicted following a certain movement in ourselves connected with, but distinct from, the mental picture presented—which is the cause of error.

For the presentations which, for example, are received in a picture or arise in dreams, or from any other form of apprehension by the mind or by the other criteria of truth, would never have resembled what we call the real and true things, had it not been for certain actual things of the kind with which we come in contact. Error would not have occurred, if we had not experienced some other movement in ourselves, conjoined with, but distinct from, the perception of what is presented. And from this movement, if it be not confirmed or be contradicted, falsehood results; while, if it be confirmed or not contradicted, truth results.

And to this view we must closely adhere, if we are not to repudiate the criteria founded on the clear evidence of sense, nor again to throw all these things into confusion by maintaining falsehood as if it were truth.

Again, hearing takes place when a current passes from the object, whether person or thing, which emits voice or sound or noise, or produces the sensation of hearing in any way whatever. This current is broken up into homogeneous particles, which at the same time preserve a certain mutual connection and a distinctive unity extending to the object which emitted them, and thus, for the most part, cause the perception in that case or, if not, merely indicate the presence of the external object. For without the transmission from the object of a certain interconnection of the parts no such sensation could arise. Therefore we must not suppose that the air itself is molded into shape by the voice emitted or something similar; for it is very far from being the case that the air is acted upon by it in this way. The blow which is struck in us when we utter a sound causes such a displacement of the particles as serves to produce a current resembling breath, and this displacement gives rise to the sensation of hearing.

Again, we must believe that smelling, like hearing, would produce no sensation, were there not particles conveyed from the object which are of the proper sort for exciting the organ of smelling, some of one sort, some of another, some exciting it confusedly and strangely, others quietly and agreeably.

Moreover, we must hold that the atoms in fact possess none of the qualities belonging to things which come under our observation, except shape, weight, and size, and the properties necessarily conjoined with shape. For every quality changes, but the atoms do not change, since, when the composite bodies are dissolved, there must needs be a permanent something, solid and indissoluble, left behind, which makes change possible: not changes into or from the non-existent. but often through differences of arrangement, and sometimes through additions and subtractions of the atoms. Hence these somethings capable of being diversely arranged must be indestructible, exempt from change, but possessed each of its own distinctive mass and configuration. This must remain.

For in the case of changes of configuration within our experience the figure is supposed to be inherent when other qualities are stripped of, but the qualities are not supposed, like the shape which is left behind, to inhere in the subject of change, but to vanish altogether from the body. Thus, then, what is left behind is sufficient to account for the differences in composite bodies, since something at least must necessarily be left remaining and be immune from annihilation.

Again, you should not suppose that the atoms have any and every size, lest you be contradicted by facts; but differences of size must be admitted; for this addition renders the facts of feeling and sensation easier of explanation. But to attribute any and every magnitude to the atoms does not help to explain the differences of quality in things; moreover, in that case atoms large enough to be seen ought to have reached us, which is never observed to occur; nor can we conceive how its occurrence should be possible, in other words that an atom should become visible.

Besides, you must not suppose that there are parts unlimited in number, be they ever so small, in any finite body. Hence not only must we reject as impossible subdivision ad infinitum into smaller and smaller parts, lest we make all things too weak and, in our conceptions of the aggregates, be driven to pulverize the things that exist, in other words the atoms, and annihilate them; but in dealing with finite things we must also reject as impossible the progression ad infinitum by less and less increments.

For when once we have said that an infinite number of particles, however small, are contained in anything, it is not possible to conceive how it could any longer be limited or finite in size. For clearly our infinite number of particles must have some size; and then, of whatever size they were, the aggregate they made would be infinite. And, in the next place, since what is finite has an extremity which is distinguishable, even if it is not by itself observable, it is not possible to avoid thinking of another such extremity next to this. Nor can we help thinking that in this way, by proceeding forward from one to the next in order, it is possible by such a progression to arrive in thought at infinity.

We must consider the minimum perceptible by sense as not corresponding to that which is capable of being traversed, that is to say is extended, nor again as utterly unlike it, but as having something in common with the things capable of being traversed, though it is without distinction of parts. But when from the illusion created by this common property we think we shall distinguish something in the minimum, one part on one side and another part on the other side, it must be another minimum equal to the first which catches our eye. In fact, we see these minima one after another, beginning with the first, and not as occupying the same space; nor do we see them touch one another's parts with their parts, but we see that by virtue of their own peculiar character (as being unit indivisibles) they afford a means of measuring magnitudes: there are more of them, if the magnitude measured is greater; fewer of them, if the magnitude measured is less.

We must recognize that this analogy also holds of the minimum in the atom; it is only in minuteness that it differs from that which is observed by sense, but it follows the same analogy. On the analogy of things within our experience we have declared that the atom has magnitude; and this, small as it is, we have merely reproduced on a larger scale. And further, the least and simplest things must be regarded as extremities of lengths, furnishing from themselves as units the means of measuring lengths, whether greater or less, the mental vision being employed, since direct observation is impossible. For the community which exists between them and the unchangeable parts (the minimal parts of area or surface) is sufficient to justify the conclusion so far as this goes. But it is not possible that these minima of the atom should group themselves together through the possession of motion.

Further, we must not assert "up" and "down" of that which is unlimited, as if there were a zenith or nadir. As to the space overhead, however, if it be possible to draw a line to infinity from the point where we stand, we know that never will this space—or, for that matter, the space below the supposed standpoint if produced to infinity—appear to us to be at the same time "up" and "down" with reference to the same point; for this is inconceivable. Hence it is possible to assume one direction of motion, which we conceive as extending upwards ad infinitum, and another downwards, even if it should happen ten thousand times that what moves from us to the spaces above our heads reaches the feet of those above us, or that which moves downwards from us the heads of those below us. None the less is it true that the whole of the motion in the respective cases is conceived as extending in opposite directions ad infinitum.

When they are traveling through the void and meet with no resistance, the atoms must move with equal speed. Neither will heavy atoms travel more quickly than small and light ones, so long as nothing meets them, nor will small atoms travel more quickly than large ones, provided they always find a passage suitable to their size. and provided also that they meet with no obstruction. Nor will their upward or their lateral motion, which is due to collisions, nor again their downward motion, due to weight, affect their velocity. As long as either motion obtains, it must continue, quick as the speed of thought, provided there is no obstruction, whether due to external collision or to the atoms' own weight counteracting the force of the blow.

Moreover, when we come to deal with composite bodies, one of them will travel faster than another, although their atoms have equal speed. This is because the atoms in the aggregates are traveling in one direction a during the shortest continuous time, albeit they move in different directions in times so short as to be appreciable only by the reason, but frequently collide until the continuity of their motion is appreciated by sense. For the assumption that beyond the range of direct observation even the minute times conceivable by reason will present continuity of motion is not true in the case before us. Our canon is that direct observation by sense and direct apprehension by the mind are alone invariably true.

Next, keeping in view our perceptions and feelings (for so shall we have the surest grounds for belief), we must recognize generally that the soul is a corporeal thing, composed of fine particles, dispersed all over the frame, most nearly resembling wind with an admixture of heat, in some respects like wind, in others like heat. But, again, there is the third part which exceeds the other two in the fineness of its particles and thereby keeps in closer touch with the rest of the frame. And this is shown by the mental faculties and feelings, by the ease with which the mind moves, and by thoughts, and by all those things the loss of which causes death. Further, we must keep in mind that soul has the greatest share in causing sensation. Still, it would not have had sensation, had it not been somehow confined within the rest of the frame. But the rest of the frame, though it provides this indispensable conditions for the soul, itself also has a share, derived from the soul, of the said quality; and yet does not possess all the qualities of soul. Hence on the departure of the soul it loses sentience. For it had not this power in itself; but something else, congenital with the body, supplied it to body: which other thing, through the potentiality actualized in it by means of motion, at once acquired for itself a quality of sentience, and, in virtue of the neighborhood and interconnection between them, imparted it (as I said) to the body also.

Hence, so long as the soul is in the body, it never loses sentience through the removal of some other part. The containing sheaths may be dislocated in whole or in part, and portions of the soul may thereby be lost; yet in spite of this the soul, if it manage to survive, will have sentience. But the rest of the frame, whether the whole of it survives or only a part, no longer has sensation, when once those atoms have departed, which, however few in number, are required to constitute the nature of soul. Moreover, when the whole frame is broken up, the soul is scattered and has no longer the same powers as before, nor the same notions; hence it does not possess sentience either.

For we cannot think of it as sentient, except it be in this composite whole and moving with these movements; nor can we so think of it when the sheaths which enclose and surround it are not the same as those in which the soul is now located and in which it performs these movements.

There is the further point to be considered, what the incorporeal can be, if, I mean, according to current usage the term is applied to what can be conceived as self-existent. But it is impossible to conceive anything that is incorporeal as self-existent except empty space. And empty space cannot itself either act or be acted upon, but simply allows body to move through it. Hence those who call soul incorporeal speak foolishly. For if it were so, it could neither act nor be acted upon. But, as it is, both these properties, you see, plainly belong to soul.

If, then, we bring all these arguments concerning soul to the criterion of our feelings and perceptions, and if we keep in mind the proposition stated at the outset, we shall see that the subject has been adequately comprehended in outline: which will enable us to determine the details with accuracy and confidence.

Moreover, shapes and colors, magnitudes and weights, and in short all those qualities which are predicated of body, in so far as they are perpetual properties either of all bodies or of visible bodies, are knowable by sensation of these very properties: these, I say, must not be supposed to exist independently by themselves (for that is inconceivable), nor yet to be non-existent, nor to be some other and incorporeal entities cleaving to body, nor again to be parts of body. We must consider the whole body in a general way to derive its permanent nature from all of them, though it is not, as it were, formed by grouping them together in the same way as when from the particles themselves a larger aggregate is made up, whether these particles be primary or any magnitudes whatsoever less than the particular whole. All these qualities, I repeat, merely give the body its own permanent nature. They all have their own characteristic modes of being perceived and distinguished, but always along with the whole body in which they inhere and never in separation from it; and it is in virtue of this complete conception of the body as a whole that it is so designated.

Again, qualities often attach to bodies without being permanent concomitants. They are not to be classed among invisible entities nor are they incorporeal. Hence, using the term "accidents" in the commonest sense, we say plainly that "accidents" have not the nature of the whole thing to which they belong, and to which, conceiving it as a whole, we give the name of body, nor that of the permanent properties without which body cannot be thought of. And in virtue of certain peculiar modes of apprehension into which the complete body always enters, each of them can be called an accident. But only as often as they are seen actually to belong to it, since such accidents are not perpetual concomitants. There is no need to banish from reality this clear evidence that the accident has not the nature of that whole—by us called body—to which it belongs, nor of the permanent properties which accompany the whole. Nor, on the other hand, must we suppose the accident to have independent existence (for this is just as inconceivable in the case of accidents as in that of the permanent properties); but, as is manifest, they should all be regarded as accidents, not as permanent concomitants, of bodies, nor yet as having the rank of independent existence. Rather they are seen to be exactly as and what sensation itself makes them individually claim to be.

There is another thing which we must consider carefully. We must not investigate time as we do the other accidents which we investigate in a subject, namely, by referring them to the preconceptions envisaged in our minds; but we must take into account the plain fact itself, in virtue of which we speak of time as long or short, linking to it in intimate connection this attribute of duration. We need not adopt any fresh terms as preferable, but should employ the usual expressions about it. Nor need we predicate anything else of time, as if this something else contained the same essence as is contained in the proper meaning of the word "time" (for this also is done by some). We must chiefly reflect upon that to which we attach this peculiar character of time, and by which we measure it. No further proof is required: we have only to reflect that we attach the attribute of time to days and nights and their parts, and likewise to feelings of pleasure and pain and to neutral states, to states of movement and states of rest, conceiving a peculiar accident of these to be this very characteristic which we express by the word "time."

After the foregoing we have next to consider that the worlds and every finite aggregate which bears a strong resemblance to things we commonly see have arisen out of the infinite. For all these, whether small or great, have been separated off from special conglomerations of atoms; and all things are again dissolved, some faster, some slower, some through the action of one set of causes, others through the action of another.

And further, we must not suppose that the worlds have necessarily one and the same shape. For nobody can prove that in one sort of world there might not be contained, whereas in another sort of world there could not possibly be, the seeds out of which animals and plants arise and all the rest of the things we see.

Again, we must suppose that nature too has been taught and forced to learn many various lessons by the facts themselves, that reason subsequently develops what it has thus received and makes fresh discoveries, among some tribes more quickly, among others more slowly, the progress thus made being at certain times and seasons greater, at others less.

Hence even the names of things were not originally due to convention, but in the several tribes under the impulse of special feelings and special presentations of sense primitive man uttered special cries. The air thus emitted was molded by their individual feelings or sense-presentations, and differently according to the difference of the regions which the tribes inhabited. Subsequently whole tribes adopted their own special names, in order that their communications might be less ambiguous to each other and more briefly expressed. And as for things not visible, so far as those who were conscious of them tried to introduce any such notion, they put in circulation certain names for them, either sounds which they were instinctively compelled to utter or which they selected by reason on analogy according to the most general cause there can be for expressing oneself in such a way.

Nay more: we are bound to believe that in the sky revolutions, solstices, eclipses, risings and settings, and the like, take place without the ministration or command, either now or in the future, of any being who it the same time enjoys perfect bliss along with immortality. For troubles and anxieties and feelings of anger and partiality do not accord with bliss, but always imply weakness and fear and dependence upon one's neighbors.

Nor, again, must we hold that things which are no more than globular masses of fire, being at the same time endowed with bliss, assume these motions at will. Nay, in every term we use we must hold fast to all the majesty which attaches to such notions as bliss and immortality, lest the terms should generate opinions inconsistent with this majesty. Otherwise such inconsistency will of itself suffice to produce the worst disturbance in our minds. Hence, where we find phenomena invariably recurring, the invariability of the recurrence must be ascribed to the original interception and conglomeration of atoms whereby the world was formed.

Further, we must hold that to arrive at accurate knowledge of the cause of things of most moment is the business of natural science, and that happiness depends on this (viz. on the knowledge of celestial and atmospheric phenomena), and upon knowing what the heavenly bodies really are, and any kindred facts contributing to exact knowledge in this respect.

Further, we must recognize on such points as this no plurality of causes or contingency, but must hold that nothing suggestive of conflict or disquiet is compatible with an immortal and blessed nature. And the mind can grasp the absolute truth of this.

But when we come to subjects for special inquiry, there is nothing in the knowledge of risings and settings and solstices and eclipses and all kindred subjects that contributes to our happiness; but those who are well-informed about such matters and yet are ignorant—what the heavenly bodies really are, and what are the most important causes of phenomena, feel quite as much fear as those who have no such special information—nay, perhaps even greater fear, when the curiosity excited by this additional knowledge cannot find a solution or understand the subordination of these phenomena to the highest causes.

Hence, if we discover more than one cause that may account for solstices, settings and risings, eclipses and the like, as we did also in particular matters of detail, we must not suppose that our treatment of these matters fails of accuracy, so far as it is needful to ensure our tranquillity and happiness. When, therefore, we investigate the causes of celestial and atmospheric phenomena, as of all that is unknown, we must take into account the variety of ways in which analogous occurrences happen within our experience; while as for those who do not recognize the difference between what is or comes about from a single cause and that which may be the effect of any one of several causes, overlooking the fact that the objects are only seen at a distance, and are moreover ignorant of the conditions that render, or do not render, peace of mind impossible—all such persons we must treat with contempt. If then we think that an event could happen in one or other particular way out of several, we shall be as tranquil when we recognize that it actually comes about in more ways than one as if we knew that it happens in this particular way.

There is yet one more point to seize, namely, that the greatest ,anxiety of the human mind arises through the belief that the heavenly bodies are blessed and indestructible, and that at the same time they have volition and actions and causality inconsistent with this belief; and through expecting or apprehending some everlasting evil, either because of the myths, or because we are in dread of the mere insensibility of death, as if it had to do with us; and through being reduced to this state not by conviction but by a certain irrational perversity, so that, if men do not set bounds to their terror, they endure as much or even more intense anxiety than the man whose views on these matters are quite vague. But mental tranquillity means being released from all these troubles and cherishing a continual remembrance of the highest and most important truths.

Hence we must attend to present feelings and sense perceptions, whether those of mankind in general or those peculiar to the individual, and also attend to all the clear evidence available, as given by each of the standards of truth. For by studying them we shall rightly trace to its cause and banish the source of disturbance and dread, accounting for celestial phenomena and for all other things which from time to time befall us and cause the utmost alarm to the rest of mankind.

Here then, Herodotus, you have the chief doctrines of Physics in the form of a summary. So that, if this statement be accurately retained and take effect, a man will, I make no doubt, be incomparably better equipped than his fellows, even if he should never go into all the exact details. For he will clear up for himself many of the points which I have worked out in detail in my complete exposition; and the summary itself, if borne in mind, will be of constant service to him.

It is of such a sort that those who are already tolerably, or even perfectly, well acquainted with the details can, by analysis of what they know into such elementary perceptions as these, best prosecute their researches in physical science as a whole; while those, on the other hand, who are not altogether entitled to rank as mature students can in silent fashion and as quick as thought run over the doctrines most important for their peace of mind.

LETTER TO MENOECEUS

Greetings!

Let no one be slow to seek wisdom when he is young nor weary in the search thereof when he is grown old. For no age is too early or too late for the health of the soul. And to say that the season for studying philosophy has not yet come, or that it is past and gone, is like saying that the season for happiness is not yet or that it is now no more. Therefore, both old and young ought to seek wisdom, the former in order that, as age comes over him, he may be young in good things because of the grace of what has been, and the latter in order that, while he is young, he may at the same time be old, because he has no fear of the things which are to come. So we must exercise ourselves in the things which bring happiness, since, if that be present, we have everything, and, if that be absent, all our actions are directed toward attaining it.

Those things which without ceasing I have declared to you, those do, and exercise yourself in those, holding them to be the elements of right life. First believe that God is a living being immortal and happy, according to the notion of a god indicated by the common sense of humankind; and so of him anything that is at agrees not with about him whatever may uphold both his happiness and his immortality. For truly there are gods, and knowledge of them is evident; but they are not such as the multitude believe, seeing that people do not steadfastly maintain the notions they form respecting them. Not the person who denies the gods worshipped by the multitude, but he who affirms of the gods what the multitude believes about them is truly impious. For the utterances of the multitude about the gods are not true preconceptions but false assumptions; hence it is that the greatest evils happen to the wicked and the greatest blessings happen to the good from the hand of the gods, seeing that they are always favorable to their own good qualities and take pleasure in people like to themselves, but reject as alien whatever is not of their kind.

Accustom yourself to believe that death is nothing to us, for good and evil imply awareness, and death is the privation of all awareness; therefore a right understanding that death is nothing to us makes the mortality of life enjoyable, not by adding to life an unlimited time, but by taking away the yearning after immortality. For life has no terror; for those who thoroughly apprehend that there are no terrors for them in ceasing to live. Foolish, therefore, is the person who says that he fears death, not because it will pain when it comes, but because it pains in the prospect. Whatever causes no annoyance when it is present, causes only a groundless pain in the expectation. Death, therefore, the most awful of evils, is nothing to us, seeing that, when we are, death is not come, and, when death is come, we are not. It is nothing, then, either to the living or to the dead, for with the living it is not and the dead exist no longer. But in the world, at one time people shun death as the greatest of all evils, and at another time choose it as a respite from the evils in life. The wise person does not deprecate life nor does he fear the cessation of life. The thought of life is no offense to him, nor is the cessation of life regarded as an evil. And even as people choose of food not merely and simply the larger portion, but the more pleasant, so the wise seek to enjoy the time which is most pleasant and not merely that which is longest. And he who admonishes the young to live well and the old to make a good end speaks foolishly, not merely because of the desirability of life, but because the same exercise at once teaches to live well and to die well. Much worse is he who says that it were good not to be born, but when once one is born to pass with all speed through the gates of Hades. For if he truly believes this, why does he not depart from life? It were easy for him to do so, if once he were firmly convinced. If he speaks only in mockery, his words are foolishness, for those who hear believe him not.

We must remember that the future is neither wholly ours nor wholly not ours, so that neither must we count upon it as quite certain to come nor despair of it as quite certain not to come.

We must also reflect that of desires some are natural, others are groundless; and that of the natural some are necessary as well as natural, and some natural only. And of the necessary desires some are necessary if we are to be happy, some if the body is to be rid of uneasiness, some if we are even to live. He who has a clear and certain understanding of these things will direct every preference and aversion toward securing health of body and tranquillity of mind, seeing that this is the sum and end of a happy life. For the end of all our actions is to be free from pain and fear, and, when once we have attained all this, the tempest of the soul is laid; seeing that the living creature has no need to go in search of something that is lacking, nor to look anything else by which the good of the soul and of the body will be fulfilled. When we are pained pleasure, then, and then only, do we feel the need of pleasure. For this reason we call pleasure the alpha and omega of a happy life. Pleasure is our first and kindred good. It is the starting-point of every choice and of every aversion, and to it we come back, inasmuch as we make feeling the rule by which to judge of every good thing. And since pleasure is our first and native good, for that reason we do not choose every pleasure whatever, but often pass over many pleasures when a greater annoyance ensues from them. And often we consider pains superior to pleasures when submission to the pains for a long time brings us as a consequence a greater pleasure. While therefore all pleasure because it is naturally akin to us is good, not all pleasure is worthy of choice, just as all pain is an evil and yet not all pain is to be shunned. It is, however, by measuring one against another, and by looking at the conveniences and inconveniences, teat all these matters must be judged. Sometimes we treat the good as an evil, and the evil, on the contrary, as a good. Again, we regard. independence of outward things as a great good, not so as in all cases to use little, but so as to be contented with little if we have not much, being honestly persuaded that they have the sweetest enjoyment of luxury who stand least in need of it, and that whatever is natural is easily procured and only the vain and worthless hard to win. Plain fare gives as much pleasure as a costly diet, when one the pain of want has been removed, while bread and water confer the highest possible pleasure when they are brought to hungry lips. To habituate one's self, therefore, to simple and inexpensive diet supplies all that is needful for health, and enables a person to meet the necessary requirements of life without shrinking and it places us in a better condition when we approach at intervals a costly fare and renders us fearless of fortune.

When we say, then, that pleasure is the end and aim, we do not mean the pleasures of the prodigal or the pleasures of sensuality, as we are understood to do by some through ignorance, prejudice, or willful misrepresentation. By pleasure we mean the absence of pain in the body and of trouble in the soul. It is not an unbroken succession of drinking-bouts and of merrymaking, not sexual love, not the enjoyment of the fish and other delicacies of a luxurious table, which produce a pleasant life; it is sober reasoning, searching out the grounds of every choice and avoidance, and banishing those beliefs through which the greatest disturbances take possession of the soul. Of all this the d is prudence. For this reason prudence is a more precious thing even than the other virtues, for ad a life of pleasure which is not also a life of prudence, honor, and justice; nor lead a life of prudence, honor, and justice, which is not also a life of pleasure. For the virtues have grown into one with a pleasant life, and a pleasant life is inseparable from them.

Who, then, is superior in your judgment to such a person? He holds a holy belief concerning the gods, and is altogether free from the fear of death. He has diligently considered the end fixed by nature, and understands how easily the limit of good things can be reached and attained, and how either the duration or the intensity of evils is but slight. Destiny which some introduce as sovereign over all things, he laughs to scorn, affirming rather that some things happen of necessity, others by chance, others through our own agency. For he sees that necessity destroys responsibility and that chance or fortune is inconstant; whereas our own actions are free, and it is to them that praise and blame naturally attach. It were better, indeed, to accept the legends of the gods than to bow beneath destiny which the natural philosophers have imposed. The one holds out some faint hope that we may escape if we honor the gods, while the necessity of the naturalists is deaf to all entreaties. Nor does he hold chance to be a god, as the world in general does, for in the acts of a god there is no disorder; nor to be a cause, though an uncertain one, for he believes that no good or evil is dispensed by chance to people so as to make life happy, though it supplies the starting-point of great good and great evil. He believes that the misfortune of the wise is better than the prosperity of the fool. It is better, in short, that what is well judged in action should not owe its successful issue to the aid of chance.

Exercise yourself in these and kindred precepts day and night, both by yourself and with him who is like to you; then never, either in waking or in dream, will you be disturbed, but will live as a god among people. For people lose all appearance of mortality by living in the midst of immortal blessings.

LETTER TO PYTHOCLES

Greetings!

Cleon has brought me your letter, in which you continue to evince towards me an affection worthy of the friendship which I have for you. You devote all your care, you tell me, to engraving in your memory those ideas which contribute to the happiness of life; and you entreat me at the same time to send you a simple abridgment and abstract of my ideas on the heavenly phenomena, in order that you may without difficulty preserve the recollection of them. For, say you, what I have written on this subject in my other works is difficult to recollect, even with continual study.

I willingly yield to your desire, and I have good hope, that in fulfilling what you ask, I shall be useful too to many others, especially to those who are as yet novices in the real knowledge of nature, and to those to whom the perplexities and the ordinary affairs of life leave but little leisure. Be careful then to seize on those precepts thoroughly, engrave them deeply in your memory, and meditate on them with the abridgment addressed to Herodotus, which I also send you.

Know then, that it is with the knowledge of the heavenly phenomena, both with those which are spoken of in contact with one another, and of those which have a spontaneous existence, as with every other science; it has no other aim but that freedom from anxiety, and that calmness which is derived from a firm belief.

It is not good to desire what is impossible, and to endeavour to enunciate a uniform theory about everything; accordingly, we ought not here to adopt the method, which we have followed in our researches into Ethics, or in the solution of problems of natural philosophy. We there said, for instance; that there are no other things, except bodies and the vacuum, that the atoms are the principles of things, and so of the rest. In a word, we gave a precise and simple explanation of every fact, conformable to appearances.

We cannot act in the same way with respect to the heavenly phenomena; these productions may depend upon several different causes, and we may give many different explanations on this subject, equally agreeing with the impressions of the senses. Besides, it is not here a question about reasoning on new principles, and of laying down, a priori, rules for the interpretation of nature; the only guides for us to follow are the appearances themselves; for that which we have in view is not a set of systems and vain opinions, but much rather a life exempt from every kind of disquietude.

The heavenly phenomena do not inspire those who give different explanations of them, conformable with appearances, instead of explaining them by hypothesis, with any alarm. But if, abandoning hypothesis, one at the same time renounces the attempt to explain them by means of analogies founded on appearances, then one is placing one's self altogether at a distance from the science of nature, in order to fall into fables.

It is possible that the heavenly phenomena may present some apparent characters which appear to assimilate them to those phenomena which we see taking place around ourselves, without there being any real analogy at the bottom. For the heavenly phenomena may depend for their production on many different causes; nevertheless, we must observe the appearances presented by each, and we must distinguish the different circumstances which attach to them, and which can be explained in different manners by means of analogous phenomena which arise under our eyes.

The world is a collection of things embraced by the heaven, containing the stars, the earth, and all visible objects. This collection, separated from the infinite, is terminated by an extremity, which is either rare, or dense, or revolving, or in a state of repose, or of a round, or triangular, or of some shape or other in fact, for it may be of any shape, the dissolution of which must bring the destruction of everything which they embrace. In fact, it can take place in every sort of way, since there is not one of those things which are seen which testifies against this world in which we cannot detect any extremity; and that such worlds are infinite in number is easily seen, and also that such a world can exist both in the world and in the space between the worlds, a huge space made up of plenum and vacuum, but not, as some philosophers pretend, an immensity of space absolutely empty. This production of a world may be explained thus: seeds suitably appropriated to such an end may emanate either from one or from several worlds, or from the space that separates them; they flow towards a particular point where they become collected together and organized; after that, other germs come to unite them together in such a way as to form a durable whole, a basis, a nucleus to which all successive additions unite themselves.

One must not content one's self in this question with saying, as one of the natural philosophers has done, that there is a reunion of the elements, or a violent motion in the vacuum under the influence of necessity, and that the body which is thus produced increases until it comes to crash against some other; for this doctrine is contrary to appearances.

The sun, the moon, and the other stars, were originally formed separately, and were afterwards comprehended in the entire total of the world. All the other objects which our world comprises, for instance, the earth and the sea, were also formed spontaneously, and subsequently gained size by the addition and violent movement of light substances, composed of elements of fire and air, or even of these two principles at once. This explanation, moreover, is in accordance with the impressions of the senses.

As to the magnitude of the sun and of the other stars, it is, as far as we are concerned, such as it appears to us to be. But, considered by itself, the sun may be a little greater or a little smaller than it appears; or it may be just such as it looks; for that is exactly the case with the fires of common occurrence among men, which are perceived by the senses at a distance. Besides, all the difficulties on this subject will be easily explained if one attends to the clear evidence of the perceptions, as I have shown in my books about Nature.

The rising and setting of the sun, of the moon, and of the stars, may depend on the fact of their becoming lighted up, and extinguished alternately, and in the order which we behold. One may also give other reasons for this phenomenon, which are not contradicted by any sensible appearances; accordingly, one might explain them by the passage of the stars above and below the earth, for the impressions of the senses agree also with this supposition.

As to their motion, one may make that depend on the circular movement of the entire heaven. One may also suppose that the stars move, while the heaven itself is immoveable; for there is nothing to prevent the idea that originally, before the formation of the world, they may have received, by the appointment of fate, an impulse from east to west, and that now their movement continues in consequence of their heat, as the fire naturally proceeds onwards in order to seek the element which suits it.

The intertropical movements of the sun and moon may depend, either on the obliquity impressed by fate on the heaven at certain determined epochs, or on the resistance of the air, or on the fact that these ignited bodies stand in need of being nourished by a matter suitable to their nature, and that this matter fails them; or finally, they may depend on the fact of their having originally received an impulse which compels them to move as they do describing a sort of spiral figure.

The sensible evidence does not in the least contradict these different suppositions, and all those of the same kind which one can form, having always a due regard to what is possible, and bringing back each phenomenon to its analogous appearances in sensible facts, without disquieting one's self about the miserable speculations of the astronomers.

The evacuations and subsequent replenishings of the moon may depend either on a conversion of this body, or on the different forms which the air when in a fiery state can adopt, or perhaps to the interposition of another body, or lastly, to some one of the causes by which one gives account of the analogous phenomena which pass under our eyes. Provided, however, that one does not obstinately adopt an exclusive mode of explanation; and that, for want of knowing what is possible for a man to explain, and what is inaccessible to his intelligence; one does not throw one's self into interminable speculations.

It may also be possibly the case that the moon has a light of her own, or that she reflects that of the sun. For we see around us many objects which are luminous of themselves, and many others which have only a borrowed light. In a word, one will not be arrested by any of the celestial phenomena, provided that one always recollects that there are many explanations possible; that one examines the principles and reasons which agree with this mode of explanation, and that one does not proceed in accounting for the facts which do not agree with this method, to suffer one's self to be foolishly carried away, and to propose a separate explanation for each phenomenon, sometimes in one way, and sometimes in another.

The appearance of a face in the orb of the moon, may depend either on a displacement of its parts, or on the interposition of some obstacle, or on any other cause capable of accounting for such an appearance. For one must not neglect to apply this same method to all the heavenly phenomena; for, from the moment when one comes to any point of contradiction to the evidence of the senses, it will be impossible to possess perfect tranquillity and happiness.

The eclipses of the sun and moon may depend either on the fact that these stars extinguish themselves, a phenomenon which we often see produced under our eyes, or on other bodies, the earth, the heaven, or something else of the same kind interposing, between them and us. Besides, we must compare the different modes of explanation appropriate to phenomena, and recollect that it is not impossible that many causes may at one and the same time concur in their production.

The regular and periodical march of these phenomena has nothing in it that ought to surprise us, if we only attend to the analogous facts which take place under our eyes. Above ill things let us beware of making the Deity interpose here, or that being we ought to suppose exempt from all occupation and perfectly happy; otherwise we shall be only giving vain explanations of the heavenly phenomena, as has happened already to a crowd of authors. Not being able to recognize what is really possible, they have fallen into vain theories, in supposing that for all phenomena there was hut one single mode of production, and in rejecting all other explanations which are founded on probability; they have adopted the most unreasonable opinions, for want of placing in the front the study of the heavenly phenomena, and of sensible facts, which ought to serve to explain the first.

The differences in the length of nights and days may arise from the fact that the passage of the sun above the earth is more or less rapid; and more or less slow, according to the length of the regions which it has to pass through. Or, again, to the fact that certain regions are passed through more rapidly than others, as is seen to be the case by our own eyes, in those things to which we can compare the heavenly phenomena. As to those who on this point admit only one explanation as possible, they put themselves in opposition to facts, and lose sight of the bounds set to human knowledge.

The prognostics which are derived from the stars may, like those which we borrow from animals, arise from a simple coincidence. They may also have other causes, for example, some change in the air; for these two suppositions both harmonize equally with facts; but it is impossible to distinguish in what case one is to attribute them to the one cause or to the other.

The clouds may be formed either by the air condensed under the pressure of the winds, or by the agency of atoms set apart for that end, or by emanations from the earth and waters, or by other causes. For there are a great number which are all equally able to produce this effect. When the clouds clash with one another, or undergo any transformation, they produce showers; and the long rains are caused by the motion of the clouds when moved from places suitable to them through the air, when a more violent inundation than usual takes place, from collections of some masses calculated to produce these effects.

Thunder possibly arises from the movement of the winds revolving in the cavities of the clouds ; of which we may see an image in vessels in our own daily use. It may also arise from the noise of fire acted upon by the wind in them, and from the tearings and ruptures of the clouds when they have received a sort of crystalline consistency. In a word, experience drawn from our senses, teaches us that all these phenomena, and that one in particular, may be produced in many different manners.

One may also assign different causes to the lightning; either the shock and collision of the clouds produce a fiery appearance, which is followed by lightning; or the lighting up of the clouds by the winds, produces this luminous appearance; or the mutual pressure of the clouds, or that of the wind against them, disengages the lightning. Or, one might say, that the interception of the light diffused from the stars, arrested for a time in the bosom of the clouds, is driven from them subsequently by their own movements, and by those of the winds, and so escapes from their sides; that the lightning is an extremely subtile light that evaporates from the clouds; that the clouds which carry the thunder are collected masses of fire; that the lightning arises from the motion of the fire, or from the conflagration of the wind, in consequence of the rapidity and continuousness of its motion. One may also attribute the luminous appearance of lightning to the rupture of the clouds under the action of the winds, or to the fall of inflammable atoms. Lastly, one may easily find a number of other explanations, if one applies to sensible facts, in order to search out the analogies which they present to the heavenly phenomena.

Lightning precedes thunder, either because it is produced at the same moment that the wind falls on the cloud, while the noise is only heard at the instant when the wind has penetrated into the bosom of the cloud; or, perhaps, the two phenomena being simultaneous, the lightning arrives among us more rapidly than the noise of the thunder-bolt, as is in fact remarked in other cases when we see at a distance the clash of two objects.

The thunderbolt may be produced either by a violent condensation of the winds, or by their rapid motion and conflagration. It may arise from the fact of the winds meeting in places which are too dense, in consequence of the accumulation of clouds, and then a portion of the current detaches itself and proceeds towards the lower situations; or else it may be caused by the fire which is contained in the bosom of the clouds precipitating itself downwards. As one may suppose that an immense quantity of fire being accumulated in the cloud dilates, violently bursting the substance which envelops it, because the resistance of the centre hinders it from proceeding further. This effect is especially produced in the neighbourhood of high mountains; and, accordingly, they are very frequently struck with the thunderbolts. In short, one may give a number of explanations of the thunderbolt; but we ought, above all things, to be on our guard against fables, and this one will easily be, if one follows faithfully the sensible phenomena in the explanation of these things, which are not perceived, except indirectly.

Hurricanes may be caused either by the presence of a cloud, which a violent wind sets in motion and precipitates with a spiral movement towards the lower regions, or by a violent gust which bears a cloud into the neighbourhood of some other current, or else by the mere agitation of the wind by itself, when air is brought together from the higher regions and compressed without being able to escape on either side, in consequence of the resistance of the air which surrounds it; when the hurricane descends towards the earth, then there result whirlwinds in proportion to the rapidity of the wind that has produced them; and this phenomenon extends over the sea also.

Earthquakes may arise from the wind penetrating into the interior of the earth, or from the earth itself receiving incessantly the addition of exterior particles, and being in incessant motion as to its constituent atoms, being in consequence disposed to a general vibration. That which permits the wind to penetrate is the fact that falls take place in the interior, or that the air being impressed by the winds insinuates itself into the subterraneous caverns. The movement which numberless falls and the re-action of the earth communicate to the earth, when this motion meets bodies of greater resistance and solidity, is sufficient to explain the earthquakes. One might, however, give an account of them in several other ways.

Winds are caused, either by the successive and regular addition of some foreign matter, or else by the re-union of a great quantity of water; and the differences of the winds may arise from the fact that some portions of this same matter fall into the numerous cavities of the earth, and are divided there.

Hail is produced by an energetic condensation acting on the ethereal particles which the cold embraces in every direction; or, in consequence of a less violent condensation acting however on aqueous particles, and accompanied by division, in such a manner as to produce, at the same time, the re-union of certain elements and of the collective masses; or by the rupture of some dense and compact mass which would explain at the same time, the numerousness of the particles and their individual hardness. As to the spherical form of the hail, one may easily account for that by admitting that the shocks which it receives in every direction make all the angles disappear, or else that at the moment when the different fragments are formed, each of them is equally embraced on all sides by aqueous or ethereal particles.

Snow may be produced by a light vapour full of moisture which the clouds allow to escape by passages intended for that end, when they are pressed, in a corresponding manner, by other clouds, and set in motion by the wind. Dew proceeds from a re-union of particles contained in the air calculated to produce this moist substance. These particles may be also brought from places which are moist or covered with water (for in those places, above all others, it is that dew is abundant). These then re-unite, again resume their aqueous form, and fall down. The same phenomenon takes place in other cases before our own eyes under many analogies.

The rainbow may be produced by the reflection of the solar rays on the moist air; or it may arise from a particular property of light and air, in virtue of which these particular appearances of colour are formed, either because the shades which we perceive result directly from this property, or because, on the contrary, it only produces one single shade, which, reflecting itself on the nearest portions of the air, communicates to them the tints which we observe. As to the circular form of the rainbow, that depends either on the fact of the sight perceiving an equal distance in every direction, or the fact of the atoms taking this form when re-uniting in the air; or it may be caused by its detaching from the air which moves towards the moon, certain atoms which, being re-united in the clouds, give rise to this circular appearance.

The lunar halo arises from the fact of the air, which moves towards the moon from all quarters, uniformly intercepting the rays emitted by this star, in such a way as to form around it a sort of circular cloud which partially veils it. It may also arise from the fact of the moon uniformly rejecting from all quarters, the air which surrounds it, in such a manner as to produce this circular and opaque covering. And perhaps this: opaqueness may be caused by some particles which some current brings from without; perhaps also, the heat communicates to the moon the property of emitting by the pores in; its surface, the particles by which this effect is produced.

Certain stars return to the same point in accomplishing their revolutions; and this arises, not only as has been sometimes believed, from the fact of the pole of the world, around which they move, being immoveable, but also from the fact that the gyrations of the air which surrounds them, hinder them from deviations like the wandering stars.

Imprint all these precepts in your memory, Pythocles, and so you will easily escape fables, and it will be easy for you to discover other truths analogous to these. Above all, apply yourself to the study of general principles, of the infinite, and of questions of this kind, and to the investigation of the different criteria and of the passions, and to the study of the chief good, with a view to which we prosecute all our researches. When these questions are once resolved, all particular difficulties will be made plain to you. As to those who will not apply themselves to these principles, they will neither be able to give a good explanation of these same questions, nor to reach that end to which all our researches tend.

PRINCIPAL DOCTRINES

By

Epicurus

THE DOCTRINES

1. That which is happy and imperishable, neither has trouble itself, nor does it cause it to anything; so that it is not subject to the feelings of either anger or gratitude; for these feelings only exist in what is weak.

2. Death is nothing to us; for that which is dissolved is devoid of sensation, and that which is devoid of sensation is nothing to us.

3. The limit of the greatness of the pleasures is the removal of everything which can give pain. And where pleasure is, as long as it lasts, that which gives pain, or that which feels pain, or both of them, are absent.

4. Pain does not abide continuously in the flesh, but in its extremity it is present only a very short time. That pain which only just exceeds the pleasure in the flesh, does not last many days. But long diseases have in them more that is pleasant than painful to the flesh.

5. It is not possible to live pleasantly without living prudently, and honourably, and justly; nor to live prudently, and honourably, and justly, without living pleasantly. But he to whom it does not happen to live prudently, honourably, and justly, cannot possibly live pleasantly.

6. For the sake of feeling confidence and security with regard to men, and not with reference to the nature of government and kingly power being a good, some men have wished to be eminent and powerful, in order that others might attain this feeling by their means; thinking that so they would secure safety as far as men are concerned. So that, if the life of such men is safe, they have attained to the nature of good; but if it is not safe, then they have failed in obtaining that for the sake of which they originally desired power according to the order of nature.

7. No pleasure is intrinsically bad: but the efficient causes of some pleasures bring with them a great many perturbations of pleasure.

8. If every pleasure were condensed, if one may so say, and if each lasted long, and affected the whole body, or the essential parts of it, then there would be no difference between one pleasure and another.

9. If those things which make the pleasures of debauched men, put an end to the fears of the mind, and to those which arise about the heavenly bodies, and death, and pain; and if they taught us what ought to be the limit of our desires, we should have no pretence for blaming those who wholly devote themselves to pleasure, and who never feel any pain or grief (which is the chief evil) from any quarter.

10. If apprehensions relating to the heavenly bodies did not disturb us, and if the terrors of death have no concern with us, and if we had the courage to contemplate the boundaries of pain and of the desires, we should have no need of physiological studies.

11. It would not be possible for a person to banish all fear about those things which are called most essential, unless he knew what is the nature of the universe, or if he had any idea that the fables told about it could be true; and therefore, it is, that a person cannot enjoy unmixed pleasure without physiological knowledge.

12. It would be no good for a man to secure himself safety as far as men are concerned, while in a state of apprehension as to all the heavenly bodies, and those under the earth, and in short, all those in the infinite.

13. Irresistible power and great wealth may, up to a certain point, give us security as far as men are concerned; but the security of men in general depends upon the tranquillity of their souls, and their freedom from ambition.

14. The riches of nature are defined and easily procurable; but vain desires are insatiable.

15. The wise man is but little favoured by fortune; but his reason procures him the greatest and most valuable goods, and these he does enjoy, and will enjoy the whole of his life.

16. The just man is the freest of all men from disquietude; but the unjust man is a perpetual prey to it.

17. Pleasure in the flesh is not increased, when once the pain arising from want is removed; it is only diversified.

18. The most perfect happiness of the soul depends on these reflections, and on opinions of a similar character on all those questions which cause the greatest alarm to the mind.

19. Infinite and finite time both have equal pleasure, if any one measures its limits by reason.

20. If the flesh could experience boundless pleasure, it would want to dispose of eternity.

21. But reason, enabling us to conceive the end and dissolution of the body, and liberating us from the fears relative to eternity, procures for us all the happiness of which life is capable, so completely that we have no further occasion to include eternity in our desires. In this disposition of mind, man is happy even when his troubles engage him to quit life; and to die thus, is for him only to interrupt a life of happiness.

22. He who is acquainted with the limits of life knows, that that which removes the pain which arises from want, and which makes the whole of life perfect, is easily procurable; so that he has no need of those things which can only be attained with trouble.

23. But as to the subsisting end, we ought to consider it with all the clearness and evidence which we refer to whatever we think and believe; otherwise, all things will be full of confusion and uncertainty of judgment.

24. If you resist all the senses, you will not even have anything left to which you can refer, or by which you may be able to judge of the falsehood of the senses which you condemn.

25. If you simply discard one sense, and do not distinguish between the different elements of the judgment, so as to know on the one hand, the induction which goes beyond the actual sensation, or, on the other, the actual and immediate notion; the affections, and all the conceptions of the mind which lean directly on the sensible representation, you will be imputing trouble into the other sense, and destroying in that quarter every species of criterion.

26. If you allow equal authority to the ideas, which, being only inductive, require to be verified, and to those which bear about them an immediate certainty, you will not escape error; for you will be confounding doubtful opinions with those which are not doubtful, and true judgments with those of a different character.

27. If, on every occasion, we do not refer every one of our actions to the chief end of nature, if we turn aside from that to seek or avoid some

other object, there will be a want of agreement between our words and our actions.

28. Of all the things which wisdom provides for the happiness of the whole life, by far the most important is the acquisition of friendship.

29. The same opinion encourages man to trust that no evil will be everlasting, or even of long duration; as it sees that, in the space of life allotted to us, the protection of friendship is most sure and trustworthy.

30. Of the desires, some are natural and necessary, some natural, but not necessary, and some are neither natural nor necessary, but owe their existence to vain opinions.

31. Those desires which do not lead to pain, if they are not satisfied, are not necessary. It is easy to impose silence on them when they appear difficult to gratify, or likely to produce injury.

32. When the natural desires, the failing to satisfy which is, nevertheless, not painful, are violent and obstinate, it is a proof that there is an admixture of vain opinion in them; for then energy does not arise from their own nature, but from the vain opinions of men.

33. Natural justice is a covenant of what is suitable, leading men to avoid injuring one another, and being injured.

34. Those animals which are unable to enter into an argument of this nature, or to guard against doing or sustaining mutual injury, have no such thing as justice or injustice. And the case is the same with those nations, the members of which are either unwilling or unable to enter into a covenant to respect their mutual interests.

35. Justice has no independent existence; it results from mutual contracts, and establishes itself wherever there is a mutual engagement to guard against doing or sustaining mutual injury.

36. Injustice is not intrinsically bad ; it has this character only because there is joined with it a fear of not escaping those who are appointed to punish actions marked with that character.

37. It is not possible for a man who secretly does anything in contravention of the agreement which men have made with one another, to guard against doing, or sustaining mutual injury, to believe that he shall always escape notice, even if he have escaped notice already ten thousand times; for, till his death, it is uncertain whether he will not be detected.

38. In a general point of view, justice is the same thing to every one; for there is something advantageous in mutual society. Nevertheless, the difference of place, and divers other circumstances, make justice vary.

39. From the moment that a thing declared just by the law is generally recognized as useful for the mutual relations of men, it becomes really just, whether it is universally regarded as such or not.

40. But if, on the contrary, a thing established by law is not really useful for the social relations, then it is not just; and if that which was just, inasmuch as it was useful, loses this character, after having been for some time considered so, it is not less true that, during that time, it was really just, at least for those who do not perplex themselves about vain words, but who prefer, in every case, examining and judging for themselves.

41. When, without any fresh circumstances arising, a thing which has been declared just in practice does not agree with the impressions of reason, that is a proof that the thing was not really just. In the same way, when in consequence of new circumstances, a thing which has been pronounced just does not any longer appear to agree with utility, the thing which was just, inasmuch as it was useful to the social relations and intercourse of mankind, ceases to be just the moment when it ceases to be useful.

42. He who desires to live tranquilly without having any thing to fear from other men, ought to make himself friends; those whom he cannot make friends of, he should, at least, avoid rendering enemies; and if that is not in his power, he should, as far as possible, avoid all intercourse with them, and keep them aloof, as far as it is for his interest to do so.

43. The happiest men are they who have arrived at the point of having nothing to fear from those who surround them. Such men live with one another most agreeably, having the firmest grounds of confidence in one another, enjoying the advantages of friendship in all their fulness, and not lamenting, as a pitiable circumstance, the premature death of their friends.

DE FINIBUS, BONORUM ET MALORUM

By

Marcus Tullius Cicero

I

To begin with what is easiest, let us first pass in review the system of Epicurus, which to most men is the best known of any. Our exposition of it, as you shall see, will be as accurate as any usually given even by the professed adherents of his school. For our object is to discover the truth, not to refute someone as an opponent.

An elaborate defense of hedonistic theory of Epicurus was once delivered by Lucius Torquatus, a student well versed in all the systems of philosophy; to him I replied, and Gaius Triarius, a youth of remarkable learning and seriousness of character, assisted at the discussion. Both of these gentlemen had called to pay me their respects at my place at Cumæ. We first exchanged a few remarks about literature, of which both were enthusiastic students.

Then Torquatus said, "As we have for once found you at leisure, I am resolved to hear the reason why you regard my master Epicurus, not indeed with hatred, as those who do not share his view mostly do, but at all events with disapproval. I myself consider him as the one person who has discerned the Truth, and who has delivered men from the gravest errors and imparted to them all there is to know about well-being and happiness. The fact is, I think that you are like our friend Triarius, and dislike Epicurus because he has neglected the graces of style that you find in you Plato, Aristotle, and Theophrastus. For I can scarcely bring myself to believe that you think his opinions untrue."

"Let me assure you, Torquatus," said I, "that you are entirely mistaken. With you master's style I have no fault to find. He expresses his meaning adequately, and gives me a plain intelligible statement. Not that I despise eloquence in a philosopher if he has to offer it, but I should not greatly insist on it if he has not. But his material I do not find so satisfactory, and that in more points than one. However, 'many men, many minds:' so it is possible that I am mistaken."

"What is it, please," he asked, "to which you take exception? For I recognize you as a just critic, provided you really know what his doctrines are."

"Oh," said I, "I know the whole of Epicurus' opinions well enough—unless you think that Phædrus or Zeno did not tell me the truth. I have heard both of them lecture, though to be sure they convinced me of nothing but their own devotion to the system. Indeed I regularly attended those professors, in company with our friend Atticus, who for his part had an admiration for them both, and a positive affection for Phædrus. Every day we used to discuss together in private what we had head at lecture, and there was never any dispute as to what I could understand; the question was, what I could accept as true."

II

"Well then, what is the point?" said he; "I should very much like to know what it is that you disagree with."

"Let me begin," I replied, "with the subject of Natural Philosophy, which is Epicurus' particular boast. Here, in the first place, he is entirely second-hand. His doctrines are those of Democritus, with a very few modifications. And as for the latter, where he attempts to improve upon his original, in my opinion he only succeeds in making things worse. Democritus believes in certain things which he terms 'atoms,' that is, bodies so solid as to be indivisible, moving about in a vacuum of infinite extent, which has neither top, bottom nor middle, neither center nor circumference. The motion of these atoms is such that they collide and so cohere together; and from this process result the whole of the things that exist and that we see. Moreover, this movement of the atoms must not be conceived as starting from a beginning, but as having gone on from all eternity. Epicurus for his part, where he follows Democritus, does not generally blunder.

Still, there is a great deal in each of them with which I do not agree, and especially this: in the study of Nature there are two questions to be asked, first, what is the matter out of which each thing is made, second, what is the force by which it is made; now Democritus and Epicurus have discussed the question of matter, but they have not considered the question of force or the effective cause. But this is a defect shared by both; I now come to the lapses peculiar to Epicurus. He believes that these same indivisible solid bodies are borne by their own weight perpendicularly downward, which he holds is the natural motion of all bodies; but thereupon this clever fellow, being met with the difficulty that if they all traveled downwards in a straight line, and, as I said, perpendicularly, no one atom would ever be able to overtake any other atom, accordingly introduced an idea of his own invention: he said that the atom makes a very tiny swerve—the smallest divergence possible; and thus produces entanglements and combinations and cohesion of atoms with atoms, which result in the creation of the world, and all its parts, and of all that in them is. Now not only is this whole affair a piece of childish fancy, but it does not even achieve the result that its author desires. The swerving is itself an arbitrary fiction; for Epicurus says the atoms swerve without cause—yet this is the capital offense in a natural philosopher, to speak of something taking place uncaused. Then also he gratuitously deprives the atoms of what he himself declared to be the natural motion of all heavy bodies, namely, movement in a straight line downwards, and yet he does not attain the object for the sake of which this fiction was devised.

For, if all the atoms swerve, none will ever come to cohere together; or if some swerve while others travel in a straight line, but their own natural tendency, in the first place this will be tantamount to assigning to the atoms their different spheres of action, some to travel straight and some sideways; while secondly (and this is a weak point with Democritus also) this riotous hurly-burly of atoms could not possibly result in the ordered beauty of the world we know. It is also unworthy of a natural philosopher to deny the infinite divisibility of matter; an error that assuredly Epicurus would have avoided, if he had been willing to let his friend Polyænus teach him geometry instead of making Polyænus himself unlearn it. Democritus, being an educated man and well versed in geometry, thinks the sun is of vast size; Epicurus considers it perhaps a foot in diameter, for he pronounces it to be exactly as large as it appears, or a little larger or smaller. Thus where Epicurus alters the doctrines of Democritus, he alters them for the worse; while for those ideas which he adopts, the credit belongs entirely to Democritus—the atoms, the void, the images, or as they call them, eidola, whose impact is the cause not only of vision but also of thought; the very conception of infinite space, apeiria as they term it, is entirely derived from Democritus; and again the countless numbers of worlds that come into existence and pass out of existence every day. For my own part I reject these doctrines altogether; but still I could wish that Democritus, whom every one else applauds, had not been vilified by Epicurus who took him as his sole guide.

III

"Turn next to the second division of philosophy, the department of Method and of Dialectic, which is termed Logic. Of the whole armor of Logic your founder, as it seems to me, is absolutely destitute. He does away with Definition; he has no doctrine of Division or Partition; he gives no rules for Deduction or Syllogistic Inference, and imparts no method for resolving Dilemmas or for detecting Fallacies of Equivocation.

The Criteria of reality he places in sensation; once let the senses accept as true something that is false, and every possible criterion of truth and falsehood seems to him to be immediately destroyed... He lays the very greatest stress upon that which, as he declares, Nature herself decrees and sanctions, that is: the feelings of pleasure and pain. These he maintains lie at the root of every act of choice and of avoidance. This is the doctrine of Aristippus, and it is upheld more cogently and more frankly by the Cyrenaics; but nevertheless it is in my judgment a doctrine in the last degree unworthy of the dignity of man. Nature, in my opinion at all events, has created and endowed us for higher ends. I may possibly be mistaken; but I am absolutely convinced that the Torquatus who first won that surname did not wrest the famous necklet from his foe in the hope of getting from it any physical enjoyment, nor did he fight the battle of the Veseris against the Latins in his third consulship for the sake of pleasure. Indeed in sentencing his son to be beheaded, it would seem that he actually deprived himself of a great deal of pleasure; for he sacrificed his natural instincts of paternal affection to the claims state and of his military office.

"Then, think of the Titus Torquatus who was consul with Gnaeus Octavius; when he dealt so sternly with the son who had passed out of his paternal control through his adoption by Decius Silanus—when he summoned him into his presence to answer to the charge preferred against him by a deputation from Macedonia, of accepting bribes while praetor in that province—when, after hearing both sides of the case, he gave judgment that he found his son guilty of having conducted himself in office in a manner unworthy of his ancestry, and banished him for ever from his sight—do you think that he had any regard for his own pleasure? But I pass over the dangers, the toils, the actual pain that all good men endure for country and for friends, not only not seeking pleasure, but actually renouncing pleasures altogether, and preferring to undergo every sort of pain rather than be false to any portion of their duty. Let us turn to matters seemingly less important, but equally conclusive. What actual pleasure do you, Torquatus, or does Triarius here, derive from literature, from history and learning, from turning the pages of the poets and committing vast quantities of verse to memory?

Do not tell me that these pursuits are in themselves a pleasure to you, and that so were the deeds I mentioned to the Torquati. That line of defense was never taken by Epicurus or Metrodorus, nor by any one of them if he possessed any intelligence or had mastered the doctrines of your school. Again, as to the questions often asked, why so many men are Epicureans, though it is not the only reason, the thing that most attracts the crowd is the belief that Epicurus declares right conduct and moral worth to be intrinsically and of themselves delightful, which means productive of pleasure. These worthy people do not realize that, if this is true, it upsets the theory altogether. If it were admitted that goodness is spontaneously and intrinsically pleasant, even without any reference to bodily feeling, then virtue would be desirable for its own sake, and so also would knowledge; but this Epicurus by no means allows.

"These then," said I, "are the doctrines of Epicurus that I cannot accept. For the rest, I could desire that he himself had been better equipped with learning (since even you must recognize that he is deficient in the liberal culture which confers on its possessor the title of an educated man) or at all events that he had not deterred others from study. Although I am aware that he has not succeeded in deterring you."

IV

I had spoken rather with the intention of drawing out Torquatus than of delivering a discourse of my own. But Triarius interposed, with a smile: "Why, you have practically expelled Epicurus altogether from the philosophic choir. What have you left to him except that, whatever his style may be, you find his meaning intelligible? His doctrines in Natural Philosophy were second-hand, and in your opinion unsound at that; and his attempts to improve on his authority only made things worse. Dialectic he had none. His identification of the Chief Good with pleasure in the first place was in itself an error, and secondly this also was not original; for it had been said before, and said better, by Aristippus. To crown all you added that Epicurus was a person of no education."

"Well, Triarius," I rejoined, "when one disagrees with a man, it is essential to say what it is that one objects to in his views. What should prevent me from being an Epicurean, if I accepted the doctrines of Epicurus? especially as the system is an exceedingly easy one to master. You must not find fault with members of opposing schools for criticizing each other's opinions; though I always feel that insult and abuse, or ill-tempered wrangling and bitter, obstinate controversy are beneath the dignity of philosophy."

"I am quite of you mind," said Torquatus; "it is impossible to debate properly without criticizing, but it is equally impossible to debate with ill-temper or obstinacy. But I have something I should like to say in reply to all this, if it will not weary you."

"Do you suppose," said I, "that I should have said what I have, unless I wanted to hear you?"

"Then would you like me to make a rapid review of the whole of Epicurus' system, or to discuss the single topic of pleasure, which is the one main subject of dispute?"

"Oh," I said, "that must be for you to decide."

"Very well then," said he, "this is what I will do, I will expound a single topic, and that the most important. Natural Philosophy we will postpone; though I will undertake to prove to you both your swerve of the atoms and size of the sun, and also that very many errors of Democritus were criticized and corrected by Epicurus. But on the present occasion I will speak about pleasure; not that I have anything original to contribute, yet I am confident that what I say will command even your acceptance."

"Be assured," I said, "that I shall not be obstinate, but will gladly own myself convinced if you can prove your case to my satisfaction."

"I shall do so," he rejoined, "provided you are as fair-minded as you promise. But I prefer to employ continuous discourse rather than question and answer."

"As you please," said I.
So he began.

V

"I will start then," he said, "in the manner approved by the author of the system himself, by settling what are the essence and qualities of the thing that is the object of our inquiry; not that I suppose you to be ignorant of it, but because this is the logical method of procedure. We are inquiring, then, what is the final and ultimate Good, which as all philosophers are agreed must be of such a nature as to be the End to which all other things are means, while it is not itself a means to anything else.

This Epicurus finds in pleasure; pleasure he holds to be that Chief Good, pain the Chief Evil. This he sets out to prove as follows: Every animal, as soon as it is born, seeks for pleasure, and delights in it as the Chief Good, while it recoils from pain as the Chief Evil, and so far as possible avoids it. This it does as long as it remains unperverted, at the prompting of Nature's own unbiased and honest verdict. Hence Epicurus refuses to admit any necessity for argument or discussion to prove that pleasure is desirable and pain to be avoided.

These facts, he thinks, are perceived by the senses, as that fire is hot, snow white, honey sweet, none of which things need be proved by elaborate argument: it is enough merely to draw attention to them. (For there is a difference, he holds, between formal syllogistic proof of a thing and a mere notice or reminder: the former is the method for discovering abstruse and recondite truths, the latter for indicating facts that are obvious and evident.) Strip mankind of sensation, and nothing remains; it follows that Nature herself is the judge of that which is in accordance with or contrary to nature. What does Nature perceive or what does she judge of, beside pleasure and pain, to guide her actions of desire and of avoidance? Some members of our school however would refine upon this doctrine; these say that it is not enough for the judgment of good and evil to rest with the senses; the facts that pleasure is in and for itself desirable and pain in and for itself to be avoided can also be grasped by the intellect and reason. Accordingly they declare that the perception in which the one is to be sought after and the other avoided is a notion naturally implanted in our minds. Others again, with whom I agree, observing that a great many philosophers do advance a vast array of reasons to prove why pleasure should not be counted as a good nor pain as an evil, consider that we had better not be too confident of our case; in their view it requires elaborate and reasoned argument, and abstruse theoretical discussion of the nature of pleasure and pain.

VI

"But I must explain to you how all this mistaken idea of reprobating pleasure and extolling pain arose. To do so, I will give you a complete account of the system, and expound the actual teachings of the great explorer of the truth, the master-builder of human happiness. No one rejects, dislikes or avoids pleasure itself, because it is pleasure, but because those who do not know how to pursue pleasure rationally encounter consequences that are extremely painful. Nor again is there anyone who loves or pursues or desires to obtain pain of itself, because it is pain, but because occasionally circumstances occur in which toil and pain can procure him some great pleasure. To take a trivial example, which of us ever undertakes laborious physical exercise, except to obtain some advantage from it? But who has any right to find fault with a man who chooses to enjoy a pleasure that has no annoying consequences, or one who avoids a pain that produces no resultant pleasure?

On the other hand, we denounce with righteous indignation and dislike men who are so beguiled and demoralized by the charms of the pleasure of the moment, so blinded by desire, that they cannot foresee the pain and trouble that are bound to ensue; and equal blame belongs to those who fail in their duty through weakness of will, which is the same as saying through shrinking from toil and pain. These cases are perfectly simple and easy to distinguish. In a free hour, when our power of choice is untrammeled and when nothing prevents our being able to do what we like best, every pleasure is to be welcomed and every pain avoided. But in certain emergencies and owing to the claims of duty or the obligations of business it will frequently occur that pleasures have to be repudiated and annoyances accepted. The wise man therefore always holds in these matters to this principle of selection: he rejects pleasures to secure other greater pleasures, or else he endures pains to avoid worse pains.

"This being the theory I hold, why need I be afraid of not being able to reconcile it with the case of the Torquati my ancestors? Your references to them just now were historically correct, and also showed your kind and friendly feeling towards myself; but all the same I am not to be bribed by your flattery of my family, and you will not find me a less resolute opponent. Tell me, please, what explanation do you put upon their actions? Do you really believe that they charged an armed enemy, or treated their children, their own flesh and blood, so cruelly, without a thought for their own interest or advantage? Why, even wild animals do not act in that way; they do not run amok so blindly that we cannot discern any purpose in their movements and their onslaughts. Can you then suppose that those heroic men performed their famous deeds without any motive at all? What their motive was, I will consider later on: for the present I will confidently assert, that if they had a motive for those undoubtedly glorious exploits, that motive was not a love of virtue in and for itself. He wrested the necklet from his foe—yes, and saved himself from death.

But he braved great danger—yes, before the eyes of an army. What did he get from it?—honor and esteem, the strongest guarantees of security in life. He sentenced his own son to death—if from no motive, then I am sorry to be the descendant of anyone so savage and inhuman; but if his purpose was, by inflicting pain upon himself, to establish his authority as a commander and to tighten the reins of discipline during a very serious war by holding over his army the fear of punishment, then his action aimed at ensuring the safety of his fellow citizens, upon which he knew his own depended. And this is a principle of wide application. People of your school, and especially yourself, who are so diligent a student of history, have found a favorite field for the display of your eloquence in recalling the stories of brave and famous men of old, and in praising their actions, not on utilitarian grounds, but on account of the splendor of abstract moral worth. But all of this falls to the ground if the principle of selection that I have just mentioned be established—the principle of forgoing pleasures for the purpose of getting greater pleasures, and enduring pains for the sake of escaping greater pains.

VII

"But enough has been said at this stage about the glorious exploits and achievements of the heroes of renown. The tendency of all of the virtues to produce pleasure is a topic that will be treated in its own place later on. At present I shall proceed to expound the essence and qualities of pleasure itself, and shall endeavor to remove the misconceptions of ignorance and to make you realize how serious, how temperate, how austere is the school that is supposed to be sensual, lax, and luxurious. The pleasure we pursue is not that kind alone which directly affects our physical being with a delightful feeling—a positively agreeable perception of the senses; on the contrary, the greatest pleasure according to us is that which is experienced as a result of the complete removal of pain. When we are released from pain, the mere sensation of complete emancipation and relief from uneasiness is in itself a source of gratification. But everything that causes gratification is a pleasure (just as everything that causes annoyance is a pain). Therefore the complete removal of pain has correctly been termed a pleasure. For example, when hunger and thirst are banished by food and drink, the mere fact of getting rid of uneasiness brings a resultant pleasure in its train. So generally, the removal of pain causes pleasure to take its place. Epicurus consequently maintained that there is no such thing as a neutral state of feeling intermediate between pleasure and pain; for the state supposed by some thinkers to be neutral, being characterized as it is by entire absence of pain, is itself, he held, a pleasure, and, what is more, a pleasure of the highest order. A man who is conscious of his condition at all must necessarily feel either pleasure or pain. But complete absence of pain Epicurus considers to be the limit and highest point of pleasure; beyond this point pleasure may vary in kind, but it cannot vary in intensity or degree. Yet at Athens, so my father used to tell me when he wanted to air his wit at the expense of the Stoics, in the Ceramicus there is actually a statue of Chrysippus seated and holding out one hand, the gesture being intended to indicate the delight which he used to take in the following little syllogism: 'Does your hand want anything, while it is in its present condition?' Answer: 'No, nothing.'—'But if pleasure were a good, it would want pleasure.'—'Yes, I suppose it would.'—'Therefore pleasure is not a good.' An argument, as my father declared, which not even a statue would employ, if a statue could speak; because though it is appropriate as an objection to the Cyrenaics, it does not touch Epicurus. For if the only kind of pleasure were that which so to speak tickles the senses, an influence permeating them with a feeling of delight, neither the hand nor any other member could be satisfied with the absence of pain unaccompanied by an agreeable and active sensation of pleasure. Whereas if, as Epicurus holds, the highest pleasure be to feel no pain, Chrysippus' interlocutor, though justified in making his first admission, that his hand in that condition wanted nothing, was not justified in his second admission, that if pleasure were a good, his hand would have wanted it. And the reason why it would not have wanted pleasure is, that to be without pain is to be in a state of pleasure.

VIII

"The truth of the proposition that pleasure is the ultimate good will most readily appear from the following illustration. Let us imagine a man living in the continuous enjoyment of numerous and vivid pleasures alike of body and of mind, undisturbed either by the presence or by the prospect of pain: what possible state of existence could we describe as being more excellent or more desirable? One so situated must possess in the first place a strength of mind that is proof against all fear of death or of pain; he will know that death means complete unconsciousness, and that pain is generally light if long and short if strong, so that its intensity is compensated by brief duration and its continuance by diminishing severity. Let such a man moreover have no dread of any supernatural power; let him never suffer the pleasures of the past to fade away, but constantly renew their enjoyment in recollection—and his lot will be one which will not admit of further improvement. Suppose on the other hand a person crushed beneath the heaviest load of mental and of bodily anguish to which humanity is liable. Grant him no hope of ultimate relief in view; also give him no pleasure either present or in prospect. Can one describe or imagine a more pitiable state? If then, a life full of pain is the thing most to be avoided, it follows that to live in pain is the highest evil; and this position implies that a life of pleasure ultimate good. In fact the mind possesses nothing in itself upon which it can rest as final. Every fear, every sorrow can be traced back to pain; there is no other thing besides pain which is of its own nature capable of causing either anxiety or distress.

"Pleasure and pain moreover supply the motives of desire and of avoidance, and the springs of conduct generally. This being so, it clearly follows that actions are right and praiseworthy only as being a means to the attainment of a life of pleasure. But that which is not itself a means to anything else, but to which all else is a means, is what the Greeks term the *telos*, the highest, ultimate or final Good. It must therefore be admitted that the Chief Good is to live happily.

IX

"Those who place the Chief Good in virtue alone are beguiled by the glamour of a name, and do not understand the true demands of nature. If they will consent to listen to Epicurus, they will be delivered from the grossest error. Your school dilates on the transcendent beauty of the virtues; but were they not productive of pleasure, who would deem them either praiseworthy or desirable? We esteem the art of medicine not for its interest as a science but for its conduciveness to health; the art of navigation is commended for its practical and not its scientific value, because it conveys the rules for sailing a ship with success. So also Wisdom, which must be considered as the art of living, if it effected no result would not be desired; but as it is, it is desired, because it is the artificer that procures and produces pleasure. (The meaning that I attach to pleasure must by this time be clear to you, and you must not be biased against my argument owing to the discreditable associations of the term.)

The great disturbing factor in man's life is ignorance of good and evil; mistaken ideas about these frequently rob us of our greatest pleasures, and torment us with the most cruel pain of mind. Hence we need the aid of Wisdom, to rid us of our fears and appetites, to root out all our errors and prejudices, and to serve as our infallible guide to the attainment of pleasure. Wisdom alone can banish sorrow from our hearts and protect us from alarm and apprehension; put yourself to school with her, and you may live in peace, and quench the glowing flames of desire. For the desires are incapable of satisfaction; they ruin not individuals only but whole families, nay often shake the very foundations of the state. It is they that are the source of hatred, quarreling and strife, of sedition and of war. Nor do they only flaunt themselves abroad, or turn their blind onslaughts solely against other; even when imprisoned within the heart they quarrel and fall out among themselves; and this cannot but render the whole of life embittered. Hence only the Wise Man, who prunes away all the rank growth of vanity and error, can possibly live untroubled by sorrow and by fear, content within the bounds that nature has set. Nothing could be more useful or more conducive to well-being than Epicurus' doctrine as to the different classes of the desires. One kind he classified as both natural and necessary, a second as natural without being necessary, and a third as neither natural nor necessary; the principle of classification being that the necessary desires are gratified with little trouble or expense; the natural desires also require by little, since nature's own riches, which suffice to content her, are both easily procured and limited in amount; but for the imaginary desires no bound or limit can be discovered.

X

If then we observe that ignorance and error reduce the whole of life to confusion, while Wisdom alone is able to protect us from the onslaughts of appetite and the menaces of fear, teaching us to bear even the affronts of fortune with moderation, and showing us all the paths that lead to calmness and to peace, why should we hesitate to avow that Wisdom is to be desired for the sake of the pleasures it brings and Folly to be avoided because of its injurious consequences?

"The same principle will lead us to pronounce that Temperance also is not desirable for its own sake, but because it bestows peace of mind, and soothes the ear with a tranquilizing sense of harmony For it is Temperance that warns us to be guided by reason what we desire and avoid. Nor is it enough to judge what it is right to do or to leave undone; we also need to abide by our judgment. Most men however lack tenacity of purpose; their resolution weakens and succumbs as soon as the fair form of pleasures meets their gaze, and they surrender themselves prisoners to their passions, failing to foresee the inevitable result. Thus for the sake of pleasure at once small in amount and unnecessary, and one which they might have procured by other means or even denied themselves altogether without pain, they incur serious disease, or loss of fortune, or disgrace, and not infrequently become liable to the penalties of the law and of the courts of justice. Those on the other hand who are resolved so to enjoy their pleasures as to avoid all painful consequences therefrom, and who retain their faculty of judgment and avoid being seduced by pleasure into course that they perceive to be wrong, reap the very highest pleasure by forgoing pleasure. Similarly also they often voluntarily endure pain, to avoid incurring greater pain by not doing so. This clearly proves that Intemperance is not undesirable for its own sake, while Temperance is desirable not because it renounces pleasures, but because it procures greater pleasures.

XI

"The same account will be found to hold good of Courage. The performance of labors, the undergoing of pains, are not in themselves attractive, nor are endurance, industry, watchfulness, nor yet that much lauded virtue, perseverance, nor even courage; but we aim at these virtues in order to live without anxiety and fear and so far as possible to be free from pain of mind and body. The fear of death plays havoc with the calm and even tenor of life, and to bow the head to pain and bear it abjectly and feebly is a pitiable thing; such weakness has caused many men to betray their parents other friends, some their country, and very many utterly to ruin themselves. So on the other hand a strong and lofty spirit is entirely free from anxiety and sorrow. It makes light of pain, and slight ones have frequent intervals of respite; while those of medium intensity lie within our own control: we can bear them if they are endurable, or if they are not, we may serenely quit life's theater, when the play has ceased to please us. These considerations prove that timidity and cowardice are not blamed, nor courage and endurance praised, on their own account; the former are rejected because they beget pain, the latter coveted because they beget pleasure.

XII

"It remains to speak of Justice, to complete the list of the virtues; but this admits of practically the same treatment as the others. Wisdom, Temperance and Courage I have shown to be so closely linked with Pleasures that they cannot possibly be severed or sundered from it. The same must be deemed to be the case with Justice. Not only does Justice never causes anyone harm, but on the contrary it always adds some benefit, partly owning to its essentially tranquilizing influence upon the mind, partly because of the hope that it warrants of a never-failing supply of the things that uncorrupted nature really needs. And just as Rashness, License and Cowardice ever torment the mind, ever awaken trouble and discord, so

Unrighteousness, when firmly rooted in the heart, causes restlessness by the mere fact of its presence; and if once it has found expression in some deed of wickedness, however secret the act, yet it can never feel assured that it will always remain undetected. The usual consequences of crime are, first suspicion, next gossip and rumor, then comes the accuser, then the judge; many wrongdoers have even turned in evidence against themselves, as happened during your consulship. And even if any think themselves well fenced and fortified against detection by their fellow-men, they still dread the eye of heaven, and fancy that the pangs of anxiety night and day gnawing at their hearts are sent by Providence to punish them.

But what can wickedness contribute towards lessening the annoyances of life, commensurate with its effect in increasing them, owing to the burden of a guilty conscience, the penalties of the law and the hatred of one's fellows? Yet nevertheless some men indulge without limit their avarice, ambition and love of power, lust gluttony and those other desires, which ill-gotten gains can never diminish but rather must inflame the more, insomuch that they appear proper subjects for restraint rather than for reformation. Men of sound natures, therefore, are summoned by the voice of true reason to justice, equity and honesty. For one without eloquence or resources, dishonesty is not good policy, since it is difficult for such a man to succeed in his designs, or to make good his success when once achieved. On the other hand, for the rich and clever generous conduct seems more in keeping, and liberality wins them affection and good will, the surest means to a life of peace; especially as there really is no motive for transgressing: since the desires that spring from nature are easily gratified without doing any man wrong, while those that are imaginary ought to be resisted, for they set their affections upon nothing that is really wanted; while there is more loss inherent in Injustice itself than there is profit in the gains it brings. Hence Justice also cannot correctly be said to be desirable in and for itself; it is so because it is so highly productive of gratification. For esteem and affection are gratifying, because they render life safer and fuller of pleasure. Hence we hold that Unrighteousness is to be avoided not simply on account of the disadvantages that result from being unrighteous, but even far more because when it dwells in a man's heart it never suffers him to breath freely or know a moment's rest.

"If then even the glory of the Virtues, on which all the other philosophers love to expatiate so eloquently, has in the last resort no meaning unless it be based on pleasure, whereas pleasure is the only thing that is intrinsically attractive and alluring, it cannot be doubted that pleasure is the one supreme and final Good and that a life of happiness is nothing else then a life of pleasure.

XIII

The doctrine thus firmly established has corollaries which I will briefly expound.

(1) The Ends of Goods and Evils themselves, that is pleasure and pain, are not open to mistake; where people go wrong is not knowing what things are productive of pleasure and pain.

(2) Again, we assert that mental pleasures and pains arise out of bodily ones (and therefore I allow your contention that any Epicureans who think otherwise put themselves out of court; and I am aware that many do, though not those who can speak with authority); but although men do experience mental pain that is annoying, yet both of these we assert arise out of and are based upon bodily sensations.

(3) Yet we maintain that this does not preclude mental pleasures and pains from being much more intense than those of the body; since the body can feel only what is present to it at the moment, whereas the mind is also cognizant of the past and of the future. For granting that pain of body is equally painful, yet our sensation of pain can be enormously increased by the belief that some evil of unlimited magnitude and duration threatens to befall us hereafter. And the same consideration may be transferred to pleasure: a pleasure is greater if not accompanied by any apprehension of evil. It therefore clearly appears that intense mental pleasure or distress contributes more to our happiness or misery than a bodily pleasure or pain of equal duration.

(4) But we do not agree that when an active sensation of pleasure is withdrawn uneasiness at once ensues, unless the pleasure happens to have been replaced by a pain: while on the other hand one is glad to lose a pain even though no active sensation of pleasure comes in its place: a fact that serves to show how great a pleasure is the mere absence of pain.

(5) But just as we are elated by the anticipation of good things, so we are delighted by their recollection. Fools are tormented by the memory of former evils; wise men have the delight of renewing in grateful remembrance the blessings of the past. We have the power both to obliterate our misfortunes in an almost perpetual forgetfulness and to summon up pleasant and agreeable memories of our successes. But when we fix our mental vision closely on the events of the past, then sorrow or gladness ensues according as these were evil or good.

XIV

"Here is indeed a royal road to happiness—open, simple, and direct! For clearly man can have no greater good than complete freedom from pain and sorrow coupled with the enjoyment of the highest bodily and mental pleasures. Notice then how the theory embraces every possible enhancement of life, every aid to the attainment of that Chief Good which is our object.

Epicurus, the man whom you denounce as a voluptuary, cries aloud that no one can live pleasantly without living wisely, honorably, and justly, and no one wisely, honorably and justly without living pleasurably. For a city rent by faction cannot prosper, nor a house whose masters are at strife; much less then can a mind divided against itself and filled with inward discord taste any particle of pure and liberal pleasure. But one who is perpetually swayed by conflicting and incompatible counsels and desires can know no peace or calm. Why, if the pleasantness of life is diminished by the more serious bodily diseases, how much more must it be diminished by the diseases of the mind! But extravagant and imaginary desires, for riches, fame, power, and also for licentious pleasures, are nothing but mental diseases. Then, too, there are grief, trouble and sorrow, which gnaw the heart and consume it with anxiety, if men fail to realize that the mind need feel no pain unconnected with some pain of body, present or to come. Yet there is no foolish man but is afflicted by some one of these diseases; therefore there is no foolish man that is not unhappy.

Moreover, there is death, the stone of Tantalus ever hanging over men's heads; and superstition, that poisons and destroys all peace of mind. Besides, they do not recollect their past nor enjoy their present blessings; they merely look forward to those of the future, and as these are of necessity uncertain, they are consumed with agony and terror; and the climax of their torment is when they perceive too late that all their dreams of wealth or station, power or fame, have come to nothing. For they never attain any of the pleasures, the hope of which inspired them to undergo all their arduous toils. Or look again at others, petty, narrow-minded men, or confirmed pessimists, or spiteful, envious, ill-tempered creatures, unsociable, abusive, brutal; others again enslaved to the follies of love, impudent or reckless, wanton, headstrong and yet irresolute, always changing their minds. Such failings render their lives one unbroken round of misery. The conclusion is that no foolish man can be happy, nor any wise man fail to be happy. This is a truth that we establish far more conclusively than do the Stoics. For they maintain that nothing is good save that vague phantom which they entitle Moral Worth, a title more splendid than substantial; and say that Virtue resting on this Moral Worth has no need of pleasure, but is herself her own sufficient happiness.

XV

"At the same time this Stoic doctrine can be stated in a form which we do not object to, and indeed ourselves endorse. For Epicurus thus presents his Wise Man who is always happy: his desires are kept within bounds; death he disregards; he has a true conception, untainted by fear, of the Divine nature; he does not hesitate to depart from life, if that would better his condition. Thus equipped he enjoys perpetual pleasure, for there is no moment when the pleasures he experiences do not outbalance the pains; since he remembers the past with gratitude, grasps the present with a full realization of its pleasantness, and does not rely upon the future; he looks forward to it, but finds his true enjoyment in the present. Also he is entirely free from the vices that I instanced a few moment ago, and he derives no inconsiderable pleasure from comparing his own existence with the life of the foolish. Moreover, any pains that the Wise Man may encounter are never so severe but that he has more cause for gladness than for sorrow. Again, it is a fine saying of Epicurus that 'the Wise Man is but little interfered with by Fortune: the great concerns of life, the things that matter, are controlled by his own Wisdom and Reason;' and that 'no greater pleasure could be derived from a life of infinite duration than is actually afforded by this existence which we know to be finite.' Logic, on which your school lays such stress, he held to be of no effect either as a guide to conduct or as an aid to thought. Natural Philosophy he deemed all-important.

This science explains to us the meaning of terms, the nature of predication, and the law of consistency and contradiction; secondly, a thorough knowledge of the facts of nature relieves us of the burden of superstition, frees us from fear of death, and shields us against the disturbing effects of ignorance, which is often in itself a cause of terrifying apprehensions; lastly, to learn what nature's real requirements are improves the moral character also. Besides, it is only by firmly grasping a well-established scientific system, observing the Rule or Canon that has fallen as it were from heaven so that all men may know it—only by making that Canon the test of all our judgments, that we can hope always to stand fast in our belief unshaken by the eloquence of any man. On the other hand, without a full understanding of the world of nature it is impossible to maintain the truth of our sense-perceptions. Further, every mental presentations has its origin in sensation: so that no certain knowledge will be possible, unless all sensations are true, as the theory of Epicurus teaches that they are. Those who deny the validity of sensation and say that nothing can be perceived, having excluded the evidence of the senses, are unable even to expound their own argument. Besides, by abolishing knowledge and science they abolish all possibility of rational life and action. Thus Natural

Philosophy supplies courage to face the fear of death; resolution to resist the terrors of religion; peace of mind, for it removes all ignorance of the mysteries of nature; self-control, for it explains the nature of the desires and distinguishes their different kinds; and, as I showed just now, the Canon or Criterion of Knowledge, which Epicurus also established, gives a method of discerning truth from falsehood.

XVI

"There remains a topic that is pre-eminently germane to this discussion, I mean the subject of Friendship. Your school maintains that if pleasure be the Chief Good, friendship will cease to exist. Now Epicurus' pronouncement about friendship is that of all the means to happiness that wisdom has devised, none is greater, none more fruitful, none more delightful than this. Nor did he only commend this doctrine by his eloquence, but far more by the example of his life and conduct. How great a thing friendship is, is shown by the mythical stories of antiquity. Review the legends from the remotest ages, and, copious and varied as they are, you will barely find in them three pairs of friends, beginning with Theseus and ending with Orestes. Yet Epicurus in single house and that a small one maintained a whole company of friends, united by the closest sympathy and affection; and this still goes on in the Epicurean school. But to return to our subject, for there is no need of personal instances: I notice that the topic of friendship has been treated by Epicureans in three ways.

(1) Some have denied that pleasures affecting our friends are in themselves to be desired by us in the same degree as we desire our own pleasures. This doctrine is thought by some critics to undermine the foundations of friendship; however, its supporters defend their position and in my opinion have no difficulty in making good their ground. They argue that friendship can no more be sundered form pleasure than can the virtues, which we have discussed already. A solitary, friendless life must be beset by secret dangers and alarms. Hence reason itself advises the acquisition of friends; their possession gives confidence, and a firmly rooted hope of winning pleasure. And just as hatred, jealousy and contempt are hindrances to pleasure, so friendship is the most trustworthy preserver and also creator of pleasure alike for our friends and for ourselves. It affords us enjoyment in the present, and it inspires us with hope for the near and distant future. Thus it is not possible to secure uninterrupted gratification in life without friendship is the most trustworthy preserver and also creator of pleasure alike for our friends and for ourselves. It affords us enjoyment in the present, and it inspires us with hopes for the near and distant future. Thus it is not possible to secure uninterrupted gratification in life without

friendship, nor yet to preserve friendship itself unless we love our friends as much as ourselves. Hence this unselfishness does occur in friendship, while also friendship is closely link with pleasure. For we rejoice in our friends' joy as much as in our own, and are equally painted by their sorrows. Therefore the Wise Man will feel exactly the same towards his friend as he does towards himself, and will exert himself as much for his friend's pleasure as he would for his own. All that has been said about the essential connection of the virtues with pleasure must be repeated about friendship. Epicurus said well (I give almost his exact words): 'The same creed that has given us courage to overcome all fear of everlasting or long-enduring evil hereafter, has discerned that friendship is our strongest safeguard in this present term of life.'—

(2) Other Epicureans though by no means lacking in insight are a little less courageous in defying the opprobrious criticism of the Academy. They fear that if we hold friendship to be desirable only for the pleasure that it affords to ourselves, it will be thought that it is crippled altogether. They therefore say that the first advances and overtures, and the original inclination to form an attachment, are promoted by the desire for pleasure, but that when the progress of intercourse has led to intimacy, the relationship blossoms into an affection strong enough to make us love our friends for their own sake, even though no practical advantage accrues from their friendship. Does not familiarity endear to us localities, temples, cities, gymnasia and playgrounds, horses and hounds, gladiatorial shows and fight with wild beasts? Then how much more natural and reasonable that this should be able to happen in our intercourse with our fellow-men!—

(3) The third view is that wise men have made a sort of compact to love their friends no less than themselves. We can understand the possibility of this, and we often see it happen. Clearly no more effective means to happiness could be found than such an alliance.

"All these considerations go to prove not only that the theory of friendship is not embarrassed by the identification of the Chief Good with pleasure, but also that without this no foundation for friendship whatsoever can be found.

XVII

"If then the doctrine I have set forth is clearer and more luminous than daylight itself; if it is derived entirely from Nature's source; if my whole discourse relies throughout for confirmation on the unbiased and unimpeachable evidence of the senses; if lisping infants, nay even dumb animals prompted by Nature's teaching, almost find voice to proclaim that there is no welfare but pleasure, no hardship but pain—and their judgment in these matters is neither sophisticated nor biased—ought we not to feel the greatest gratitude to him who caught this utterance of Nature's voice, and grasped its import so firmly and so fully that he has guided all sane-minded men into the paths of peace and happiness, calmness and repose? You are disposed to think him uneducated. The reason is that he refused to consider any education worth the name that did not help to school us in happiness. Was he to spend his time, as you encourage Triarius and me to do, in perusing poets, who give us nothing solid and useful, but merely childish amusement? Was he to occupy himself like Plato with music and geometry, arithmetic and astrology, which starting from false premises cannot be true, and which moreover if they were true would contribute nothing to make our lives pleasanter and therefore better? Was he, I say, to study arts like these, and neglect the master art, so difficult and correspond so fruitful, the art of living? No! Epicurus was not uneducated: the real philistines are those who ask us to go on studying till old age the subjects that we ought to be ashamed not to have learnt in boyhood."

Thus concluding, he added: "I have explained my own view, but solely with the object of learning what your verdict is. I have never hitherto had a satisfactory opportunity of hearing it."

UPON THE GARDEN OF EPICURUS

By

William Temple

The same faculty of reason, which gives mankind the great advantage and prerogative over the rest of the creation, seems to make the greatest default of human nature; and subjects it to more troubles, miseries, or at least disquiets of life, than any of its fellow creatures: it is this which furnishes us with such variety of passions, and consequently of wants and desires, that none other feels and these followed by infinite designs and endless pursuits, and improved by that restlessness of thought which is natural to most men, give him a condition of life suitable to that of his birth; so that, as he alone is born crying, he lives complaining and dies disappointed.

Since we cannot escape the pursuit of passions and perplexity of thoughts which our reason furnishes us, there is no way left, but to endeavour all we can either to subdue or to divert them. This last is the common business of common men, who seek it by all sorts of sports, pleasures, play, or business. But, because the two first are of short continuance, soon ending with weariness, or decay of vigour and appetite, the return whereof must be attended before the others can be renewed; and because play grows dull if it be not enlivened with the hopes of gain, the general diversion of mankind seems to be business, or the pursuit of riches in one kind or other; which is an amusement that has this one advantage above all others, that it lasts those men who engage in it to the very ends of their lives; none ever- growing too old for the thoughts and desires of increasing his wealth and fortunes, either for himself, his friends, or his posterity.

In the first and most simple ages of each country, the conditions and lives of men seem to have been very near of kin with the rest of the creatures: they lived by the hour, or by the day, and satisfied their appetite with what they could get from the herbs, the fruits, the springs they met with when they were hungry or dry; then, with what fish, fowl, or beasts they could kill, by swiftness or strength, by craft or contrivance, by their hands, or such instruments as wit helped or necessity forced them to invent. When a man had got enough for the day, he laid up the rest for the morrow, and spent one day in labour that he might pass the other at ease; and lured on by the pleasure of this bait, when he was in vigour, and his game fortunate, he would provide for as many days as he could, both for himself and his children, that were too young to seek out for themselves. Then he cast about, how by sowing of grain, and by pasture of the tamer cattle, to provide for the whole year. After this, dividing the lands necessary for these uses, first among children, and then among servants, he reserved to himself a proportion of their gain, either in the native stock, or something equivalent, which brought in the use of money; and where this once came in, none was to be satisfied, without having enough for himself and his family, and all his and their posterity for ever; so that I know a certain Lord who professes to value no lease, though for an hundred or a thousand years, nor any estate or possession of land, that is not for ever and ever.

From such small beginnings have grown such vast and extravagant designs of poor mortal men: yet none could ever answer the naked Indian, why one man should take pains, and run hazards by sea and land all his life, that his children might be safe and lazy all theirs: and the precept of taking no care for tomorrow, though never minded as impracticable in the world, seems but to reduce mankind to their natural and original condition of life. However, by these ways and degrees, the endless increase of riches seems to be grown the perpetual and general amusement or business of mankind.

Some few in each country make those higher flights after honour and power, and to these ends sacrifice their riches, their labour, their thought, and their lives; and nothing diverts nor busies men more than these pursuits, which are usually covered with the pretences of serving a man's country, and of public good. But the true service of the public is a business of so much labour and so much care, that though a good and wise man may not refuse it, if he be called to it by his Prince or his country, and thinks he can be of more than vulgar use, yet he will seldom or never seek it, but leaves it commonly to men who, under the disguise of public good, pursue their own designs of wealth, power, and such bastard honours as usually attend them, not that which is the true, and only true reward of virtue.

The pursuits of ambition, though not so general, yet are as endless as those of riches, and as extravagant; since none ever yet thought he had power or empire enough: and what Prince so ever seems to be so great, as to live and reign without any further desires or fears, falls into the life of a private man, and enjoys but those pleasures and entertainments which a great many several degrees of private fortune will allow, and as much as human nature is capable of enjoying.

The pleasures of the senses grow a little more choice and refined: those of imagination are turned upon embellishing the scenes he chooses to live in; ease, conveniency, elegancy, magnificence, are sought in building first, and then in furnishing houses or palaces: the admirable imitations of nature are introduced by pictures, statues, tapestry, and other such achievements of arts. And the most exquisite delights of sense are pursued, in the contrivance and plantation of gardens; which, with fruits, flowers, shades, fountains, and the music of birds that frequent such happy places, seem to furnish all the pleasures of the several senses, and with the greatest, or at least the most natural perfections.

Thus the first race of Assyrian Kings, after the conquests of Ninus and Semiramis, passed their lives, till their empire fell to the Medes. Thus the

Caliphs of Egypt, till deposed by their Mamalukes. Thus passed the latter parts of those great lives of Scipio, Lucullus, Augustus, Dioclesian. Thus turned the great thoughts of Henry II. of France, after the end of his wars with Spain. Thus the present King of Morocco, after having subdued all his competitors, passes his life in a country villa, gives audience in a grove of orange-trees planted among purling streams. And thus the King of France, after all the successes of his councils or arms, and in the mighty elevation of his present greatness and power, when he gives himself leisure from such designs or pursuits, passes the softer and easier parts of his time in country houses and gardens, in building, planting, or adorning the scenes, or in the common sports and entertainments of such kind of lives. And those mighty Emperors, who contented not themselves with these pleasures of common humanity, fell into the frantic or the extravagant; they pretended to be Gods or turned to be Devils, as Caligula and Nero, and too many others known enough in story.

Whilst mankind is thus generally busied or amused, that part of them, who have had either the justice or the luck to pass in common opinion for the wisest and the best part among them, have followed another and very different scent; and instead of the common designs of satisfying their appetites and their passions, and making endless provisions for both, they have chosen what they thought a nearer and a surer way to the ease and felicity of life, by endeavoring to subdue, or at least to temper their passions, and reduce their appetites to what nature seems only to ask and to need. And this design seems to have brought philosophy into the world, at least that which is termed moral, and appears to have an end not only desirable by every man, which is the ease and happiness of life, but also in some degree suitable to the force and reach of human nature: for, as to that part of philosophy which is called natural, I know no end it can have, but that of either busying a man's brains to no purpose, or satisfying the vanity so natural to most men of distinguishing themselves, by some way or other, from those that seem their equals in birth and the common advantages of it; and whether this distinction be made by wealth or power, or appearance of knowledge, which gains esteem and applause in the world, is all a case. More than this I know no advantage mankind has gained by the progress of natural philosophy, during so many ages it has had vogue in the world, excepting always, and very justly, what we owe to the mathematics, which is in a manner all that seems valuable among the civilized nations, more than those we call barbarous, whether they are so or no, or, more so than ourselves.

How ancient this natural philosophy has been in the world is hard to know; for we find frequent mention of ancient philosophers in this kind, among the most ancient now extant with us. The first who found out the vanity of it seems to have been Solomon, of which discovery he has left such admirable strains in Ecclesiastes. The next was Socrates, who made it the business of his life to explode it, and introduce that which we call moral in its place, to busy human minds to better purpose. And indeed, whoever reads with thought what these two, and Marcus Antoninus, have said upon the vanity of all that mortal man can ever attain to know of nature, in its originals or operations, may save himself a great deal of pains, and justly conclude, that the knowledge of such things is not our game; and (like the pursuit of a stag by a little spaniel) may serve to amuse and to weary us, but will never be hunted down. Yet I think those three I have named may justly pass for the wisest triumvirate that are let us upon the records of story or of time.

After Socrates, who left nothing in writing, many sects of philosophers began to spread in Greece, who entered boldly upon both parts of natural and moral philosophy. The first with the greatest disagreement, and the most eager contention that could be upon the greatest subjects: as, whether the world were eternal, or produced at some certain time? whether, if produced, it was by some eternal Mind, and to some end, or by the fortuitous concourse of atoms, or some particles of eternal matter? whether there was one world, or many? whether the soul of man was a part of some ethereal and eternal substance, or was corporeal? whether, if eternal, it was so before it came into the body, or only after it went out? There were the same contentions about the motions of the heavens, the magnitude of the celestial bodies, the faculties of the mind, and the judgment of the senses. But all the different schemes of nature - that have been drawn of old, or of late, by Plato, Aristotle, Epicurus, Des Cartes, Hobbs, or any other that I know of, seem to agree but in one thing, which is, the want of demonstration or satisfaction to any thinking and unpossessed man; and seem more or less probable one than another, according to the wit and eloquence of the authors and advocates that raise or defend them; like jugglers tricks, that have more or less appearance of being real, according to the dexterousness and skill of him that plays them; whereas perhaps, if we were capable of knowing truth and nature, these fine schemes would prove like rover shots, some nearer and some further off; but all at great distance from the mark; it may be, none in sight.

Yet, in the midst of these and many other such disputes and contentions in their natural philosophy, they seemed to agree much better in their moral; and, upon their inquires after the ultimate end of man, which was his happiness, their contentions or differences seemed to be rather in words, than in the sense of their opinions, or in the true meaning of their several authors or masters of their sects: all concluded that happiness was the chief good, and ought to be the ultimate end of man; that, as this was the end of wisdom, so wisdom was the way to happiness. The question then was, in what this happiness consisted? The contention grew warmest between the Stoics and Epicureans; the other sects, in this point, siding in a manner with one or the other of these in their conceptions or expressions. The Stoics would have it to consist in virtue, and the Epicureans in pleasure; yet the most reasonable of the Stoics made the pleasure of virtue to be the greatest happiness, and the best of the Epicureans made the greatest pleasure to consist in virtue; and the difference between these two seems not easily discovered. All agreed; the greatest temper, if not the total subduing of passion, and exercise of reason, to be the state of the greatest felicity; to live without desires or fears, or those perturbations of mind and thought which passions raise; to place true riches in wanting little, rather than in possessing much; and true pleasure in temperance, rather than in satisfying the senses; to live with indifference to the common enjoyments and accidents of life, and with constancy upon the greatest blows of fate or of chance; not to disturb our minds with sad reflexions upon what is past, nor with anxious cares or raving hopes about what is to come; neither to disquiet life with the fears of death, nor death with the desires of life; but in both, and in all things else, to follow nature, seem to be the precepts most agreed among them.

Thus reason seems only to have been called in to allay those disorders which itself had raised, to cure its own wounds, and pretends to make us wise no other way than; by rendering us insensible. This at least was the profession of many rigid Stoics, who would have had a wise man, not only without any sort of passion, but without any sense of pain as well as pleasure; and to enjoy himself in the midst of diseases and torments, as well as of health and ease: a principle, in my mind, against common nature and common sense; and which might have told us in fewer words, or with less, circumstance, that a man, to be wise, should not be a man; and this perhaps might have been easy enough believe, but nothing so hard as the other.

The Epicureans were more intelligible in their notion, and fortunate in their expression, when they placed a man's happiness in the tranquillity of mind and indolence of body; for while we are composed of both, I doubt both must have a share in the good or ill we feel. As men of several languages say the same things in very different words; so in several ages, countries, constitutions of laws and religion, the same thing seems to be meant by very different expressions: what is called by the Stoics apathy, or dispassion; by the Sceptics indisturbance; by the Molinists quietism; by common men peace of conscience; seems all to mean but great tranquillity of mind, though it be made to proceed from so diverse causes, as human wisdom, innocence of life; or resignation to the will of God. An old usurer had the same notion, when he said, "No man could have peace of conscience, that run out of his estate;" not comprehending what else was meant by that phrase, besides true quiet and content of mind; which, however expressed, is, I suppose, meant by all to be the best account that can be given of the happiness of man, since no man can pretend to be happy without it.

I have often wondered how such sharp and violent invectives came to be made go generally against Epicurus by the ages that followed him, whose admirable wit, felicity of expression, excellence of nature, sweetness of conversation, temperance of life, and constancy of death, made him so beloved by his friends, admired by his scholars, and honoured by the Athenians. But this injustice may be fastened chiefly upon the envy and malignity of the Stoics at first, then upon the mistakes of some gross pretenders to his sect (who took pleasure only to be sensual) and afterwards, upon the piety of the primitive Christians, who esteemed his principles of natural philosophy more opposite to those of our religion, than either the Platonists, the Peripatetics; or Stoics themselves: yet, I confess, I do not know why the account given by Lucretius of the Gods, should be thought more impious than that given by Homer, who makes them not only subject to all the weakest passions, but perpetually busy in all the worst or meanest actions men.

But Epicurus has found so great advocates of his virtue, as well as learning and inventions, that there need no more; and the testimonies of Diogenes Laertius alone seem too sincere and impartial to be disputed, or to want the assistance of modern authors: if all failed, he would be but too well defended by the excellence of so many of his sect in all ages, and especially of those who lived in the compass of one, but the greatest in story, both as to persons and events: I need name no more than Cæsar, Atticus, Mæcenas, Lucretius, Virgil, Horace all admirable in their several kinds, and perhaps unparalleled in story.

Cæsar, if considered in all lights, may justly challenge the first place in the registers we have of mankind, equal only to himself, and surpassing all others of his nation and his age, in the virtues and excellencies of a statesman, a captain, an orator, an historian; besides all these, a poet, a philosopher, when his leisure allowed him; the greatest man of counsel and of action, of design and execution; the greatest nobleness of birth, of person, and of countenance; the greatest humanity and clemency of nature, in the midst of the greatest provocations, occasions, and examples of cruelty and revenge: it is true, he overturned the laws and constitutions of his country, yet it was after so many others had not only begun, but proceeded very far, to change, and violate them; so as, in what he did, he seems rather to have prevented others, than to have done what he himself designed; for though his ambition was vast, yet it seems to have been raised to those heights, rather by the insolence of his enemies than by his own temper; and that what was natural to him was only a desire of true glory, and to acquire it by good actions as well as great, by conquests of barbarous nations, extent of the Roman empire; defending at first the liberties of the plebeians, opposing the faction that had begun in Sulla and ended in Pompey; and, in the whole course of his victories and successes, seeking all occasions of bounty to his friends, and clemency to his enemies.

Atticus appears to have been one of the wisest and best of the Romans; learned without pretending, good without affectation, bountiful without design, a friend to all men in misfortune, a flatterer to no man in greatness or power, a lover of mankind, and beloved by them all; and by these virtues and dispositions, he passed safe and untouched through all the flames of civil dissentions that ravaged his country the greatest part of his life; and, though he never entered into any public affairs or particular factions of his state, yet he was favoured, honoured, and courted by them all, from Sylla to Augustus.

Mæcenas was - the wisest counselor, the truest friend both of his Prince and his country, the best Governor of Rome, the happiest and ablest negotiator, the best judge of learning and virtue, the choicest in his friends, and thereby the happiest in his conversation that has been known in story; and I think, to his conduct in. civil, and Agrippa's in military affairs, may be truly ascribed all the fortunes and greatness of Augustus, so much celebrated in' the world.

For Lucretius, Virgil, and Horace, they deserve, in my opinion, the honour of the greatest philosophers, as well as the best poets of their nation or age. The two first, besides what looks like something more than human in their poetry, were very great naturalists, and admirable in their morals: and Horace, besides the sweetness and elegancy of his Lyrics, appears, in the rest of his writings, so great a master of life, and of true sense in the conduct of it, that I know none beyond him. It was no mean strain of his philosophy, to refuse being Secretary to Augustus, when so great an emperor so much desired it. But all the different sects of philosophies seem to have agreed in the opinion of a wise man abstaining from public affairs, which is thought the meaning of Pythagoras's precept, to abstain from beans, by which the affairs or public resolutions in Athens were managed. They thought that sort of business too gross and material for the abstracted fineness of their speculations. They esteemed it too sordid and too artificial for the cleanness and simplicity of their manners and lives. They would have no part in the faults of a government; and they knew too well, that the nature and passions of men made them incapable of any that was perfect and good; and therefore thought all the service they could do to the state they lived under, was to mend the lives and manners of particular men that composed it. But where, factions were once entered and rooted in a state, they thought it madness for good men to meddle with public affairs; which made them turn their thoughts and entertainments to any thing rather than this; and Heraclitus, having, upon the factions of the citizens, quitted the government of his city, and amusing himself to play with the boys in the porch of the temple, asked those who wondered at him, Whether it was not better to play with such boys, than govern such men? But above all, they esteemed public business the most contrary of all others to that tranquillity of mind, which they esteemed and taught to be the only true felicity of man.

For this reason, Epicurus passed his life wholly in his garden: there he studied, there he exercised, there he taught his philosophy; and, indeed, no other sort of abode seems to contribute so much to both the tranquility of mind and indolence of body, which he made his chief ends. The sweetness of air, the pleasantness of smell, the verdure of plants, the cleanness and lightness, of food, the exercises of working or walking; but above all, the exemption from cares and solicitude, seem equally to favour and improve both contemplation and health, the enjoyment of sense and imagination, and thereby the quiet and ease both of the body and mind.

Though Epicurus be said to have been the first that had a garden in Athens, whose citizens before him had theirs' in their villas or farms without the city; yet the use of gardens seems to have been the most ancient and most general of any sorts of possession among mankind, and to have, preceded those of corn or of cattle as yielding the easier, the pleasanter, and more natural food. As it has been the inclination of Kings and the choice of philosophers, so it has been the common favourite of public and private men; a pleasure of the greatest, and the care of the meanest; and indeed an employment and a possession, for which no man is too high nor too low.

If we believe the Scripture, we must allow that God Almighty esteemed the life of a man in a garden--the happiest he could give him, or else he would not have placed Adam in that of Eden; that it was the state of innocence and pleasure; and that the life of husbandry and cities came after the fall, with guilt and with labour.

Where paradise was, has been much debated, and little agreed; but what sort of place is meant by it may perhaps easier be conjectured. It seems to have been a Persian word, since Xenophon and other Greek authors mention it, as what was much in use and delight among the Kings of those eastern countries. Strabo, describing Jericho, says, "Ibi est palmentum, cui immixtæ sunt etiam aliæ stirpes, hortenses, locus ferax, palmis abundans, spatio stadiorum centum, totus iriguus, ibi est Regiet Balsami paradisus." He, mentions, another place, to be "prope Libanum et Paradisum." And Alexander is written to have seen Cyrus's tomb in paradise, being tower not very great, and covered with a shade of trees about it. So that a paradise, among them seems to have been a large space of ground adorned and beautified with all sorts of trees, both of fruits and of forest, either found there before it was inclosed, or planted after; either cultivated like gardens, for shades and for walks, with fountains or streams, and all sorts of plants usual in the climate, and pleasant to the eye, the smell, or the taste; or else employed like our parks, for inclosure and harbour of all sorts of wild beasts, as well, as for the pleasure of riding and walking: and so they were of more or less extent, and of different entertainment, according to the several humours of the Princes that ordered and inclosed them.

Semiramis is the first we are told of in story, that brought them in use through her empire, and was so fond of them, as to take one where-ever she built, and in all, or most of the provinces she subdued; which are said to have been from Babylon as far as India. The Assyrian Kings continued this custom and care, or rather this pleasure, till one of them brought in the use of smaller and more regular gardens: for having married a wife he was fond of, out of one of the provinces, where, such paradises or gardens were much in use, and the country lady not well bearing the air or inclosure of the palace in Babylon, to which the Assyrian, Kings used to confine themselves, he made her gardens, not only within the palaces, but upon terraces raised with earth, over the arched roofs, and even upon the top of the highest tower, planted them with all sorts of fruit-trees, as well as other plants and flowers, the most pleasant of that country; and thereby made at least the most airy gardens, as well as the most costly, that have been heard of in the world. This lady may probably have been native of the provinces of Chasimer or of Damascus, which have in all times been the happiest regions for fruits of all the East, by the excellence of soil, the position of mountains, the frequency of streams, rather than the advantages of climate. And it is great pity we do not yet see the history of Chasimer, which Monsieur Bernier assured me he had translated out of Persian, and intended to publish; and of which he has given such a taste, in his excellent Memoirs of the Mogul's country.

The next gardens we read of are those of Solomon, planted with all sorts of fruit-trees, and watered with fountains; and though we have no more particular description of them yet we may find, they were the places where he passed the times of his leisure and delight, where the houses as well as grounds were adorned with all that could be of pleasing and elegant, and were the retreats and entertainments of those among his wives that he loved the best; and it is not improbable, that the paradises mentioned by Strabo were planted by this great and wisest Wing. But the idea of the garden must be very great, if it answer at all to that of the gardener, who must have employed a great deal of his care and of his study, as well as of his leisure and thought, in these entertainments, since he wrote of all plants, from the cedar to the shrub.

What the gardens of the Hesperides' were,' we have little or no account, further than the mention of them, and thereby the testimony of their having been in use and request in such remoteness of place and antiquity of time.

The garden of Alcinous, described by Homer, seems wholly poetical, and made at the pleasure of the painter; like the rest of the romantic palaces in that little barren island of Phæcia or Corfu. Yet, as all the pieces of this transcendent genius are composed with excellent knowledge, as well as fancy; so they seldom fail of instruction as well as delight, to all that read him. The seat of this garden, joining to the gates of the palace, the compass of the inclosure being four acres, the tall trees of shade, as well as those of fruit, the two fountains, the one for the use of the garden, and the other of the pa. lace, the continual succession of fruits throughout the whole year, are, for aught I know, the best rules or provision that can go towards composing the best gardens; nor is it unlikely, that Homer may have drawn this picture after the life of some he had seen in Ionia, the country and usual abode of this divine oet; and indeed, the region of the most refined pleasure and luxury, as well as invention and wit: for the humour and custom of gardens may have descended earlier into the Lower Asia, from Damascus, Assyria, and other parts of the eastern empires, though they seem to have made late entrance and smaller improvement in those of Greece and Rome; at least in no proportion to their other inventions or refinements of pleasure and luxury.

The long and flourishing peace of the two first empires gave earlier rise and growth to learning and civility, and all the consequences of them, in magnificence and elegancy of building and gardening; whereas Greece and Rome were almost perpetually engaged in quarrels and wars either abroad or at home, and so were busy in actions that were done under the sun, rather than those under the shade. These were the entertainments of the softer nations, that fell under the virtue and prowess of the two last empires, which from those conquests brought home mighty increases both of riches and luxury, and so perhaps lost more than they got by the spoils of the East.

There may be another reason for the small advance of gardening in those excellent and more temperate climates, where the air and soil were so apt of themselves to produce the best sorts of fruits, without the necessity of cultivating them by labour and care; whereas the hotter climates, as well as the cold, are forced upon industry and skill, to produce or improve many fruits that grow of themselves in the more temperate regions. However it were, we have very little mention of gardens in old Greece or in old Rome, for pleasure or with, elegance. nor of much curiousness or care, to introduce the fruits of foreign climates, contenting themselves with those which were, native of their own; and these were the vine, the olive, the fig, the pear, and the apple: Cato, as I remember, mentions no more; and their gardens were then but the necessary part of their farms, intended particularly for the cheap and easy food of their hinds or slaves employed in their agriculture, and so were turned chiefly to all the common sorts of plants, herbs, or legumes (as the French call them) proper for common nourishment; and the name of *Hortus* is taken to be from ortus, because it perpetually furnishes some rise or production of some-thing new in the world.

Lucullus, after the Mithridatic war, first brought cherries -from Pontus into Italy, which so generally pleased, and were so easily propagated in all climates, that within the space of about an hundred years, having traveled westward with the Roman conquests, they grew common as far as the Rhine, and passed over into Britain. After the conquest of Africa, Greece, the Lesser Asia, and Syria, were brought into Italy all the sorts of their mala, which we interpret as apples, and might signify no more at first, but were afterwards applied to many other foreign fruits: the apricots, coming from Empire, were called mala Epirotica; peaches from Persia, mala Persica; citrons of Media, Medica; pomegranates from Carthage, Punica; quinces, Cathonea, from a small island in the Grecian seas; their best pears were brought from Alexandria, Numidia, Greece, and Numantia; as appears by their several appellations: their plums, from Armenia, Syria, but chiefly from Damascus. The kinds of these are reckoned, in Nero's time, to have been near thirty, as well as of figs; and many of them were entertained at Rome with so great applause and so general vogue, that the great Captains, and even consular men, who first brought them over, took pride in giving them their own names, (by which they run a great while in Rome) as in memory of some great service or pleasure they had done their country; so that not only laws and battles, but several sorts of apples or mala, and of pears were called Marilian and Claudian, Pompeian and Tiberian, and by several other such noble names.

Thus the fruits of Rome, in about an hundred years, came from countries as far as their conquests had reached; and, like learning, architecture, painting, and statuary, made their great advances in Italy about the Augustan age. What was of most request in their common gardens in Virgil's time, Or at least in his youth, may be conjectured by the description of his old Corycian's gardens in the fourth of the Georgics; which begins,

Namque sub Oebaliae memini turribus altis.

Among flowers, the roses had the first place, especially a kind which bore twice a-year; and none other sorts are here mentioned besides the Narcissus, though the violet and the lily were very common, and the next in esteem; especially the breve Illium, which was the tuberose. The plants he mentions are the apium, which though commonly interpreted parsley, yet comprehends all sorts of smallage, whereof celery is one; cucumis, which takes in all sorts of melons, as well as cucumbers; olus, which is a common word for all sorts of pot-herbs and legumes; verbenas, which signifies all kinds of sweet or sacred plants that were used for adorning the altars; as bays, olive, rosemary, myrtle: the acanthus seems to be what we called pericanthe; but what their hederæ were, that deserved place in a garden, I cannot guess, unless they had sorts of ivy unknown to us; nor what his vescum papaver was, since poppies with us are of no use in eating. The fruits mentioned are only apples, pears, and plums; for olives, vines, and figs, were grown to be fruits of their fields, rather than of their gardens. The shades were the elm, the pine, the lime-tree, and the platanus, or plane-tree: whose leaf and shade, of all others, was the most in request; and, having been brought out of Persia, was such an inclination among the Greeks and Romans, that they usually fed it with wine instead of water; they believed this tree loved that liquor, as well as those that used to drink under its shade; which was a great humour and custom, and perhaps gave rise to the other, by observing the growth of the tree, or largeness of the leaves, where much wine was spilt or left, and thrown upon the roots.

It is a great pity that the haste which Virgil seems here to have been in, should have hindered him from entering farther into the account or instructions, of gardening, which he said he could have given, and which he seems to have so much esteemed and loved, by that admirable picture of this old man s felicity, which he draws like so great a master, with one stroke of a pencil in those four words:

Regum æquabat opes animis.

That in the midst of these small possessions, upon a few acres of barren ground, yet he equaled all the wealth and opulence of Kings, in the ease, content, and freedom of his mind.

I am not satisfied with tile common acceptation of the mala aurea for oranges; nor do I find any passage in the authors of that age, which gives me the opinion, that these were otherwise known to the Romans than as fruits of the eastern climates. I should take their mala aurea to be - rather some kind of apples, so called from the golden colour, as some are amongst us; for otherwise, the orange-tree is too noble in the beauty, taste, and smell of its fruit; in the perfume and virtue of its flowers; in the perpetual verdure of its leaves, and in the excellent uses of all, these, both for pleasure and health; not to have deserved any particular mention in the writings of an age and nation so refined and exquisite in all sorts of delicious luxury.

The charming description Virgil makes of the happy apple, must be intended either for the citron, or for some sort of orange growing in Media, which was either so proper to that country as not to grow in any other, (as a certain sort of fig was to Damascus) or to have lost its virtue by changing soils, or to have had its effect of curing some sort of poison that was usual in that country, but particular to it: I cannot forbear inserting those few lines out of the second of Virgil's Georgics, not having ever heard any body else take notice of them.

Media fert tristes succos, tardumque saporem
Felicis mali; quo non præsentius ullum,

Pocula si quandò sævæ infecere novercæ,
Auxilium venit, ac membris agit atra venena
Ipsa ingens arbos, faciemque simillima lauro;
Et, si non alios late jactaret odores,
Laurus erit: folia haud ullis labentia ventis;
Flos apprirna tenax: animas et olentia Medi
Ora fovent illo, ac senibus medicantur anhelis.

Media brings pois'nous herbs, and the flat taste
Of the bless'd apple, than which ne'er was found
A help more present, when curs'd step-dames mix
Their mortal cups, to drive the Venom out:
'Tis a large tree, and like a bays in hue;
And, did it not such odours cast about,
'Twould be a bays; the leaves with no winds fall,
The flowers all excel: with these the Medes
Perfume their breaths, and cure old pursy men.

The tree being so like a bays or laurel, the slow or dull taste of the apple, the virtue of it against poison, seem to describe the citron: the perfume of the flowers and virtues of them, to, cure ill scents of mouth or breath, or shortness of wind in pursy old men, seem to agree most with the orange: if *flos apprima tenax* mean only the excellence of the flower above all others, it may be intended for the orange; if it signifies the flowers growing most upon the tops of the trees, it may be rather the citron; for I have been so curious as to bring up a citron from a kernel, which at twelve years of age began to flower; and I observed all the flowers to grow upon the top branches of the tree, but to be nothing so high or sweet-scented as the orange. On the other side, I have always heard oranges to proper soil, being there extended under the best climate for the production of all sorts of the best fruits; which seems to be from about twenty-five, to about thirty-five degrees of latitude. Now the regions under this climate in the present Persian empire (which comprehends most of the other two, called anciently Assyria and Media) are composed of many Provinces full of great and fertile plains, bounded by high mountains, especially to the north; watered naturally with many rivers, and those, by art and labour, derived into many more and smaller streams, which all conspire to form a country, in all circumstances, the most proper and agreeable for production of the best and noblest fruits. Whereas if we survey the regions of the western world, lying in the same latitude between twenty-five and thirty-five degrees, we shall find them extend either over the Mediterranean sea, the ocean, or the sandy barren countries of Africa; and that no part of the continent of Europe lies so southward as thirty-five degrees. Which may serve to discover the true genuine reason, why the fruits of the East have been always observed and agreed to transcend those of the West.

In our north-west climates, our gardens are very different from what they were in Greece and Italy, and from what they are now in those regions in Spain or the southern parts of France. And as most general customs in countries grow from the different nature of climate, soils, or situations, and from the necessities or industry they impose, so do these.

In the warmer regions, fruits and flowers of the best sorts are so common and of so easy production, that they grow in fields, and are not worth the cost of inclosing, or the care of more than ordinary cultivating. On the other side, the great pleasures of those climates are coolness of air, and whatever looks cool even to the eyes, and relieves them from the unpleasant sight of dusty streets, or parched fields. This makes the gardens of those countries to be chiefly valued by largeness of extent (which gives greater play and openness of air) by shades of trees, by frequency of living streams or fountains, by perspectives, by statues, and by pillars and obelisks of stone scattered up and down, which all conspire to make any place look fresh and cool. On the contrary, the more northern climates, as they suffer little by heat, make little provision against it, and are careless of shade, and seldom curious in fountains. Good statues are in the reach of few men, and common ones are generally and justly despised or neglected. But no sorts of good fruits or flowers, being natives of the climates, or usual among us nor indeed the best sort of plants, herbs, salads for our kitchen gardens themselves and the best fruits, not ripening without the advantage of walls and palisades, by reflexion of the faint heat we receive from the sun, our gardens are made of smaller compass, seldom exceeding four, six, or eight acres; in closed with walls, and laid out in a manner wholly for advantage of fruits, flowers, and the product of kitchen gardens in all sorts of herbs, salads, plants, and legumes, for the common use of tables.

These are usually the gardens of England and Holland, as the first sort are those of Italy, and were so of old. In the more temperate parts of France, and in Brabant (where I take gardening to be at its greatest height), they are composed of both sorts, the extent more spacious than ours; part laid out for flowers, others for fruits; some standards, some against walls or palisades, some for forest trees, and groves for shade, some parts wild, some exact; and fountains much in request among them.

But after so much ramble into ancient times, and remote places, to return home and consider the present way and humour of our gardening in England; which seem to have grown into such vogue, and to have been so mightily improved in three or four and twenty years of his Majesty's reign, that perhaps few countries are before us, either in the elegance of our gardens, or in the number of our plants; and, I believe, none equal us in the variety of fruits which may be justly called good; and from the earliest cherry and strawberry, to the last apples and pears, may furnish every day of the circling year. For the taste and perfection of what we esteem the best, I may truly say, that the French, who have eaten my peaches and grapes at Sheen, in no very ill year, have generally concluded, that the last are as good as any they have eaten in France, on this side Fontainebleau; and the first as good as any they have eaten in Gascony; I mean those which come from the stone, and are properly called peaches, not those which are hard, and are termed pavies; for these cannot grow in too warm a climate, nor ever be good in a cold; and are better at Madrid, than in Gascony itself. Italians have agreed, my white figs to be as good as any of that sort in Italy, which is the earlier kind of white fig there; for in the latter kind, and the blue, we cannot come near the warm climates, no more than in the Fontignac or Muscat grape.

My orange-trees are as large as any I saw when I was young in France, except those of Fontainebleau, or what I have seen since in the Low-Countries, except some very old ones of the Prince of Orange's; as laden with 'flowers as any can well be, as full of fruit as I suffer or desire them: and as well tasted as are commonly brought over, except the best sorts of Seville and Portugal. And thus much I could not but say in defence of our climate, which is so much and so generally decried abroad, by those who never saw it; or, if they have been here, have yet perhaps seen no more of it, than what belongs to inns, or to taverns and ordinaries; who accuse our country for their own defaults, and speak ill, not only of our gardens and houses, but of our humours, our breeding, our customs and manners of life, by what they have observed of the meaner and baser sort of mankind, and of company among us, because they wanted themselves, perhaps, either fortune or birth, either quality or merit, to introduce them among the good.

I must needs add one thing more in favour of our climate, which I heard the King say, and I thought new and right, and truly like a King of England, that loved and esteemed his own country: it was in reply to some of the company that were reviling our climate, and extolling those of Italy and Spain, or at least of France: he said, he thought that was the best climate, where he could be abroad in the air with pleasure, or at least without trouble or inconvenience, the most days of the year, and the most hours of the day; and this, he thought, he could be in England, more than in any country he knew of in Europe. And I believe it is true, not only of the hot and the cold, but even among our neighbours in France, and the Low-Countries themselves; where the heats or the colds, and changes of seasons, are less treatable than they are with us.

The truth is, our climate wants no heat to produce excellent fruits; and the default of it is only the short season of our heats or summers, by which many of the latter are left behind, and imperfect with us. But all such as are ripe before the end of August, are, for aught I know, as good with us as any where else. This makes me esteem the true region of gardens in England, to be the compass of ten miles about London; where the accidental warmth of air, from the fires and steams of so vast a town, makes fruits, as well as corn, a great deal forwarder than in Hampshire or Wiltshire, though more southward by a full degree.

There are, besides the temper of our climate, two things particular to us, that contribute much to the beauty and elegance of our gardens, which are the gravel of our walks, and the fineness and almost perpetual greenness of our turf. The first is not known anywhere else, which leaves all their dry walks, in other countries, very unpleasant and uneasy. The other cannot be found in France or in Holland as we have it, the soil not admitting that fineness of blade in Holland, nor the sun that greenness in France, during most of the summer; nor indeed is it to be found but in the finest of our soils.

Whoever begins a garden, ought in the first place and above all to consider the soil, upon which the taste of not only his fruits, but his legumes, and even herbs and sail ads, will wholly depend; and the default of soil is without remedy: for, although all borders of fruit may be made with what earth you please (if you will be at the charge), yet it must be renewed in two or three years, or it runs into the nature of the ground where it is brought. Old trees, spread their roots further than any body's care extends, or the forms of the garden will allow; and, after all, where the soil about you is ill, the air is so too in a degree, and has influence upon the taste of fruit. What Horace says of the productions of kitchen-gardens, under the name of caulis, is true of all the best sorts of fruits, and may determine the choice of soil for all gardens.

> Caule suburbano, qui siccis crevit in agris,
> Dulcior; irriguis nihil est elutius hortis.

> *Plants from dry fields those of the town excel;*
> *Nothing more tasteless is than watered grounds.*

Any man had better throw away his care and his money upon any thing else, than upon a garden in wet or moist ground. Peaches and grapes will have no taste but upon a sand or gravel; but the richer these are, the better; and neither salads, peas, or beans, have at all the taste upon a clay or rich earth, as they have upon either of the others, though the size and colour of fruits and plants may, perhaps, be more upon the worse soils.

Next to your choice of soil, is to suit your plants to your ground, since of this every one is not master; though perhaps Varro's judgment, upon this case, is the wisest and the best; for to one that asked him what he should do if his father or ancestors had left him a seat in an ill air, or upon an ill soil?

he answered, "Why sell it, and buy another in good." "But what if I cannot get half the worth?" "Why, then take a quarter; but however sell it for any thing, rather than live upon it."

Of all sorts of soil, the best is that upon a sandy gravel, or a rosiny sand; whoever lies upon either of these may run boldly into all the best sort of peaches and grapes, how shallow so ever the turf be upon them; and whatever other tree will thrive in these soils, the fruits shall be of a much finer taste than any other: a richer soil will do well enough for apricots, plums, pears, or figs; but still the more of the sand in your earth the better, and the worse the more of the clay, which is proper for oaks, and no other tree that I know of.

Fruits should be suited to the climate among us, as well as the soil; for there are degrees of one and the other in England, where it is to little purpose to plant any of the best fruits, as peaches or grapes, hardly I doubt beyond Northamptonshire, at the furthest northwards; and I thought it very prudent in a Gentleman of my friends in Staffordshire, who is a great lover of his garden, to pretend no higher, though his soil be good enough, than to the perfection of plums; and in these (by bestowing south walls upon them) he has very well succeeded, which he could never have done in attempts upon peaches and grapes; and a good plum is certainly better than an ill peach.

When I was at Cosevelt, with that Bishop of Munster that made so much noise in his time, I observed no other trees but cherries in a great garden he had made. He told me the reason was, because he found no other fruit would ripen well in that climate, or upon that soil; and therefore, instead of being curious in others, he had only been so in the sorts of that, whereof he had so many, as never to be without them from May to the end of September.

As to the size of a garden, which will perhaps, in time, grow extravagant among us, I think from four or five to seven or eight acres is as much as any Gentleman need design, and will furnish as much of all that is expected from it, as any Nobleman will have occasion to use in his family.

In every garden, four things are necessary to be provided for, flowers, fruit, shade, and water; and whoever lays out a garden, without all these, must not pretend it in any perfection: it ought to lie to the best parts of the house, or to those of the master's commonest use, so as to be but like one of the rooms out of which you step into another. The part of your garden next to your house (besides the walks that go round it) should be a parterre for flowers, or grass-plots bordered with flowers; or if, according to the newest mode, it be cast all into grass-plots and gravel walks, the dryness of these should be relieved with fountains, and the plainness of those with statues; otherwise, if large, they have an ill effect upon the eye. However, the part next to the house should be open, and no other fruit but upon the walls. If this take up one half of the garden, the other should be fruit-trees, unless some grove for shade lie in the middle. If it take up a third part only, then the next third may be dwarf-trees, and the last standard-fruit; or else, the second part fruit-trees, and the third all sorts of winter greens, which provide for all seasons of the year.

I will not enter upon any account of flowers, having only pleased myself with seeing or smelling them, and not troubled myself with the care, which is more the ladies' part than the men's; but the success is wholly in the gardener. For fruit, the best we have in England, or, I believe, can ever hope for, are, of peaches, the white and red maudlin, the minion, the chevereuse, the ramboullet, the musk, the admirable, which is late; all the rest are either varied by names, or not to be named with these, nor worth troubling a garden, in my opinion. Of the pavies, or hard peaches, I know none good here but the Newington, nor will that easily hang till it is full ripe. The forward peaches are to be esteemed only because they are early, but should find room in a good garden, at least the white and brown nutmeg, the Persian, and the violet musk. The only good nectarins, are the murry and the French; of these there are two sorts, one very round, and the other something long, but the round is the best: of the murry there are several sorts, but, being all hard, they are seldom well ripened with us.

Of grapes, the best are the chasselas, which is the better sort of our white muscadine (as the usual name was about Sheen); it is called the pearl-grape, and ripens well enough in common years, but not so well as the common black, or currand, which is something a worse grape. The parsley is good, and proper enough to our climate; but all white frontiniacs are difficult, and seldom ripe, unless in extraordinary summers.

I have had the honour of bringing over four sorts into England; the arboyse, from the Franche Compté, which is a small white grape, or rather runs into some small and some great upon the same bunch; it agrees well with our climate, but is very choice in soil, and must have a sharp gravel; it is the most delicious of all grapes that are not muscat. The Burgundy, which is a grizelin or pale red, and of all others is surest to ripen in our climate, so that I have never known them to fail one summer these fifteen years, when all others have; and have had it very good upon an east wall. A black muscat, which is called the dowager, and ripens as well as the common white grape. And the fourth is the grizelin frontignac, being of that colour, and the highest of that taste, and the noblest of all grapes I ever ate in England; but requires the hottest wall and the sharpest gravel; and must be favoured by the summer too, to be very good. All these are, I suppose, by this time, pretty common among some gardeners in my neighbourhood, as well as several persons of quality; for I have ever thought all things of this kind, the commoner they are made, the better.

Of figs there are among us the white, the blue, and the tawny: the last is very small, bears ill, and I think but a bauble. Of the blue there are two or three sorts, but little different, one something longer than the other; but that kind which smells most is ever the best. Of the white I know but two sorts, and both excellent, one ripe in the beginning of July, the other in the end of September, and is yellower than the first; but this is hard to be found among us, and difficult to raise, though an excellent fruit.

Of apricots, the best are the common old sort, and the largest masculine; of which this last is much improved by budding upon a peach stock. I esteem none of this fruit but the Brussels apricot, which grows a standard, and is one of the best fruits we have; and which I first brought over among us.

The number of good pears, especially summer, is very great, but the best are the blanquet, robin, rousselet, rosati, sans, pepin, jargonel. Of the autumn, the buree, the vertelongue, and the bergamot. Of the winter, the vergoluz, chasseray, St. Michael, St. Germain, and ambret. I esteem the bon-cretien with us good for nothing but to bake.

Of plums, the best are St. Julian, St. Catherine, white and blue pedrigon, queen-mother, Sheen plum, and cheston.

Beyond the sorts I have named, none I think need trouble himself, but multiply these rather than make room for more kinds; and I am content to leave this register, having been so often desired it by my friends, upon their designs of gardening.

I need say nothing of apples, being so well known among us; but the best of our climate, and I believe of all others, is the golden pippin; and for all sorts of uses: the next is the Kentish pippin; but these I think are as far from their perfection with us as grapes, and yield to those of Normandy, as these to those in Anjou, and even these to those in Gascony. In other fruits the defect of sun is in a great measure supplied by the advantage of walls.

The next care to that of suiting trees with the soil, is that of suiting fruits to the position of walls: grapes, peaches, and winter-pears, to be good, must be planted upon full south, or south-east; figs are -best upon south-east, but will do well upon east and south-west: the west are proper for cherries, plums, or apricots; but all of them are improved by a south wall both as to early and taste: north, northwest, or north-east, deserve nothing but greens: these should be divided by woodbines or jessamines between every green, and the other walls by a vine between every fruit-tree; the best sorts upon the south walls, the common white and black upon east and west, because the other trees. being many of them (especially peaches) very transitory; some apt to die with hard winters, others to be cut down and make room for new fruits: without this method the walls are left for several years unfurnished; whereas the vines on each side cover the void space in one summer, and when the other trees are grown, make only a pillar between them of two or three foot broad.

Whoever would have the best fruits, in the most perfection our climate will allow, should not only take care of giving them as much sun, but also as much air as he can; no tree, unless dwarf, should be suffered to grow within forty foot of your best walls, but the farther they lie open is still the better. Of all others, this care is most necessary in vines, which are observed abroad to make the best wines, where they lie upon sides of hills, and so most exposed to the air and the winds. The way of pruning them too is best learned from the vineyards, where you see nothing in winter, but what looks like a dead stump; and upon our walls they should be left but like a ragged staff, not above two or three eyes at most upon the bearing branches; and the lower the vine and fewer the branches, the grapes will be still the better.

The best figure of a garden is either a square or an oblong, and either upon a flat or a descent; they have all their beauties, but the best I esteem an oblong upon a descent. The beauty, the air, the view makes amends for the expense, which is very great in finishing and supporting the terrace-walks, in leveling the parterres, and in the stone stairs that are necessary from one to the other.

The perfectest figure of a garden I ever saw, either at home or abroad, was that of Moor-Park in Hertfordshire, when I knew it about thirty years ago. It was made by the Countess of Bedford, esteemed among the greatest wits of her time, and celebrated by Doctor Donne; and with very great care, excellent contrivance, and much cost; but greater sums may be thrown away without effect or honour, if there want sense in proportion to money, or if nature be not followed; which I take to be the great rule in this, and perhaps in every thing else, as far as the conduct not only of our lives, but our governments. And whether the greatest of mortal men should attempt the forcing of nature, may best be judged by observing how seldom God Almighty does it himself, by so few true and undisputed miracles as we see or hear of in the world. For my own part, know not three wiser precepts for the conduct either of Princes or private men, than

...*Servare modum, finernque tueri,*
Naturarnque sequi.

Because I take the garden I have named to have been in all kinds the most beautiful and perfect, at least in the figure and disposition, that I have ever seen, I will describe it for a model to those that meet with such a situation, and are above the regards of common expense. It lies on the side of a hill (upon which the house stands) but not very steep. The length of the house, where the best rooms and of most use or pleasure are, lies upon the breadth of the garden, the great parlour opens into the middle of a terraced gravel-walk that lies even with it, and which may be, as I remember, about three hundred paces long, and broad in proportion; the border set with standard laurels, and at large distances, which have the beauty of orange-trees, out of flower and fruit: from this walk are three descents by many stone steps, in the middle and at each end, into a very large parterre. This is divided into quarters by gravel walks, and adorned with two fountains and eight statues in the several quarters; at the end of the terrace-walk are two summer-houses, and the sides of the parterre are ranged with two large cloisters, open to the garden, upon arches of stone, and ending with two other summer-houses even with the cloisters, which are paved with stone, and designed for walks of shade, there being none other in the whole parterre. Over these two cloisters are two terraces covered with lead, and fenced with balusters; and the passage into these airy walks is out of the two summer-houses, at the end of the first terrace-walk. The cloister facing the south is covered with vines, and would have been proper for an orange-house, and the other for myrtles, or other more common greens; and had, I doubt not, been cast for that purpose, if this piece of gardening had been then in as much vogue as it is now.

From the middle of the parterre is a descent by many steps flying on each side 'of a grotto that lies between them (covered with lead, and flat) into the lower garden, which is all fruit-trees, ranged about the several quarters of a wilderness which is very shady; the walks here are all green, the grotto embellished with figures of shell-rock-work, fountains, and water-works. If the hill had not ended with the lower garden, and the wall were not bounded by a common way that goes through the park, they might have added a third quarter of all greens; but this want is supplied by a garden on the other side the house, which is all of that sort, very wild, shady, and adorned with rough rock-work and fountains.

This was Moor-Park when I was acquainted with it, and the sweetest place, I think, that I have seen in my life, either before or since, at home or abroad; what it is now, I can give little account, having passed through several hands' that have made great changes in gardens as well as houses; but the remembrance of what it was is too pleasant ever to forget, and therefore I do not believe to have mistaken the figure of it, which may serve for a pattern to the best gardens of our manner, and that are most roper for our country and climate.

What I have said, of the best forms of gardens, is meant only of such as are in some sort regular; for there may be other forms wholly irregular that may, for aught I know, have more beauty than any of the others; but they must owe it to some extraordinary dispositions of nature in the seat, or some great race of fancy or judgment in the contrivance, which may reduce many disagreeing parts into some figure, which shall yet, upon the whole, be very agreeable. Something of this I have seen in some places, but heard more of it from others who have lived much among the Chinese; a people, whose way of thinking seems to lie as wide of ours in Europe, as their country does. Among us, the beauty of building and planting is placed chiefly in some certain proportions, symmetries, or uniformities; our walks and our trees ranged so as to answer one another, and at exact distances. The Chinese scorn this way of planting, and say, a boy, that can tell an hundred, may plant walks of trees in straight lines, and over-against one another, and to what length and extent he pleases. But their greatest reach of imagination is employed in contriving figures, where the beauty shall be great, and strike the eye, but without any order or disposition of parts that shall be commonly or easily observed: and, though we have hardly any notion of this sort of beauty, yet they have a particular word to express it, and, where they find it hit their eye at first sight, they say the sharawadgi is fine or is admirable, or any such expression of esteem. And whoever observes the work upon the best India gowns, or the painting upon their best screens or porcelains, will find their beauty is all of this kind (that is) without order. But I should hardly advise any of these attempts in the figure of gardens among us; they are adventures of too hard achievement for any common hands; and, though there may be more honour if they succeed well, yet there is more dishonour if they fail, and it is twenty to one they will; whereas, in regular figures, it is hard to make any great and remarkable faults.

The picture I have met with in some relations of a garden made by a Dutch Governor of their colony, upon the cape de Bonne Esperance, is admirable, and described to be of an oblong figure, very large extent, and divided into four quarters, by long and cross walks, ranged with all sorts of orange-trees, lemons, limes, and citrons; each of these four quarters is planted with the trees, fruits, flowers, and plants that are native and proper to each of the four parts of the world; so as in this one inclosure are to be found the several gardens of Europe, Asia, Africa, and America. There could not be, in my mind, a greater thought of a gardener, nor a nobler idea of a garden, nor better suited or chosen for the climate, which is about thirty degrees, and may pass for the Hesperides of our age, whatever or where-ever the other was. Yet this is agreed by all to have been in the islands or continent upon the south-west of Africa: but what their forms or their fruits were, none, that I know, pretend to tell; nor whether their golden apples were for taste, or only for sight, as those of Montezuma were in Mexico, who had large trees, with stocks, branches, leaves, and fruits, all admirably composed and wrought of gold; but this was only stupendous in cost and art, and answers not at all, in my opinion, the delicious varieties of nature in other gardens.

What I have said of gardening is perhaps enough for any Gentleman to know, so as to make no great faults, nor be much imposed upon in the designs of that kind, which I think ought to be applauded, and encouraged in all countries; that and building being a sort of creation, that raise beautiful fabrics and figures out of nothing, that make the convenience and pleasure of all private habitations, that employ many hands, and circulate much money among the poorer sort and artisans, that are a public service to one's country, by the example as well as effect, which adorn the scene, improve the earth, and even the air itself in some degree. The rest that belongs to this subject must be a gardener's part; upon whose skill, diligence, and care, the beauty of the grounds and excellence of the fruits will much depend. Though if the soil and sorts be well chosen, well suited, and disposed to the walls, the ignorance or carelessness of the servants can hardly leave the master disappointed.

I will not enter further upon his trade, than by three short directions or advices: first, in all plantations, either for his master or himself, to draw his trees out of some nursery that is upon a leaner and lighter soil than his own where he removes them: without this care they will not thrive in several years, perhaps never; and must make way for new, which should be avoided all that can be; for life is too short and uncertain, to be renewing often your plantations. The walls of your garden, without their furniture, look as ill as those of your house; so that you cannot dig up your garden too often, nor too seldom cut them down.

The second is, in all trees you raise, to have some regard to the stock, as well as the graft or bud; for the first will have a share in giving taste and season to the fruits it produces, how little so ever it is usually observed by our gardeners. I have found grafts of the same tree, upon a bon-cretien stock bring chasseray pears that lasted till March, but with a rind green and rough: and others, upon a metre-john-stock, with a smooth and yellow skin„ which were rotten in November. 1 am apt to think, all the difference between the St. Michael and the ambrette pear (which has puzzled our gardeners) is only what comes from this variety of the stocks; and by this, perhaps, as well as by raising from stones and kernels, most of the new fruits are produced every age. So the grafting a crab upon a white thorn brings the lazarolli, a fruit esteemed at Rome, though I do not find it worth cultivating here; and I believe the cidrato (or hermaphrodite) came from budding a citron upon an orange. The best peaches are raised by buds of the best fruits upon stocks growing from stones of the best peaches; and so the best apples and pears, from the best kinds grafted upon stocks from kernels also of the best sorts, with respect to the season, as well as beauty and taste. And I believe so many excellent winter-pears, as have come into France since forty years, may have been -found out by grafting summer-pears of the finest taste and most water upon winter-stocks.

The third advice is, to take the greatest care and pains in preserving your trees from the worst disease, to which those of the best fruits are subject in the best soils, and upon the best walls. It is what has not been (that I know of) taken notice of with us, till I was forced to observe it by the experience of my gardens, though I have since met with it in books both ancient and modern. I found my vines, peaches, apricots, and plums upon my best south-walls, and sometimes upon my west, apt for several years to a soot or smuttiness upon their leaves first, and then upon their fruits, which were good for nothing the years they were so affected. My orange-trees were likewise subject to it, and never prospered while they were so: and I have known some collections quite destroyed by it. But I cannot say that ever I found either my figs or pears infected with it, nor any trees upon my eastwails, though I do not well conjecture at the reason. The rest were so spoiled with it, that I complained to several of the oldest and best gardeners of England, who knew nothing of it, but that they often fell into the same misfortune, and esteemed it some blight of the spring. I observed after some years, that the diseased trees had very frequent, upon their stocks and branches, a small insect of a dark-brown colour, figured like a shield, and about the size of a large wheat-corn; they stuck close to the bark, and in many places covered it, especially about the joints: in winter they are dry, and thin-shelled, but in spring they begin to grow soft, and to fill with moisture, and to throw a spawn like a black dust upon the stocks, as well as the leaves and fruits.

I met afterwards with the mention of this disease, as known among orange-trees, in a book written upon that subject in Holland, and since in Pausanias, as a thing so much taken notice of in Greece, that the author describes a certain sort of earth which cures pediculos vitis, or, the lice of the vine. This is of all others the most pestilent disease of the best fruit trees, and upon the very best soils of gravel and sand (especially where they are too hungry): and is so contagious, that it is propagated to new plants raised from old trees that are infected, and spreads to new ones that are planted near them which makes me imagine, that it lies in the root, and that the best cure were by application there. But I have tried all sorts of soil without effect, and can prescribe no other remedy, than to prune your trees as close as you can, especially the tainted wood, then to wash them very clean with a wet brush, so as not to leave one shell upon them that you can discern: and upon our oranges to pick off every one that you can find by turning every leaf, as well as brushing clean the stocks and branches. Without these cares and diligences, you had better root up any trees that are infected, renew all the mould in your borders or boxes, and plant new sound trees, rather than suffer the disappointments and vexation of your old ones.

I may perhaps be allowed to know something of this trade, since I have so long allowed myself to be good for nothing else, which few men will do, or enjoy their gardens, without often looking abroad to see how other matters play, what motions in the State, and what invitations they may hope for into other scenes.

For my own part, as the country life, and this part of it more particularly, were the inclination of my youth itself, so they are the pleasure of my age; and I can truly say, that, among many great employments that have fallen to my share, I have never asked or sought for any one of them, but often endeavoured to escape from them, into the ease and freedom of a private scene, where a man may go his own way and his own pace, in the common paths or circles of life.

> Inter cuncta leges et per cunctabere doctos
> Qua ratione queas traducere leniter ævum,
> Quid minuat curæ, quid te tibi reddet amicum,
> Quid pure tranquiliet, honos, an dulce lucellum,
> An secretum iter, et fallentis sernita vitæ.

> *But above all the learned read, and ask*
> *By what means you may gently pass your age,*
> *What lessons care, what makes thee thine own friend,*
> *What truly cares the mind; honour, or wealth,*
> *Or else a private path of stealing life.*

These are questions that a man ought at least to ask himself, whether he asks others or not, and to choose his course of life rather by his own humour and temper, than by common accidents, or advice of friends; at least if the Spanish proverb be true, that a fool knows more in his own house than a wise man in another's.

The measure of choosing well is, whether a man likes what he has chosen; which, I thank God, has befallen me; and though, among the follies of my life, building and planting have not been the least, and have cost me more than I have the confidence to own; yet they have been fully recompensed by the sweetness and satisfaction of this retreat, where, since my resolution taken of never entering again into any public employments, I have passed five years without ever going once to town, though I am almost in sight of it, and have a house there always ready to receive me. Nor has this been any sort of affectation, as some have thought it, but a mere want of desire or humour to make so small a remove; for when I am in this corner, I can truly say with Horace,

> Me quoties reficit gelidus Digentia rivus,
> Quid sentire putas, quid credis, amice, precari?
> Sit mihi, quod nunc est, etiam minus, ut mihi vivam
> Quod superest ævi, si quid superesse volunt Di.
> Sit bona librorum, et provisæ frugis in annum
> Copia, ne fluitem dubiæ spe pendulus horæ,

Hoc satis est orasse Jovern, qui donat et aufert.

Me when the cold Digentian stream revives,
What does my friend believe I think or ask?
Let me yet less possess, so I may live,
Whate'er of life remains, unto myself.
May I have books enough, and one year's store,
Not to depend upon each doubtful hour;
This is enough of mighty Jove to pray,
Who, as he pleases, gives and takes away.

That which makes the cares of gardening more necessary, or at least more excusable, is, that all men eat fruit that can get it; so as the choice is only, whether one will eat good or ill; and between these the difference is not greater in point of taste and delicacy, than it is of health: for the first I will only say, that whoever has used to eat good will do very great penance when lie comes to ill: and for the other, I think nothing is more evident, than as ill or unripe fruit is extremely unwholesome, and causes so many untimely deaths, or so much sickness about autumn, in all great cities where it is greedily sold as well as eaten; so no, part of diet, in any season, is so healthful, so natural, and so agreeable to the stomach, as good and well-ripened fruits; for this I make the measure of their being good: and, let the kinds be what they will, if they will not ripen perfectly in our climate, they are better never planted, or never eaten. I can say it for myself at least, and all my friends, that the season of summer fruits is ever the season of health with us, which I reckon from the beginning of June to the end of September: and for all sicknesses of the stomach (from which most others are judged to proceed), I do not think any that are, like me, the most subject to them, shall complain, whenever they eat thirty or forty cherries before meals, or the like proportion of strawberries, white figs, soft peaches, or grapes perfectly ripe. But these after Michaelmas I do not think wholesome with us, unless attended by some fit of hot and dry weather; more than is usual after that season: when the frosts or the rain hath taken them, they grow dangerous, and nothing but the autumn and winter-pears are to be reckoned in season, besides apples, which, with cherries, are of all others the most innocent food, and perhaps the best physic. Now whoever will be sure to eat good fruit, must do it out of a garden of his own; for, besides the choice so necessary in the sorts, the soil, and so many other circumstances that go to compose a good garden, or produce good fruits, there is something very nice in gathering them, and choosing the best, even from the same tree. The best sorts of all among us, which I esteem the white figs and the soft peaches, will not carry without suffering. The best fruit that is bought, has no more of the Master's care, than how to raise the greatest gains; his business is to have as much fruit as he can upon a few trees; whereas the way to have it excellent is to have but little upon many trees. So that for all things out of a garden, either of salads or fruits, a poor man will eat better, that has one of his own, than a rich man that has none. And this is all I think of necessary and useful to be known upon this subject.

STOICS VS EPICUREANS

by

Robert Drew Hicks

Epicurus was an Athenian citizen and was known as the Gargettian sage. The few simple facts and dates of his uneventful career as a teacher and writer are particularly well established.

He was born in the year 341 BC, in the lunar month Gamelion, the tenth day of which was kept in his honour. Probably it was three days earlier, on the seventh of the month, that he first saw the light. The Attic civil year began, theoretically, with the summer solstice, and Gamelion, the seventh month, would naturally fall after the winter solstice, in our January. Epicurus was born in Samos, whither his father, Neocles, had gone out from Athens to settle as a colonist. His father bore the same name as the father of Themistocles, a fact which led Menander to compose an epigram comparing the achievements of their respective sons. The son of one Neocles had freed his country from slavery; Epicurus, the son of the other, from the worse bondage of superstitious folly. Many philosophers and founders of religion have aimed at emancipation, deliverance—in a word, freedom. Seldom has the world seen one who went to the same lengths in this direction as Epicurus.

In the extreme individualism of his ethical no less than of his physical doctrine, and his refusal to base the cooperation of his units on anything else but voluntary consent, he would seem to anticipate the principles professed by modern anarchists, when these latter pride themselves on their distinction from collectivist socialists. The family of Neocles was never well-to-do; his occupation was that of an elementary schoolmaster. The gossip of a later day affirmed that, when a boy, the son helped the father in his duties and prepared ink for the pupils. From the same perhaps untrustworthy source we learn that his mother, Chaerestrata, performed certain dubious rites, half religious, half magical, intended to propitiate the deities and avert disease and misfortune by charms and incantations. At these rites, celebrated at the cottages of her neighbours, it was the boy's part to assist his mother by reading the incantations. If this story is true, the employment must have been singularly uncongenial to one who all his life long hated falsehood, deceit, and superstition.

In 323 B. C. he proceeded to Athens to be enrolled as a citizen and to undergo that training in military duties which the constitution assigned to youths between the ages of eighteen and twenty. In this service he made the acquaintance of the poet Menander, who, born in the same year as himself, became his friend and admirer. The spirit of the Epicurean philosophy may be said to pervade the works of this great dramatist of the New Comedy. About this time Xenocrates was teaching in the Academy and Theophrastus in the Lyceum; Aristotle had retired to Chalcis, where in the next year he died.

But events marched apace. The death of Alexander was followed by the unfortunate Lamian war, and in 322 BC Perdiccas expelled the Athenian colonists from their holdings in Samos. Epicurus joined his father, now more than ever a broken man, at Colophon. Of the next dozen years we have little information, but we find him in 310 BC, in his thirty-second year, at Mitylene, where he came forward as a teacher of philosophy. Even as a schoolboy he is said to have given proofs of an inquiring mind. When reading in Hesiod how all things had their origin in Chaos, he puzzled the master by asking, "Whence came Chaos?" In after days he boasted that he had been self-taught. His writings and conversation were enlivened with scoffs, gibes, and sneers at all other schools of so-called wisdom, a precedent of liberty which in the later Epicureans ran to unbounded licence. "The followers of Plato he used to call 'the flatterers of Dionysius' and Plato himself 'the man of gold' and Aristotle 'a profligate who, after squandering his patrimony, joined the army and sold drugs.'

Protagoras he called 'the porter' and 'the copyist of Democritus' and said that 'he taught grammar in villages.' Heraclitus he called 'the confusion-maker' and Democritus 'the babbler.' It is quite certain, however, that he studied the system of Democritus with unusual care, and there is no ground for rejecting the story that he was for some time a pupil of the Democritean Nausiphanes of Teos, whom he sarcastically styled a "mollusc," to express contempt for his want of backbone. At Mitylene, Epicurus gained over Hermarchus, afterward his successor, and at Lampsacus, on the Hellespont, he made the most enduring friendships of his life. Here he became acquainted with Idomeneus and Leonteus, men of great influence in that town, who were his patrons and lifelong correspondents and, with Metrodorus and Polyaenus, the ablest among his disciples.

Though his teaching in Asia had been eminently successful, he must have felt the attraction of the home of philosophy. Athens was still the centre of intellectual activity and social intercourse for the ancient world, as Paris for the modern world. Here was the most refined society, the greatest possibilities for the aesthetic enjoyment of life. Accordingly, about 306 B C, Epicurus removed with his pupils to Athens, which he never afterward quitted except for short visits to Asia Minor. Of one such visit we have a charming memorial, unearthed, like so much besides of Epicurean literature, from beneath the ashes of Herculaneum. It is a letter written by the master to a little child, possibly the daughter of Metrodorus, of whom more hereafter. We may premise that Themista was the wife of Leonteus, of Lampsacus, and Matron obviously a domestic in charge of the child.

"We came to Lampsacus, Pythocles, Hermarchus, Ctesippus, and myself, and we are quite well. We found there Themista and our other friends, and they are quite well. I hope you are well, too, and your mamma, and that you obey her and papa and Matron in

everything, as you used to do. For you know quite well, my pet, that I and all the others love you very much, because you are obedient to them in everything."

For more than thirty years, Epicurus resided continuously in Athens. He founded a school by the simple expedient of purchasing for eighty minae a house and garden in the quarter known as Melite, where his friends and disciples might have easy access to him. Hence his followers were often known as the Garden Philosophers. The little society was united together by no other tie than that of a common affection to their teacher. Friends and admirers quickly gathered round him, among them his three brothers, who almost worshipped him. Nor were women excluded, and even slaves were numbered among his pupils. Though leading the life of a recluse and holding aloof from political parties, he enjoyed intercourse with the best minds of the day.

These years were not spent idly. Like Democritus, Plato, and Aristotle before him, he was an indefatigable and voluminous author. He wrote some three hundred separate treatises, being surpassed in the wealth of his philosophic output by Chrysippus alone among the ancients. At the same time he kept up a vigorous correspondence with friends at a distance who shared his aims. As we know from Herculaneum, selections were published from the letters of Epicurus, Metrodorus, Polyaenus, Hermarchus, and their acquaintance. His great work, *On Nature*, in thirty-seven books or rolls, occupied him for several years. It had reached Book XV in 300-299 BC, while Book XXVIII was finished in 296-5 BC. In the production of a quantity of literature so prodigious, something had to be sacrificed. Ancient critics complain sadly that the qualities of elegance and lucid arrangement so conspicuous in his three great predecessors above mentioned were totally wanting in him. Yet even Cicero admits that, crude and commonplace as his ideas were, the meaning was always plain; and probably this was all their author cared for. He was too much in earnest to cultivate the graces of style, and he looked down with contempt upon the accomplishments of an ordinary Athenian education, in which high-flown rhetoric and hair-splitting logic played a leading part.

The last years of Epicurus were clouded. His favourite disciple, Metrodorus, died in 277 BC, at the age of fifty-three, and another able pupil, Polyaenus, predeceased him. The former left a son and daughter, the latter a son, and Epicurus must have deemed himself in a special sense responsible for the education and future welfare of these orphans, to whom he was probably guardian. By his will his executors are charged to provide for their maintenance in consultation with Hermarchus, and in due course to provide a dowry for the girl on her marriage. Epicurus had always been in delicate health. In his boyhood, if we may trust Suidas, he had to be lifted down from his chair, was bleary-eyed, and of so sensitive a skin that he could not bear any clothing heavier than a tunic. He was long subject to gout and dropsy, for many years he was unable to walk, and finally renal calculus carried him off in 270 BC, in his seventy-second year. These painful disorders he endured with the utmost fortitude. Scraps have come down to us from two letters written by him in his last illness, the one to his successor Hermarchus, the other to Idomeneus, of Lampsacus. The latter runs as follows:

"On this last, yet blessed, day of my life, I write to you. Pains and tortures of body I have to the full, but there is set over against these the joy of my heart at the memory of our happy conversations in the past. Do you, if you would be worthy of your devotion to me and philosophy, take care of the children of Metrodorus."

To the members of his little society he seems to have been at all times extremely generous in contributions from his own means, though he scouted the notion of a common purse, as savouring too much of mistrust and suspicion between friends. It appears from his letters that the aged philosopher had accepted annual contributions sent for his support from his wealthy friends in Lampsacus and possibly from other quarters. Here we are reminded of the pecuniary help which Auguste Comte received from his friends and admirers. In the character of Epicurus the conspicuous traits are sympathy, generosity, and sweet reasonableness. No man was ever more vilely slandered or more cruelly misunderstood, but the severest critics of his teaching, Cicero, Seneca, Plutarch, in the most honourable way dissociate themselves entirely from the aspersions cast upon his personal character.

"Of his unequalled consideration toward all there is ample testimony," says an ancient writer. "I appeal to his native country, which honoured him with a statue, to the great number of his friends, who could be counted by whole cities, to the followers attracted and held fast by the siren-charms of his doctrines, to the long continuance and perpetuation of his school in strong contrast to the checkered fortunes of its rivals, to his gratitude to his parents, his generosity to his brothers, his gentleness to his slaves, as attested by his will and also by the fact that slaves were among his pupils—in fact, to his universal kindness to all men."

No less positive is the evidence as to his frugality and abstemious mode of life. "Send me some cheese of Cythnos," he writes to a friend, "that I may be able to fare sumptuously when I like." He was usually contented with mere bread and water. The school made experiments in frugal living. In a letter to Polyaenus the master tells him that, while Metrodorus had only reduced his expenses to four pence a day, he himself had contrived to subsist on less. Whatever else he was, such a man was at all events no epicure. At the same time such abstemiousness, if practised universally, would not be without its dangers. It has often happened that to raise the standard of comfort and so to create wants is the first step in social advance. What satisfied Epicurus would fail to satisfy all men, or even the average man. He must be credited with a certain lack of imagination if he did not perceive this. Similarly with another characteristic trait, his quietism. The love of adventure, the thirst for honour, the cravings of ambition found no response in his breast; but neither would his own love of study, meditation, and retirement ever appeal to any but a small section of men, invalids, the elderly or the disillusioned. One detail serves to illustrate the practical turn of his mind.

He foresaw that many would be curious to learn the main outlines of his system without possessing the leisure, inclination, or ability to master its details. Instead of repelling the advances of such honest folk, as Plato had done when he inscribed over the portals of the Academy "Let no one enter here who is ignorant of geometry," Epicurus is careful, even anxious, to cater for their peculiar needs. He brought out an epitome of his doctrines, itself a work of considerable length, known as the "larger" epitome. As scholars now recognise, this was the work which the poet Lucretius made the basis of his poem in six books and over seven thousand lines. But this was not enough. A shorter summary was prepared and possibly the extant epistles to Herodotus and Menoeceus formed part of this. They may, however, be distinct compilations. Lastly, either the master himself or some authorities of the school picked out a selection of golden sentences or maxims, articles of belief, which the members of the society were exhorted to commit to memory, to recite, and make the subject of meditation. The Epicurean literature is full of allusions to them. Not only are they preserved in the pages of Diogenes Laertius, but they were actually discovered a few years ago inscribed on the walls of the market-place of (Enoanda, an obscure Pisidian town in the heart of Asia Minor, where they might best catch the eye alike of the rustic from the country and of the cultured traveller.

Thus, though the three hundred treatises of the master are either wholly lost or survive only in the buried treasures of Herculaneum, yet, as a result of these precautions, we are better informed upon most points of Epicurean doctrine than upon the system of any ancient philosopher with the sole exception of Plato and Plotinus. But in fact the subsequent history of the school is in itself a sufficient proof of its founder's talent for organisation. Elsewhere we find contending influences at work, perpetual change of view and shifting of opinion, particularly when a succession of teachers interpreted, enlarged, or violently combated the doctrines bequeathed to them. The Academy was not content to preserve the tenets of Plato unaltered, but passed by violent reactions from dogmatism to scepticism, and probabilism, and back to dogmatism again. In the

Epicurean society there was nothing comparable to this. From first to last its members were united by a common reverence for their founder, and hardly a trace is to be discovered of any serious dissent. It is their constant boast that they frequently won adherents from the rival schools, but that no Epicurean had gone over to another school. To this rule there are only one or two exceptions, the most conspicuous being Timocrates, who seems, on personal grounds, to have had a feud with his brother Metrodorus. Numenius compared the school of Epicurus to a republic free from party strife, having only one mind, one opinion, in which an innovation would have been regarded as an impiety. When Lucretius speaks of himself as repeating oracles more holy, and far more certain than those of the Pythian prophetess, he merely voices the convictions of the whole brotherhood. Their reverence for the writings of their master is the counterpart of the attitude of evangelical Protestants toward the Bible.

It is now time to inquire into the nature of that teaching which met with such an enthusiastic reception and was greeted almost like a revelation. Philosophy was defined by Epicurus as "a daily business of speech and thought to secure a happy life." Here is struck the note of intense earnestness characteristic alike of Epicurus and his age. Philosophy is a practical concern; it deals with the health of the soul. It is a life and not merely a doctrine. It holds out the promise of well-being and happiness. This is the one thing needful. Literature, art, and the other embellishments of life are not indispensable. The wise man lives poems instead of making them.

"It need not trouble anyone," said Metrodorus, "if he had never read a line of Homer and did not know whether Hector was a Trojan or a Greek." Accordingly, as we have seen, Epicurus regarded with indifference the ordinary routine education of the day in grammar, rhetoric, dialectic, and music, and for mere erudition he had a hearty contempt. The only study absolutely necessary for a philosopher was the study of nature, or what we now call natural science, and this must be cultivated, not for its own sake, but merely as the indispensable means to a happy life. Unless and until we have learned the natural causes of phenomena, we are at the mercy of superstition, fears, and terrors.

We must defer to a subsequent chapter the consideration of the steps by which Epicurus was led to the conclusion that the external world is a vast machine built up by the concourse of atoms in motion without an architect or plan. Suppose, however, this conclusion firmly established; what has our philosopher to tell us respecting human life and action? In what consists the happiness which is our being's end and aim? This had, by the time of Epicurus, become the chief question of philosophy, and, strange as it may appear, the answer is no new doctrine, but one which had often been proposed and discussed in the ancient schools. He identifies happiness, at least nominally, with pleasure, and he means the pleasure of the agent. His is a system of Egoistic Hedonism. Verbally, then, he is in agreement with Aristippus, the founder of the Cyrenaics, with the Socrates of Plato's Protagoras, and with Eudoxus, whose doctrine of pleasure is criticised by Aristotle in the Nicomachean Ethics. The same doctrine is discussed in more than one of Plato's dialogues, sometimes apparently with approval, sometimes with disapproval. The historical Socrates never, so far as we know, reached a final definition of Good. He knew no good, he said, which was not good for somebody or something. His teaching would serve equally well as an introduction to Egoistic Hedonism, to Universal Hedonism, to Utilitarianism, or to Eudaemonism. The difficulty at once occurs; if pleasure and good are identical, why is it that some pleasures are approved as good and others condemned as evil? Why, on this hypothesis, should life ever present conflicting alternatives in which we are called upon to choose between doing what is good and doing what is pleasurable? Every hedonistic system must face this problem. Some progress had been made by Plato in the Protagoras. There his spokesman, Socrates, maintains that since every one desires what is best for himself, and since he further identifies good with pleasure, evil with pain, he avoids pleasure when it is the source of still greater pain, and only chooses pain when a greater amount of pleasure results from it.

In this Epicurus heartily concurred. He never recedes from the position that pleasure is always a good and pain always an evil, but it does not follow that pleasure is always to be chosen, pain to be shunned. For experience shows that certain pleasures are attended by painful consequences, certain pains by salutary results, and it is necessary to measure or weigh these after-effects one against the other before acting. "No one beholding evil chooses it, but, being enticed by it as by a bait, and believing it to contain more good than I evil, he is ensnared."

We now get a clearer notion of the end of action, which turns out to be the maximum of pleasure to the agent after subtraction of whatever pain is involved in securing the pleasure or directly attends upon it. At this point Epicurus parts company with Aristippus, whose crude presentation of hedonistic doctrine identified the end with the pleasure of the moment. So soon as conditions and consequences are taken into account, pleasure tends to become an ideal element capable of being realised in a series of actions, or in the whole of life, but not to be exhausted at any given point of the series. More important, however, for determining the exact significance of this conception is the incursion which Epicurus makes into the psychology of desire. Desire is prompted by want; unsatisfied want is painful. When we act in order to gratify our desires, we are seeking to remove the pain of want, but the cessation of the want brings a cessation of mental trouble or unrest, and this must carefully be distinguished from positive pleasure.

In this negative conception of happiness as freedom from pain, whether of body or mind, Epicurus must have been influenced by the ethical teaching of Democritus, who also made happiness in its essential nature consist in the cheerfulness and well-being, the right disposition, harmony, and unalterable peace of mind which enable a man to live a calm and steadfast life. Democritus also exalted mental above bodily pleasures and pains, and laid stress upon ignorance, fear, folly, and superstition as causes of those mental pains which tend most to disturb life. With Epicurus the great obstacle to happiness is neither pain nor poverty, nor the absence of the ordinary good things of life; it is rather whatever contributes to disturb our serenity and mental satisfaction, whatever causes fear, anxiety—in a word, mental trouble. A letter to Menoeceus sets forth the ethical doctrine of Epicurus in a convenient summary as follows:

"Let no one be slow to seek wisdom when he is young nor weary in the search thereof when he is grown old. For no age is too early or too late for the health of the soul. And to say that the season for philosophy has not yet come, or that it is passed and gone, is like saying that the season for happiness is not yet or that it is now no more. Therefore, both old and young ought to seek wisdom, that so a man as age comes over him may be young in good things, because of the grace of what has been, and while he is young may likewise be old, because he has no fear of the things which are to come. So we must exercise ourselves in the things which bring happiness, since, if that be present, we have everything and, if that be absent, all our actions are directed toward attaining it.

"Those things which without ceasing I have declared unto thee, those do and exercise thyself therein, holding them to be the elements of right life. First, believe that God is a being blessed and immortal, according to the notion of a God commonly held amongst men; and so believing, thou shalt not affirm of him aught that is contrary to immortality or that agrees not with blessedness, but shalt believe about him whatsoever may uphold both his blessedness and his immortality. For verily there are gods, and the knowledge of them is manifest; but they are not such as the multitude believe, seeing that men do not steadfastly maintain the notions they form respecting them. Not the man who denies the gods worshipped by the multitude, but he who affirms of the gods what the multitude believes about them, is truly impious. For the utterances of the multitude about the gods are not true preconceptions but false assumptions, according to which the greatest evils happen to the wicked and the greatest blessings happen to the good from the hand of the gods, seeing that they are always favourable to their own good qualities and take pleasure in men like unto themselves, but reject as alien whatever is not of their kind.

"Accustom thyself to believe that death is nothing to us, for good and evil imply sentience and death is the privation of all sentience; therefore, a right understanding that death is nothing to us makes enjoyable the mortality of life, not by adding to life an illimitable time, but by taking away the yearning after immortality. For life has no terrors for him who has thoroughly apprehended that there are no terrors for him in ceasing to live. Foolish, therefore, is the man who says that he fears death, not because it

will pain when it comes, but because it pains in the prospect. Whatsoever causes no annoyance when it is present causes only a groundless pain in the expectation. Death, therefore, the most awful of evils, is nothing to us, seeing that when we are, death is not come, and when death is come, we are not. It is nothing, then, either to the living or the dead, for with the living it is not and the dead exist no longer. But in the world, at one time men shun death as the greatest of all evils and at another time choose it as a respite from the evils in life. The wise man does not deprecate life nor does he fear the cessation of life. The thought of life is no offence to him nor is the cessation of life regarded as an evil. And even as men choose of good, not merely and simply the larger portion, but the more pleasant, so the wise seek to enjoy the time which is most pleasant and not merely that which is longest.

And he who admonishes the young to live well and the old to make a good end, speaks foolishly, not merely because of the desirableness of life, but because the same exercise at once teaches to live well and to die well. Much worse is he who says that it were good not to be born, but when once one is born to pass with all speed through the gates of Hades. If he, in truth, believes this, why does he not depart from life? It were easy for him to do so if once he is firmly convinced. If he speaks only in mockery his words are foolishness, for those who hear believe him not.

"And since pleasure is our first and native good, for that reason we do not choose every pleasure whatsoever, but oft times pass over many pleasures when a greater annoyance ensues from them. And oft times we consider pains superior to pleasures when submission to the pains for a long time brings us as its consequence a greater pleasure. While, therefore, all pleasure because it is naturally akin to us is good, not all pleasure is choice worthy, just as all pain is an evil but all pain is not to be shunned. It is, however, by measuring one against another, and by looking at the conveniences and inconveniences, that all these matters must be judged. Sometimes we treat the good as an evil and the evil, on the contrary, as a good. Again, we regard independence of outward things as a great good, not so as in all cases to use little, but so as to be contented with little if we have not much, being honestly persuaded that they have the sweetest enjoyment of luxury who stand least in need of it, and that whatever is natural is easily procured and only the vain and worthless hard to win. Plain fare is not more distasteful than a costly diet, when once the pain of want has been removed, while bread and water confer the highest possible pleasure when they are brought to hungry lips. To habituate one's self, therefore, to simple and inexpensive diet supplies all that is needful for health, and enables a man to meet the necessary requirements of life without shrinking, and it places us in a better condition when we approach at intervals a costly fare and renders us fearless of fortune.

"Wherefore, prudence is a more precious thing even than philosophy; from it spring all the other virtues, for it teaches that we cannot lead a life of pleasure which is not also a life of prudence, honour, and justice; nor lead a life of prudence, honour, and justice which is not also a life of pleasure. For the virtues have grown into one with a pleasant life, and a pleasant life is inseparable from them.

"Who, then, is superior, in thy judgment, to such a man? He holds a holy belief concerning the gods, and is altogether free from the fear of death. He has diligently *considered the end fixed by nature, and understands how easily the limit of good things can be procured and attained; that as for evils either their duration or their poignancy is but slight. Destiny, which some introduce as sovereign over all things, he laughs to scorn, affirming that certain things happen of necessity, others by chance, others through our own agency. For he sees that necessity destroys responsibility and that chance or fortune is inconstant; whereas our own actions are free, and it is to them that praise and blame naturally attach. It were better, indeed, to accept the legends of the gods than to bow beneath that yoke of destiny which the natural philosophers have imposed. The one holds out some faint hope that we may escape by honouring the gods, while the necessity of the philosophers is deaf to all supplications. Nor does such an one make chance a god, as the world in general does (for in the acts of God nothing is irregular), nor yet regard it as a vacillating cause, for he believes that chance dispenses to men no good or evil which can make life blessed though it furnishes means and occasions for great good and great evil. He believes that the misfortune of the wise is better than the prosperity of the fool. It is better, in short, that what is well judged in action should not owe its successful issue to the aid of chance.*

"Exercise thyself in these and kindred precepts day and night, both by thyself and with him who is like unto thee; then never, either in waking or in dream, wilt thou be disturbed but wilt live as a god amongst men. For by living in the midst of immortal blessings man loses all semblance of mortality."

In this document scientific ethics, as the term is now understood, is overlaid with a variety of other topics. The practical exordium, the dogmatic inculcation of moral precepts, the almost apostolic fervour and seriousness of tone find their nearest counterpart in the writings of religious teachers. We are reminded by turns of the Proverbs of Solomon and of the Epistles of St. Paul. The rejection of the popular religion and the denial of divine retribution are coupled with an emphatic affirmation of the existence of blessed and immortal gods. The instinctive fear of death is declared to be groundless; and here the writer enlarges upon a theme, first started by the sophist Prodicus, that death is nothing to us. Incidentally, the value of life is vindicated and the folly of pessimism exposed. The limitation of desire is seen to involve habituation to an almost ascetic bodily discipline, in order that the wise man may become self-sufficing, that is, independent of external things. Lastly, the freedom of human action is stoutly maintained in opposition to the doctrine of natural necessity first promulgated by the earlier Atomists Leucippus and Democritus, but at the time of Epicurus developed with the utmost rigour and consistency by the Stoics. On the main question there is no uncertainty. The pleasure of the agent is the foundation upon which Epicurus, like many after him, sought to construct a theory of morality which would explain scientifically the judgments of praise and blame passed by the ordinary man. All systems allow that there are self-regarding virtues and self-regarding duties, and when he has given his peculiar interpretation of pleasure, Epicurus has no great difficulty with these. But the case is different when we come to the social virtues and the duties which a man owes to his neighbour. In a system which makes self-love the centre of all virtues, and in which all duties must be self-regarding, if we accept, as he did, as a psychological truth that by instinct and nature all are led to pursue their own pleasure and avoid their own pain, how can any conduct savouring of dis interestedness find rational justification?

This was the great problem of the English and French moralists in that age of enlightenment, the eighteenth century. As then, so two thousand years before in Greece, extreme individualism was the order of the day. The primary fact is individual man as he is given by nature, and all that lies outside this, all that he has been made by institutions like the family and the state, all the relations that go beyond the individual are subsequent, secondary, derivative, requiring to be explained from him and to justify their validity to the reason. Take a concrete instance. Whence came the rules of justice? What makes actions just and how is my obedience to such rules, enjoined by Epicurus, an indispensable means to my own happiness? In short, how does disinterested conduct arise under a selfish system? The answer given to this question was often repeated later. It reappears in Hobbes and Rousseau. Before dealing with it, it is necessary to consider briefly the Epicurean conception of the growth of human civilisation from the earliest times.

Looking back at the past history of our planet, Epicurus derives all organisms, first plants, then animals, from mother earth. The species with which we are familiar are those which, being adapted, to their environment, prospered in the struggle for existence. They were preceded by many uncouth creatures and ill-contrived monsters, many races of living things, which have since died out from lack of food or some similar cause. Apart from the undeniable suggestion of one feature in the doctrine of evolution, the account of the origin of life is in its details wholly unscientific and even repulsive. But with surer insight primitive man is described as hardier than now: destitute of clothing and habitation, he lived a roving life like the beasts with whom he waged ceaseless warfare, haunting the woods and caves, insensible to hardship and privation. The first step in advance was the discovery of fire, due to accident. Afterward man learned to build huts and clothe himself with skins. Then the progress of culture is traced with the beginnings of domestic life through the discovery and transmission of useful arts. As comforts multiplied, the robust strength of the state of nature was gradually impaired by new disabilities, particularly susceptibility to disease. Language was not the outcome of convention, but took its rise from the cries which, like the noises of animals, are the instinctive expression of the feelings and emotions. Experience is the mother of invention and of all the arts. They are all due to the intelligent improvement of what was offered or suggested to man by natural occasions. None of the blessings of civilisation are due to the adventitious aid of divine agency. Man raised himself from a state of primitive rudeness and barbarism and gradually widened the gulf which separated him from other animals. From the stage when men and women lived on the wild fruits of the wood and drank the running stream, when their greatest fear was of the claws and fangs of savage beasts, to the stage when they formed civic communities and obeyed laws and submitted to the ameliorating influences of wedlock and friendship, all has been the work of man, utilising his natural endowments and natural circumstances. Religion has been rather a hindrance than a help in the course of civilisation. Next to the use of money, the baleful dread of supernatural powers has been the most fruitful source of evil.

In this historical survey, where shall we find the origin of law and justice? Epicurus was fully convinced that in the present state of society "the just man enjoys the greatest peace of mind, the unjust is full of the utmost disquietude"; and yet injustice is not in itself an evil, and in the state of nature man is predatory. The explanation tendered by Epicurus, as by Hobbes and Hume, is that of a compact which, once made, is ever afterward strictly observed. Yet it is not easy to discover why men should carry out a compact made in their natural, that is, predatory state. Why should the wise man observe it if he find secret injustice possible and convenient? Epicurus frankly admits that the only conceivable motive which can deter him is self-interest, the desire to avoid the painful anxieties that the perpetual dread of discovery would entail. Even if the compact could be evaded, prudential considerations forbid it, since the risk of detection is enormous and the mere possibility of discovery is an ever-present evil sufficient to poison all the goods of life. That such motives do not weigh with criminals is irrelevant; we are dealing now with the wise and prudent man.

"Natural justice is a contract of expediency, to prevent one man from harming or being harmed by another."

"Those animals which were incapable of making compacts with one another, to the end that they might neither inflict nor suffer harm, are without either justice or injustice. Similarly those tribes which either could not or would not form mutual covenants to the same end are in the like case."

Justice, then, is artificial, not natural. The view could not be more clearly expressed. This is just the position taken up by modern international law and just the attitude adopted by Christian nations; in historical times to those outside the pale of civilisation, who are assumed to have no rights. So, too, Hume holds that we should not, properly speaking, lie under any restraint of justice with regard to rational beings who were so much weaker than ourselves that we had no reason to fear their resentment. There never was an absolute justice," says one of the golden sentences, "but only a convention made in mutual inter course, in whatever region, from time to time, providing against the infliction or suffering of harm."

"Injustice is not in itself an evil, but only in its con sequence, viz., the terror which is excited by apprehension that those appointed to punish such offences will discover the injustice."

"It is impossible for the man who secretly violates any article of the social compact to feel confident that he will remain undiscovered, even if he has already escaped ten thousand times; for until his death he is never sure he will not be detected." It was easy for the Stoics to present this in an unfavourable light as does Epictetus when he says: "Not even does Epicurus himself declare, stealing to be bad, but he admits that detection is, and because it is impossible to have security against detection, for this reason he says, Do not steal."

"Taken generally," to quote another Epicurean saying, "justice is the same for all, but in its application to particular cases of territory or the like, it varies under different circumstances." In other words, justice is the foundation of all positive law, but the positive law of one state will differ from that of another.

"Whatever in conventional law is attested to be expedient in the needs arising out of mutual intercourse is by its nature just, whether the same for all or not, and in case any law is made and does not prove suitable to the expediency of mutual intercourse, then this is no longer just. And should the expediency which is expressed by the law vary and only for a time correspond with the notion of justice, nevertheless, for the time being, it was just, so long as we do not trouble ourselves about empty terms but look broadly at facts."

Thus a law judged to be inexpedient is no longer binding. The old sophistical quibble that no positive law can be unjust Epicurus, from his stand-point, can easily expose, and he is equally well able to meet the conservative dislike and dread of legislative innovation as something essentially immoral. "Where without any change in circumstances the conventional laws when judged by their consequences were seen not to correspond with the notion of justice, such laws were not really just; but wherever the laws have ceased to be expedient in consequence of a change in circumstances, in that case the laws were for the time being just, when they were expedient for the mutual intercourse of the citizens, and ceased subsequently to be just when they ceased to be expedient." "He who best insured safety from external foes made into one nation all the folk capable of uniting together, and those incapable of such union he assuredly did not treat as aliens; if there were any whom he could not even on such terms incorporate, he excluded them from intercourse whenever this suited with his own interests."

Thus civilisation is an advance upon the condition of primitive man; nor does Epicurus ever contemplate the possibility of undoing what has been done. Applying the standard of human good in his own conception of it as tranquil enjoyment, he pronounces government to be a benefit to the wise so far as it protects them from harm. But it does not therefore follow that they should themselves take part in political administration; they are only advised to do so in circumstances where it is necessary and so far as it is necessary for their own safety. Experience shows that as a rule the private citizen lives more calmly and safely than the public man. The burdens of office are a hinderance rather than an aid to the end of life.

"The Epicureans," says Plutarch, "shun politics as the ruin and confusion of true happiness."

An unobtrusive life is the ideal. To strive at power without attaining one's own personal security is an act of folly certain to entail lasting discomfort. Moreover, as Philodemus remarks, " If any one were to inquire which influence is of all others the most hostile to friendship and the most productive of enmity, he would find it to be politics, because of the envy of one's rivals and the ambition natural in those so engaged and the discord recurring when opposite notions are proposed."

Restless spirits, however, who cannot find satisfaction in retirement are permitted to face the risks of public activity. To all forms of government the Epicureans were theoretically indifferent, but the impossibility of pleasing the multitude and the necessity of strong control inclined them to favour the monarchical principle. Under all circumstances they recommended unconditional obedience. The traditions of the old republican life of petty Greek states demanded from the citizen far more than this—active co-operation, personal sacrifice, enthusiasm for the common cause.

Judged by this standard, the Epicurean would seem to take an unfair advantage of the state. He got all the protection it afforded and shirked as much as he could of its burdens. But, in reality, what he was prepared to contribute would fully satisfy the demands of the modern territorial state. To obey the laws, to pay taxes, to assist by an occasional vote in the formation of public opinion constitutes nowadays the whole of civic duty for the vast majority of citizens. Under existing conditions how can it be otherwise? For, in order to integrate, as it were, these multitudinous infinitesimals, organisation is required; but division of responsibility and specialisation of function circumscribe personal effort. Again, when the popular cry has been adequately voiced by press or platform and has taken effect through proportional representation or other constitutional means, the greatness of the results secured and the very perfection of the machinery for securing them leave less and less scope to private initiative.

The consistent application of individualist principles might enjoin a severance, so far as is possible, from the ties of the family no less than of the state, and the picture of the wise man represents him as shirking these responsibilities also. But such a counsel of perfection has regard to special circumstances, and in all fairness the actual conduct of the man should be allowed to correct the supposed tendency of his system. Now, by his kindness to his brothers, his gratitude to his parents, and his tender solicitude for his wards, Epicurus is proved to have cherished warm family affection himself. Nor is it reasonable to presume that the philosopher who deprecated suicide, except in extreme cases, and set the example by so cheerfully enduring severe physical pain, can ever seriously have intended race suicide. Political association, even if originally based upon a contract, has its present sanction in pains and penalties. It is at best a compromise, a pis aller of only relative and subsidiary value. Men submit to the compulsion and constraint which it entails for fear of finding something worse. The true form of association is that in which man surrenders nothing of his original freedom, and this Epicurus believed to be realised in friendship, upon which he set the highest value. The only duties that Epicurus recognises are those voluntarily accepted on reasonable grounds, not from natural instinct or compulsion of circumstances.

"No one," says Epicurus, "loves another except for his own interest."

"Human nature alone does not give natural affection for nothing, nor can it love without advantage to itself."

"Of all things which wisdom provides for the happiness of a lifetime, by far the greatest is the acquisition of friendship."

The terms in which it is extolled recall the eulogies lavished upon the Christian grace of charity or love. It was the signal characteristic of the little society in the founder's lifetime, and it continued a prominent trait of the sect to the latest times. Upon its own principles no ethical system which starts with self-love can recognise disinterested conduct. Nor did Epicurus anticipate Hume's discovery and call in sympathy as a necessary supplement to self-interest. He is, therefore, obliged to maintain that friendship, like justice, is based solely upon mutual utility. The services rendered have the same selfish motive which prompts the farmer to commit the seed to the soil in expectation of a future harvest. So alone the theory is consistent; friendship, like the cynic's gratitude, must needs be a lively sense of favours yet to come. There is, of course, a difficulty at the beginning. Someone must make the start. "Neither those who are over-ready nor those who are too slow to enter into friendships are to be approved; one must even run some risk in order to make friends."

"To do good," says Epicurus, "is not only more noble, but also more pleasant" (mark the predicate) "than to receive good."

Benevolence would cease to be a virtue if it ceased to be self-regarding. Yet it was upon this unsound basis that devoted friendships were based. When we are told that the wise man will, upon occasion, even die for his friend, the suggestion of disinterested action, however inconsistent, can hardly be dismissed.

"The wise man suffers no more pain when on the rack himself than when his friend is upon it; but if any man suspects his friend, his whole life will by his distrust be con founded and turned upside down."

And there are other utterances to the same effect. "What we require is not so much to have our needs supplied by our friends as to be assured that our needs will be supplied by them."

"The wise man, when brought into distress in company with others, shows himself a comrade ready to give rather than to receive; so great a treasure of self-reliance has he found."

In the foregoing sketch the main questions of ethics have come before us and the answers of Epicurus have been indicated in outline. Like his rivals the Stoics, he made his appeal to the world primarily as a moral teacher, an inquirer whose aim was to deal comprehensively and systematically with moral problems.

On The Nature of Things

By Lucretius

BOOK I

PROEM

Mother of Rome, delight of Gods and men,
Dear Venus that beneath the gliding stars
Makest to teem the many-voyaged main
And fruitful lands—for all of living things
Through thee alone are evermore conceived,
Through thee are risen to visit the great sun—
Before thee, Goddess, and thy coming on,
Flee stormy wind and massy cloud away,
For thee the daedal Earth bears scented flowers,
For thee waters of the unvexed deep
Smile, and the hollows of the serene sky
Glow with diffused radiance for thee!
For soon as comes the springtime face of day,
And procreant gales blow from the West unbarred,
First fowls of air, smit to the heart by thee,
Foretoken thy approach, O thou Divine,
And leap the wild herds round the happy fields
Or swim the bounding torrents. Thus amain,
Seized with the spell, all creatures follow thee
Whithersoever thou walkest forth to lead,
And thence through seas and mountains and swift streams,
Through leafy homes of birds and greening plains,
Kindling the lure of love in every breast,
Thou bringest the eternal generations forth,
Kind after kind. And since 'tis thou alone
Guidest the Cosmos, and without thee naught
Is risen to reach the shining shores of light,
Nor aught of joyful or of lovely born,
Thee do I crave co-partner in that verse
Which I presume on Nature to compose
For Memmius mine, whom thou hast willed to be
Peerless in every grace at every hour—
Wherefore indeed, Divine one, give my words
Immortal charm. Lull to a timely rest
O'er sea and land the savage works of war,
For thou alone hast power with public peace
To aid mortality; since he who rules
The savage works of battle, puissant Mars,

How often to thy bosom flings his strength
O'ermastered by the eternal wound of love—
And there, with eyes and full throat backward thrown,
Gazing, my Goddess, open-mouthed at thee,
Pastures on love his greedy sight, his breath
Hanging upon thy lips. Him thus reclined
Fill with thy holy body, round, above!
Pour from those lips soft syllables to win
Peace for the Romans, glorious Lady, peace!
For in a season troublous to the state
Neither may I attend this task of mine
With thought untroubled, nor mid such events
The illustrious scion of the Memmian house
Neglect the civic cause.
Whilst human kind
Throughout the lands lay miserably crushed
Before all eyes beneath Religion—who
Would show her head along the region skies,
Glowering on mortals with her hideous face—
A Greek it was who first opposing dared
Raise mortal eyes that terror to withstand,
Whom nor the fame of Gods nor lightning's stroke
Nor threatening thunder of the ominous sky
Abashed; but rather chafed to angry zest
His dauntless heart to be the first to rend
The crossbars at the gates of Nature old.
And thus his will and hardy wisdom won;
And forward thus he fared afar, beyond
The flaming ramparts of the world, until
He wandered the unmeasurable All.
Whence he to us, a conqueror, reports
What things can rise to being, what cannot,
And by what law to each its scope prescribed,
Its boundary stone that clings so deep in Time.
Wherefore Religion now is under foot,
And us his victory now exalts to heaven.
I know how hard it is in Latian verse
To tell the dark discoveries of the Greeks,
Chiefly because our pauper-speech must find
Strange terms to fit the strangeness of the thing;
Yet worth of thine and the expected joy
Of thy sweet friendship do persuade me on
To bear all toil and wake the clear nights through,

Seeking with what of words and what of song
I may at last most gloriously uncloud
For thee the light beyond, wherewith to view
The core of being at the centre hid.
And for the rest, summon to judgments true,
Unbusied ears and singleness of mind
Withdrawn from cares; lest these my gifts, arranged
For thee with eager service, thou disdain
Before thou comprehendest: since for thee
I prove the supreme law of Gods and sky,
And the primordial germs of things unfold,
Whence Nature all creates, and multiplies
And fosters all, and whither she resolves
Each in the end when each is overthrown.
This ultimate stock we have devised to name
Procreant atoms, matter, seeds of things,
Or primal bodies, as primal to the world.
I fear perhaps thou deemest that we fare
An impious road to realms of thought profane;
But 'tis that same religion oftener far
Hath bred the foul impieties of men:
As once at Aulis, the elected chiefs,
Foremost of heroes, Danaan counsellors,
Defiled Diana's altar, virgin queen,
With Agamemnon's daughter, foully slain.
She felt the chaplet round her maiden locks
And fillets, fluttering down on either cheek,
And at the altar marked her grieving sire,
The priests beside him who concealed the knife,
And all the folk in tears at sight of her.
With a dumb terror and a sinking knee
She dropped; nor might avail her now that first
'Twas she who gave the king a father's name.
They raised her up, they bore the trembling girl
On to the altar—hither led not now
With solemn rites and hymeneal choir,
But sinless woman, sinfully foredone,
A parent felled her on her bridal day,
Making his child a sacrificial beast
To give the ships auspicious winds for Troy:
Such are the crimes to which Religion leads.
And there shall come the time when even thou,
Forced by the soothsayer's terror-tales, shalt seek

To break from us. Ah, many a dream even now
Can they concoct to rout thy plans of life,
And trouble all thy fortunes with base fears.
I own with reason: for, if men but knew
Some fixed end to ills, they would be strong
By some device unconquered to withstand
Religions and the menacings of seers.
But now nor skill nor instrument is theirs,
Since men must dread eternal pains in death.
For what the soul may be they do not know,
Whether 'tis born, or enter in at birth,
And whether, snatched by death, it die with us,
Or visit the shadows and the vast caves
Of Orcus, or by some divine decree
Enter the brute herds, as our Ennius sang,
Who first from lovely Helicon brought down
A laurel wreath of bright perennial leaves,
Renowned forever among the Italian clans.
Yet Ennius too in everlasting verse
Proclaims those vaults of Acheron to be,
Though thence, he said, nor souls nor bodies fare,
But only phantom figures, strangely wan,
And tells how once from out those regions rose
Old Homer's ghost to him and shed salt tears
And with his words unfolded Nature's source.
Then be it ours with steady mind to clasp
The purport of the skies—the law behind
The wandering courses of the sun and moon;
To scan the powers that speed all life below;
But most to see with reasonable eyes
Of what the mind, of what the soul is made,
And what it is so terrible that breaks
On us asleep, or waking in disease,
Until we seem to mark and hear at hand
Dead men whose bones earth bosomed long ago.

SUBSTANCE IS ETERNAL

This terror, then, this darkness of the mind,
Not sunrise with its flaring spokes of light,
Nor glittering arrows of morning can disperse,
But only Nature's aspect and her law,
Which, teaching us, hath this exordium:
Nothing from nothing ever yet was born.
Fear holds dominion over mortality
Only because, seeing in land and sky
So much the cause whereof no wise they know,
Men think Divinities are working there.
Meantime, when once we know from nothing still
Nothing can be create, we shall divine
More clearly what we seek: those elements
From which alone all things created are,
And how accomplished by no tool of Gods.
Suppose all sprang from all things: any kind
Might take its origin from any thing,
No fixed seed required. Men from the sea
Might rise, and from the land the scaly breed,
And, fowl full-fledged come bursting from the sky;
The horned cattle, the herds and all the wild
Would haunt with varying offspring tilth and waste;
Nor would the same fruits keep their olden trees,
But each might grow from any stock or limb
By chance and change. Indeed, and were there not
For each its procreant atoms, could things have
Each its unalterable mother old?
But, since produced from fixed seeds are all,
Each birth goes forth upon the shores of light
From its own stuff, from its own primal bodies.
And all from all cannot become, because
In each resides a secret power its own.
Again, why see we lavished o'er the lands
At spring the rose, at summer heat the corn,
The vines that mellow when the autumn lures,
If not because the fixed seeds of things
At their own season must together stream,
And new creations only be revealed
When the due times arrive and pregnant earth
Safely may give unto the shores of light
Her tender progenies? But if from naught

Were their becoming, they would spring abroad
Suddenly, unforeseen, in alien months,
With no primordial germs, to be preserved
From procreant unions at an adverse hour.
Nor on the mingling of the living seeds
Would space be needed for the growth of things
Were life an increment of nothing: then
The tiny babe forthwith would walk a man,
And from the turf would leap a branching tree—
Wonders unheard of; for, by Nature, each
Slowly increases from its lawful seed,
And through that increase shall conserve its kind.
Whence take the proof that things enlarge and feed
From out their proper matter. Thus it comes
That earth, without her seasons of fixed rains,
Could bear no produce such as makes us glad,
And whatsoever lives, if shut from food,
Prolongs its kind and guards its life no more.
Thus easier 'tis to hold that many things
Have primal bodies in common (as we see
The single letters common to many words)
Than aught exists without its origins.
Moreover, why should Nature not prepare
Men of a bulk to ford the seas afoot,
Or rend the mighty mountains with their hands,
Or conquer Time with length of days, if not
Because for all begotten things abides
The changeless stuff, and what from that may spring
Is fixed forevermore? Lastly we see
How far the tilled surpass the fields untilled
And to the labour of our hands return
Their more abounding crops; there are indeed
Within the earth primordial germs of things,
Which, as the ploughshare turns the fruitful clods
And kneads the mould, we quicken into birth.
Else would ye mark, without all toil of ours,
Spontaneous generations, fairer forms.
Confess then, naught from nothing can become,
Since all must have their seeds, wherefrom to grow,
Wherefrom to reach the gentle fields of air.
Hence too it comes that Nature all dissolves
Into their primal bodies again, and naught
Perishes ever to annihilation.

For, were aught mortal in its every part,
Before our eyes it might be snatched away
Unto destruction; since no force were needed
To sunder its members and undo its bands.
Whereas, of truth, because all things exist,
With seed imperishable, Nature allows
Destruction nor collapse of aught, until
Some outward force may shatter by a blow,
Or inward craft, entering its hollow cells,
Dissolve it down. And more than this, if Time,
That wastes with eld the works along the world,
Destroy entire, consuming matter all,
Whence then may Venus back to light of life
Restore the generations kind by kind?
Or how, when thus restored, may daedal Earth
Foster and plenish with her ancient food,
Which, kind by kind, she offers unto each?
Whence may the water-springs, beneath the sea,
Or inland rivers, far and wide away,
Keep the unfathomable ocean full?
And out of what does Ether feed the stars?
For lapsed years and infinite age must else
Have eat all shapes of mortal stock away:
But be it the Long Ago contained those germs,
By which this sum of things recruited lives,
Those same infallibly can never die,
Nor nothing to nothing evermore return.
And, too, the selfsame power might end alike
All things, were they not still together held
By matter eternal, shackled through its parts,
Now more, now less. A touch might be enough
To cause destruction. For the slightest force
Would loose the weft of things wherein no part
Were of imperishable stock. But now
Because the fastenings of primordial parts
Are put together diversely and stuff
Is everlasting, things abide the same
Unhurt and sure, until some power comes on
Strong to destroy the warp and woof of each:
Nothing returns to naught; but all return
At their collapse to primal forms of stuff.
Lo, the rains perish which Ether-father throws
Down to the bosom of Earth-mother; but then

Upsprings the shining grain, and boughs are green
Amid the trees, and trees themselves wax big
And lade themselves with fruits; and hence in turn
The race of man and all the wild are fed;
Hence joyful cities thrive with boys and girls;
And leafy woodlands echo with new birds;
Hence cattle, fat and drowsy, lay their bulk
Along the joyous pastures whilst the drops
Of white ooze trickle from distended bags;
Hence the young scamper on their weakling joints
Along the tender herbs, fresh hearts afrisk
With warm new milk. Thus naught of what so seems
Perishes utterly, since Nature ever
Upbuilds one thing from other, suffering naught
To come to birth but through some other's death.

And now, since I have taught that things cannot
Be born from nothing, nor the same, when born,
To nothing be recalled, doubt not my words,
Because our eyes no primal germs perceive;
For mark those bodies which, though known to be
In this our world, are yet invisible:
The winds infuriate lash our face and frame,
Unseen, and swamp huge ships and rend the clouds,
Or, eddying wildly down, bestrew the plains
With mighty trees, or scour the mountain tops
With forest-crackling blasts. Thus on they rave
With uproar shrill and ominous moan. The winds,
'Tis clear, are sightless bodies sweeping through
The sea, the lands, the clouds along the sky,
Vexing and whirling and seizing all amain;
And forth they flow and pile destruction round,
Even as the water's soft and supple bulk
Becoming a river of abounding floods,
Which a wide downpour from the lofty hills
Swells with big showers, dashes headlong down
Fragments of woodland and whole branching trees;
Nor can the solid bridges bide the shock
As on the waters whelm: the turbulent stream,
Strong with a hundred rains, beats round the piers,
Crashes with havoc, and rolls beneath its waves
Down-toppled masonry and ponderous stone,
Hurling away whatever would oppose.

Even so must move the blasts of all the winds,
Which, when they spread, like to a mighty flood,
Hither or thither, drive things on before
And hurl to ground with still renewed assault,
Or sometimes in their circling vortex seize
And bear in cones of whirlwind down the world:
The winds are sightless bodies and naught else—
Since both in works and ways they rival well
The mighty rivers, the visible in form.
Then too we know the varied smells of things
Yet never to our nostrils see them come;
With eyes we view not burning heats, nor cold,
Nor are we wont men's voices to behold.
Yet these must be corporeal at the base,
Since thus they smite the senses: naught there is
Save body, having property of touch.
And raiment, hung by surf-beat shore, grows moist,
The same, spread out before the sun, will dry;
Yet no one saw how sank the moisture in,
Nor how by heat off-driven. Thus we know,
That moisture is dispersed about in bits
Too small for eyes to see. Another case:
A ring upon the finger thins away
Along the under side, with years and suns;
The drippings from the eaves will scoop the stone;
The hooked ploughshare, though of iron, wastes
Amid the fields insidiously. We view
The rock-paved highways worn by many feet;
And at the gates the brazen statues show
Their right hands leaner from the frequent touch
Of wayfarers innumerable who greet.
We see how wearing-down hath minished these,
But just what motes depart at any time,
The envious nature of vision bars our sight.
Lastly whatever days and nature add
Little by little, constraining things to grow
In due proportion, no gaze however keen
Of these our eyes hath watched and known. No more
Can we observe what's lost at any time,
When things wax old with eld and foul decay,
Or when salt seas eat under beetling crags.
Thus Nature ever by unseen bodies works.

THE VOID

But yet creation's neither crammed nor blocked
About by body: there's in things a void—
Which to have known will serve thee many a turn,
Nor will not leave thee wandering in doubt,
Forever searching in the sum of all,
And losing faith in these pronouncements mine.
There's place intangible, a void and room.
For were it not, things could in nowise move;
Since body's property to block and check
Would work on all and at an times the same.
Thus naught could evermore push forth and go,
Since naught elsewhere would yield a starting place.
But now through oceans, lands, and heights of heaven,
By divers causes and in divers modes,
Before our eyes we mark how much may move,
Which, finding not a void, would fail deprived
Of stir and motion; nay, would then have been
Nowise begot at all, since matter, then,
Had staid at rest, its parts together crammed.
Then too, however solid objects seem,
They yet are formed of matter mixed with void:
In rocks and caves the watery moisture seeps,
And beady drops stand out like plenteous tears;
And food finds way through every frame that lives;
The trees increase and yield the season's fruit
Because their food throughout the whole is poured,
Even from the deepest roots, through trunks and boughs;
And voices pass the solid walls and fly
Reverberant through shut doorways of a house;
And stiffening frost seeps inward to our bones.
Which but for voids for bodies to go through
'Tis clear could happen in nowise at all.
Again, why see we among objects some
Of heavier weight, but of no bulkier size?
Indeed, if in a ball of wool there be
As much of body as in lump of lead,
The two should weigh alike, since body tends
To load things downward, while the void abides,
By contrary nature, the imponderable.
Therefore, an object just as large but lighter
Declares infallibly its more of void;

Even as the heavier more of matter shows,
And how much less of vacant room inside.
That which we're seeking with sagacious quest
Exists, infallibly, commixed with things—
The void, the invisible inane.
Right here
I am compelled a question to expound,
Forestalling something certain folk suppose,
Lest it avail to lead thee off from truth:
Waters (they say) before the shining breed
Of the swift scaly creatures somehow give,
And straightway open sudden liquid paths,
Because the fishes leave behind them room
To which at once the yielding billows stream.
Thus things among themselves can yet be moved,
And change their place, however full the Sum—
Received opinion, wholly false forsooth.
For where can scaly creatures forward dart,
Save where the waters give them room? Again,
Where can the billows yield a way, so long
As ever the fish are powerless to go?
Thus either all bodies of motion are deprived,
Or things contain admixture of a void
Where each thing gets its start in moving on.
Lastly, where after impact two broad bodies
Suddenly spring apart, the air must crowd
The whole new void between those bodies formed;
But air, however it stream with hastening gusts,
Can yet not fill the gap at once—for first
It makes for one place, ere diffused through all.
And then, if haply any think this comes,
When bodies spring apart, because the air
Somehow condenses, wander they from truth:
For then a void is formed, where none before;
And, too, a void is filled which was before.
Nor can air be condensed in such a wise;
Nor, granting it could, without a void, I hold,
It still could not contract upon itself
And draw its parts together into one.
Wherefore, despite demur and counter-speech,
Confess thou must there is a void in things.

And still I might by many an argument

Here scrape together credence for my words.
But for the keen eye these mere footprints serve,
Whereby thou mayest know the rest thyself.
As dogs full oft with noses on the ground,
Find out the silent lairs, though hid in brush,
Of beasts, the mountain-rangers, when but once
They scent the certain footsteps of the way,
Thus thou thyself in themes like these alone
Can hunt from thought to thought, and keenly wind
Along even onward to the secret places
And drag out truth. But, if thou loiter loth
Or veer, however little, from the point,
This I can promise, Memmius, for a fact:
Such copious drafts my singing tongue shall pour
From the large well-springs of my plenished breast
That much I dread slow age will steal and coil
Along our members, and unloose the gates
Of life within us, ere for thee my verse
Hath put within thine ears the stores of proofs
At hand for one soever question broached.

NOTHING EXISTS per se EXCEPT ATOMS AND THE VOID

But, now again to weave the tale begun,
All nature, then, as self-sustained, consists
Of twain of things: of bodies and of void
In which they're set, and where they're moved around.
For common instinct of our race declares
That body of itself exists: unless
This primal faith, deep-founded, fail us not,
Naught will there be whereunto to appeal
On things occult when seeking aught to prove
By reasonings of mind. Again, without
That place and room, which we do call the inane,
Nowhere could bodies then be set, nor go
Hither or thither at all—as shown before.
Besides, there's naught of which thou canst declare
It lives disjoined from body, shut from void—
A kind of third in nature. For whatever
Exists must be a somewhat; and the same,
If tangible, however fight and slight,

Will yet increase the count of body's sum,
With its own augmentation big or small;
But, if intangible and powerless ever
To keep a thing from passing through itself
On any side, 'twill be naught else but that
Which we do call the empty, the inane.
Again, whate'er exists, as of itself,
Must either act or suffer action on it,
Or else be that wherein things move and be:
Naught, saving body, acts, is acted on;
Naught but the inane can furnish room. And thus,
Beside the inane and bodies, is no third
Nature amid the number of all things—
Remainder none to fall at any time
Under our senses, nor be seized and seen
By any man through reasonings of mind.
Name o'er creation with what names thou wilt,
Thou'lt find but properties of those first twain,
Or see but accidents those twain produce.
A property is that which not at all
Can be disjoined and severed from a thing
Without a fatal dissolution: such,
Weight to the rocks, heat to the fire, and flow
To the wide waters, touch to corporal things,
Intangibility to the viewless void.
But state of slavery, pauperhood, and wealth,
Freedom, and war, and concord, and all else
Which come and go whilst nature stands the same,
We're wont, and rightly, to call accidents.
Even time exists not of itself; but sense
Reads out of things what happened long ago,
What presses now, and what shall follow after:
No man, we must admit, feels time itself,
Disjoined from motion and repose of things.
Thus, when they say there "is" the ravishment
Of Princess Helen, "is" the siege and sack
Of Trojan Town, look out, they force us not
To admit these acts existent by themselves,
Merely because those races of mankind
(Of whom these acts were accidents) long since
Irrevocable age has borne away:
For all past actions may be said to be
But accidents, in one way, of mankind,—

In other, of some region of the world.
Add, too, had been no matter, and no room
Wherein all things go on, the fire of love
Upblown by that fair form, the glowing coal
Under the Phrygian Alexander's breast,
Had ne'er enkindled that renowned strife
Of savage war, nor had the wooden horse
Involved in flames old Pergama, by a birth
At midnight of a brood of the Hellenes.
And thus thou canst remark that every act
At bottom exists not of itself, nor is
As body is, nor has like name with void;
But rather of sort more fitly to be called
An accident of body, and of place
Wherein all things go on.

CHARACTER OF THE ATOMS

Bodies, again,
Are partly primal germs of things, and partly
Unions deriving from the primal germs.
And those which are the primal germs of things
No power can quench; for in the end they conquer
By their own solidness; though hard it be
To think that aught in things has solid frame;
For lightnings pass, no less than voice and shout,
Through hedging walls of houses, and the iron
White-dazzles in the fire, and rocks will burn
With exhalations fierce and burst asunder.
Totters the rigid gold dissolved in heat;
The ice of bronze melts conquered in the flame;
Warmth and the piercing cold through silver seep,
Since, with the cups held rightly in the hand,
We oft feel both, as from above is poured
The dew of waters between their shining sides:
So true it is no solid form is found.
But yet because true reason and nature of things
Constrain us, come, whilst in few verses now
I disentangle how there still exist
Bodies of solid, everlasting frame—
The seeds of things, the primal germs we teach,

Whence all creation around us came to be.
First since we know a twofold nature exists,
Of things, both twain and utterly unlike—
Body, and place in which an things go on—
Then each must be both for and through itself,
And all unmixed: where'er be empty space,
There body's not; and so where body bides,
There not at all exists the void inane.
Thus primal bodies are solid, without a void.
But since there's void in all begotten things,
All solid matter must be round the same;
Nor, by true reason canst thou prove aught hides
And holds a void within its body, unless
Thou grant what holds it be a solid. Know,
That which can hold a void of things within
Can be naught else than matter in union knit.
Thus matter, consisting of a solid frame,
Hath power to be eternal, though all else,
Though all creation, be dissolved away.
Again, were naught of empty and inane,
The world were then a solid; as, without
Some certain bodies to fill the places held,
The world that is were but a vacant void.
And so, infallibly, alternate-wise
Body and void are still distinguished,
Since nature knows no wholly full nor void.
There are, then, certain bodies, possessed of power
To vary forever the empty and the full;
And these can nor be sundered from without
By beats and blows, nor from within be torn
By penetration, nor be overthrown
By any assault soever through the world—
For without void, naught can be crushed, it seems,
Nor broken, nor severed by a cut in twain,
Nor can it take the damp, or seeping cold
Or piercing fire, those old destroyers three;
But the more void within a thing, the more
Entirely it totters at their sure assault.
Thus if first bodies be, as I have taught,
Solid, without a void, they must be then
Eternal; and, if matter ne'er had been
Eternal, long ere now had all things gone
Back into nothing utterly, and all

We see around from nothing had been born—
But since I taught above that naught can be
From naught created, nor the once begotten
To naught be summoned back, these primal germs
Must have an immortality of frame.
And into these must each thing be resolved,
When comes its supreme hour, that thus there be
At hand the stuff for plenishing the world.

So primal germs have solid singleness
Nor otherwise could they have been conserved
Through aeons and infinity of time
For the replenishment of wasted worlds.
Once more, if nature had given a scope for things
To be forever broken more and more,
By now the bodies of matter would have been
So far reduced by breakings in old days
That from them nothing could, at season fixed,
Be born, and arrive its prime and top of life.
For, lo, each thing is quicker marred than made;
And so whate'er the long infinitude
Of days and all fore-passed time would now
By this have broken and ruined and dissolved,
That same could ne'er in all remaining time
Be builded up for plenishing the world.
But mark: infallibly a fixed bound
Remaineth stablished 'gainst their breaking down;
Since we behold each thing soever renewed,
And unto all, their seasons, after their kind,
Wherein they arrive the flower of their age.

Again, if bounds have not been set against
The breaking down of this corporeal world,
Yet must all bodies of whatever things
Have still endured from everlasting time
Unto this present, as not yet assailed
By shocks of peril. But because the same
Are, to thy thinking, of a nature frail,
It ill accords that thus they could remain
(As thus they do) through everlasting time,
Vexed through the ages (as indeed they are)
By the innumerable blows of chance.

So in our programme of creation, mark
How 'tis that, though the bodies of all stuff
Are solid to the core, we yet explain
The ways whereby some things are fashioned soft—
Air, water, earth, and fiery exhalations—
And by what force they function and go on:
The fact is founded in the void of things.
But if the primal germs themselves be soft,
Reason cannot be brought to bear to show
The ways whereby may be created these
Great crags of basalt and the during iron;
For their whole nature will profoundly lack
The first foundations of a solid frame.
But powerful in old simplicity,
Abide the solid, the primeval germs;
And by their combinations more condensed,
All objects can be tightly knit and bound
And made to show unconquerable strength.
Again, since all things kind by kind obtain
Fixed bounds of growing and conserving life;
Since Nature hath inviolably decreed
What each can do, what each can never do;
Since naught is changed, but all things so abide
That ever the variegated birds reveal
The spots or stripes peculiar to their kind,
Spring after spring: thus surely all that is
Must be composed of matter immutable.
For if the primal germs in any wise
Were open to conquest and to change, 'twould be
Uncertain also what could come to birth
And what could not, and by what law to each
Its scope prescribed, its boundary stone that clings
So deep in Time. Nor could the generations
Kind after kind so often reproduce
The nature, habits, motions, ways of life,
Of their progenitors.
And then again,
Since there is ever an extreme bounding point
Of that first body which our senses now
Cannot perceive: That bounding point indeed
Exists without all parts, a minimum
Of nature, nor was e'er a thing apart,
As of itself,—nor shall hereafter be,

Since 'tis itself still parcel of another,
A first and single part, whence other parts
And others similar in order lie
In a packed phalanx, filling to the full
The nature of first body: being thus
Not self-existent, they must cleave to that
From which in nowise they can sundered be.
So primal germs have solid singleness,
Which tightly packed and closely joined cohere
By virtue of their minim particles—
No compound by mere union of the same;
But strong in their eternal singleness,
Nature, reserving them as seeds for things,
Permitteth naught of rupture or decrease.
Moreover, were there not a minimum,
The smallest bodies would have infinites,
Since then a half-of-half could still be halved,
With limitless division less and less.
Then what the difference 'twixt the sum and least?
None: for however infinite the sum,
Yet even the smallest would consist the same
Of infinite parts. But since true reason here
Protests, denying that the mind can think it,
Convinced thou must confess such things there are
As have no parts, the minimums of nature.
And since these are, likewise confess thou must
That primal bodies are solid and eterne.
Again, if Nature, creatress of all things,
Were wont to force all things to be resolved
Unto least parts, then would she not avail
To reproduce from out them anything;
Because whate'er is not endowed with parts
Cannot possess those properties required
Of generative stuff—divers connections,
Weights, blows, encounters, motions, whereby things
Forevermore have being and go on.

CONFUTATION OF OTHER PHILOSOPHERS

And on such grounds it is that those who held
The stuff of things is fire, and out of fire
Alone the cosmic sum is formed, are seen
Mightily from true reason to have lapsed.
Of whom, chief leader to do battle, comes
That Heraclitus, famous for dark speech
Among the silly, not the serious Greeks
Who search for truth. For dolts are ever prone
That to bewonder and adore which hides
Beneath distorted words, holding that true
Which sweetly tickles in their stupid ears,
Or which is rouged in finely finished phrase.
For how, I ask, can things so varied be,
If formed of fire, single and pure? No whit
'Twould help for fire to be condensed or thinned,
If all the parts of fire did still preserve
But fire's own nature, seen before in gross.
The heat were keener with the parts compressed,
Milder, again, when severed or dispersed—
And more than this thou canst conceive of naught
That from such causes could become; much less
Might earth's variety of things be born
From any fires soever, dense or rare.
This too: if they suppose a void in things,
Then fires can be condensed and still left rare;
But since they see such opposites of thought
Rising against them, and are loath to leave
An unmixed void in things, they fear the steep
And lose the road of truth. Nor do they see,
That, if from things we take away the void,
All things are then condensed, and out of all
One body made, which has no power to dart
Swiftly from out itself not anything—
As throws the fire its light and warmth around,
Giving thee proof its parts are not compact.
But if perhaps they think, in other wise,
Fires through their combinations can be quenched
And change their substance, very well: behold,
If fire shall spare to do so in no part,
Then heat will perish utterly and all,

And out of nothing would the world be formed.
For change in anything from out its bounds
Means instant death of that which was before;
And thus a somewhat must persist unharmed
Amid the world, lest all return to naught,
And, born from naught, abundance thrive anew.
Now since indeed there are those surest bodies
Which keep their nature evermore the same,
Upon whose going out and coming in
And changed order things their nature change,
And all corporeal substances transformed,
'Tis thine to know those primal bodies, then,
Are not of fire. For 'twere of no avail
Should some depart and go away, and some
Be added new, and some be changed in order,
If still all kept their nature of old heat:
For whatsoever they created then
Would still in any case be only fire.
The truth, I fancy, this: bodies there are
Whose clashings, motions, order, posture, shapes
Produce the fire and which, by order changed,
Do change the nature of the thing produced,
And are thereafter nothing like to fire
Nor whatso else has power to send its bodies
With impact touching on the senses' touch.
Again, to say that all things are but fire
And no true thing in number of all things
Exists but fire, as this same fellow says,
Seems crazed folly. For the man himself
Against the senses by the senses fights,
And hews at that through which is all belief,
Through which indeed unto himself is known
The thing he calls the fire. For, though he thinks
The senses truly can perceive the fire,
He thinks they cannot as regards all else,
Which still are palpably as clear to sense—
To me a thought inept and crazy too.
For whither shall we make appeal? for what
More certain than our senses can there be
Whereby to mark asunder error and truth?
Besides, why rather do away with all,
And wish to allow heat only, then deny
The fire and still allow all else to be?—

Alike the madness either way it seems.
Thus whosoe'er have held the stuff of things
To be but fire, and out of fire the sum,
And whosoever have constituted air
As first beginning of begotten things,
And all whoever have held that of itself
Water alone contrives things, or that earth
Createth all and changes things anew
To divers natures, mightily they seem
A long way to have wandered from the truth.
Add, too, whoever make the primal stuff
Twofold, by joining air to fire, and earth
To water; add who deem that things can grow
Out of the four—fire, earth, and breath, and rain;
As first Empedocles of Acragas,
Whom that three-cornered isle of all the lands
Bore on her coasts, around which flows and flows
In mighty bend and bay the Ionic seas,
Splashing the brine from off their gray-green waves.
Here, billowing onward through the narrow straits,
Swift ocean cuts her boundaries from the shores
Of the Italic mainland. Here the waste
Charybdis; and here Aetna rumbles threats
To gather anew such furies of its flames
As with its force anew to vomit fires,
Belched from its throat, and skyward bear anew
Its lightnings' flash. And though for much she seem
The mighty and the wondrous isle to men,
Most rich in all good things, and fortified
With generous strength of heroes, she hath ne'er
Possessed within her aught of more renown,
Nor aught more holy, wonderful, and dear
Than this true man. Nay, ever so far and pure
The lofty music of his breast divine
Lifts up its voice and tells of glories found,
That scarce he seems of human stock create.
Yet he and those forementioned (known to be
So far beneath him, less than he in all),
Though, as discoverers of much goodly truth,
They gave, as 'twere from out of the heart's own shrine,
Responses holier and soundlier based
Than ever the Pythia pronounced for men
From out the triped and the Delphian laurel,

Have still in matter of first-elements
Made ruin of themselves, and, great men, great
Indeed and heavy there for them the fall:
First, because, banishing the void from things,
They yet assign them motion, and allow
Things soft and loosely textured to exist,
As air, dew, fire, earth, animals, and grains,
Without admixture of void amid their frame.
Next, because, thinking there can be no end
In cutting bodies down to less and less
Nor pause established to their breaking up,
They hold there is no minimum in things;
Albeit we see the boundary point of aught
Is that which to our senses seems its least,
Whereby thou mayst conjecture, that, because
The things thou canst not mark have boundary points,
They surely have their minimums. Then, too,
Since these philosophers ascribe to things
Soft primal germs, which we behold to be
Of birth and body mortal, thus, throughout,
The sum of things must be returned to naught,
And, born from naught, abundance thrive anew—
Thou seest how far each doctrine stands from truth.
And, next, these bodies are among themselves
In many ways poisons and foes to each,
Wherefore their congress will destroy them quite
Or drive asunder as we see in storms
Rains, winds, and lightnings all asunder fly.
Thus too, if all things are create of four,
And all again dissolved into the four,
How can the four be called the primal germs
Of things, more than all things themselves be thought,
By retroversion, primal germs of them?
For ever alternately are both begot,
With interchange of nature and aspect
From immemorial time. But if percase
Thou think'st the frame of fire and earth, the air,
The dew of water can in such wise meet
As not by mingling to resign their nature,
From them for thee no world can be create—
No thing of breath, no stock or stalk of tree:
In the wild congress of this varied heap
Each thing its proper nature will display,

And air will palpably be seen mixed up
With earth together, unquenched heat with water.
But primal germs in bringing things to birth
Must have a latent, unseen quality,
Lest some outstanding alien element
Confuse and minish in the thing create
Its proper being.
But these men begin
From heaven, and from its fires; and first they feign
That fire will turn into the winds of air,
Next, that from air the rain begotten is,
And earth created out of rain, and then
That all, reversely, are returned from earth—
The moisture first, then air thereafter heat—
And that these same ne'er cease in interchange,
To go their ways from heaven to earth, from earth
Unto the stars of the aethereal world—
Which in no wise at all the germs can do.
Since an immutable somewhat still must be,
Lest all things utterly be sped to naught;
For change in anything from out its bounds
Means instant death of that which was before.
Wherefore, since those things, mentioned heretofore,
Suffer a changed state, they must derive
From others ever unconvertible,
Lest an things utterly return to naught.
Then why not rather presuppose there be
Bodies with such a nature furnished forth
That, if perchance they have created fire,
Can still (by virtue of a few withdrawn,
Or added few, and motion and order changed)
Fashion the winds of air, and thus all things
Forevermore be interchanged with all?
"But facts in proof are manifest," thou sayest,
"That all things grow into the winds of air
And forth from earth are nourished, and unless
The season favour at propitious hour
With rains enough to set the trees a-reel
Under the soak of bulking thunderheads,
And sun, for its share, foster and give heat,
No grains, nor trees, nor breathing things can grow."
True—and unless hard food and moisture soft
Recruited man, his frame would waste away,

And life dissolve from out his thews and bones;
For out of doubt recruited and fed are we
By certain things, as other things by others.
Because in many ways the many germs
Common to many things are mixed in things,
No wonder 'tis that therefore divers things
By divers things are nourished. And, again,
Often it matters vastly with what others,
In what positions the primordial germs
Are bound together, and what motions, too,
They give and get among themselves; for these
Same germs do put together sky, sea, lands,
Rivers, and sun, grains, trees, and breathing things,
But yet commixed they are in divers modes
With divers things, forever as they move.
Nay, thou beholdest in our verses here
Elements many, common to many worlds,
Albeit thou must confess each verse, each word
From one another differs both in sense
And ring of sound—so much the elements
Can bring about by change of order alone.
But those which are the primal germs of things
Have power to work more combinations still,
Whence divers things can be produced in turn.
Now let us also take for scrutiny
The homeomeria of Anaxagoras,
So called by Greeks, for which our pauper-speech
Yieldeth no name in the Italian tongue,
Although the thing itself is not o'erhard
For explanation. First, then, when he speaks
Of this homeomeria of things, he thinks
Bones to be sprung from littlest bones minute,
And from minute and littlest flesh all flesh,
And blood created out of drops of blood,
Conceiving gold compact of grains of gold,
And earth concreted out of bits of earth,
Fire made of fires, and water out of waters,
Feigning the like with all the rest of stuff.
Yet he concedes not any void in things,
Nor any limit to cutting bodies down.
Wherefore to me he seems on both accounts
To err no less than those we named before.
Add too: these germs he feigns are far too frail—

If they be germs primordial furnished forth
With but same nature as the things themselves,
And travail and perish equally with those,
And no rein curbs them from annihilation.
For which will last against the grip and crush
Under the teeth of death? the fire? the moist?
Or else the air? which then? the blood? the bones?
No one, methinks, when every thing will be
At bottom as mortal as whate'er we mark
To perish by force before our gazing eyes.
But my appeal is to the proofs above
That things cannot fall back to naught, nor yet
From naught increase. And now again, since food
Augments and nourishes the human frame,
'Tis thine to know our veins and blood and bones
And thews are formed of particles unlike
To them in kind; or if they say all foods
Are of mixed substance having in themselves
Small bodies of thews, and bones, and also veins
And particles of blood, then every food,
Solid or liquid, must itself be thought
As made and mixed of things unlike in kind—
Of bones, of thews, of ichor and of blood.
Again, if all the bodies which upgrow
From earth, are first within the earth, then earth
Must be compound of alien substances.
Which spring and bloom abroad from out the earth.
Transfer the argument, and thou may'st use
The selfsame words: if flame and smoke and ash
Still lurk unseen within the wood, the wood
Must be compound of alien substances
Which spring from out the wood.
Right here remains
A certain slender means to skulk from truth,
Which Anaxagoras takes unto himself,
Who holds that all things lurk commixed with all
While that one only comes to view, of which
The bodies exceed in number all the rest,
And lie more close to hand and at the fore—
A notion banished from true reason far.
For then 'twere meet that kernels of the grains
Should oft, when crunched between the might of stones,
Give forth a sign of blood, or of aught else

Which in our human frame is fed; and that
Rock rubbed on rock should yield a gory ooze.
Likewise the herbs ought oft to give forth drops
Of sweet milk, flavoured like the uddered sheep's;
Indeed we ought to find, when crumbling up
The earthy clods, there herbs, and grains, and leaves,
All sorts dispersed minutely in the soil;
Lastly we ought to find in cloven wood
Ashes and smoke and bits of fire there hid.
But since fact teaches this is not the case,
'Tis thine to know things are not mixed with things
Thuswise; but seeds, common to many things,
Commixed in many ways, must lurk in things.
"But often it happens on skiey hills" thou sayest,
"That neighbouring tops of lofty trees are rubbed
One against other, smote by the blustering south,
Till all ablaze with bursting flower of flame."
Good sooth—yet fire is not ingraft in wood,
But many are the seeds of heat, and when
Rubbing together they together flow,
They start the conflagrations in the forests.
Whereas if flame, already fashioned, lay
Stored up within the forests, then the fires
Could not for any time be kept unseen,
But would be laying all the wildwood waste
And burning all the boscage. Now dost see
(Even as we said a little space above)
How mightily it matters with what others,
In what positions these same primal germs
Are bound together? And what motions, too,
They give and get among themselves? how, hence,
The same, if altered 'mongst themselves, can body
Both igneous and ligneous objects forth—
Precisely as these words themselves are made
By somewhat altering their elements,
Although we mark with name indeed distinct
The igneous from the ligneous. Once again,
If thou suppose whatever thou beholdest,
Among all visible objects, cannot be,
Unless thou feign bodies of matter endowed
With a like nature,—by thy vain device
For thee will perish all the germs of things:
'Twill come to pass they'll laugh aloud, like men,

Shaken asunder by a spasm of mirth,
Or moisten with salty tear-drops cheeks and chins.

THE INFINITY OF THE UNIVERSE

Now learn of what remains! More keenly hear!
And for myself, my mind is not deceived
How dark it is: But the large hope of praise
Hath strook with pointed thyrsus through my heart;
On the same hour hath strook into my breast
Sweet love of the Muses, wherewith now instinct,
I wander afield, thriving in sturdy thought,
Through unpathed haunts of the Pierides,
Trodden by step of none before. I joy
To come on undefiled fountains there,
To drain them deep; I joy to pluck new flowers,
To seek for this my head a signal crown
From regions where the Muses never yet
Have garlanded the temples of a man:
First, since I teach concerning mighty things,
And go right on to loose from round the mind
The tightened coils of dread religion;
Next, since, concerning themes so dark, I frame
Songs so pellucid, touching all throughout
Even with the Muses' charm—which, as 'twould seem,
Is not without a reasonable ground:
But as physicians, when they seek to give
Young boys the nauseous wormwood, first do touch
The brim around the cup with the sweet juice
And yellow of the honey, in order that
The thoughtless age of boyhood be cajoled
As far as the lips, and meanwhile swallow down
The wormwood's bitter draught, and, though befooled,
Be yet not merely duped, but rather thus
Grow strong again with recreated health:
So now I too (since this my doctrine seems
In general somewhat woeful unto those
Who've had it not in hand, and since the crowd
Starts back from it in horror) have desired
To expound our doctrine unto thee in song
Soft-speaking and Pierian, and, as 'twere,

To touch it with sweet honey of the Muse—
If by such method haply I might hold
The mind of thee upon these lines of ours,
Till thou see through the nature of all things,
And how exists the interwoven frame.
But since I've taught that bodies of matter, made
Completely solid, hither and thither fly
Forevermore unconquered through all time,
Now come, and whether to the sum of them
There be a limit or be none, for thee
Let us unfold; likewise what has been found
To be the wide inane, or room, or space
Wherein all things soever do go on,
Let us examine if it finite be
All and entire, or reach unmeasured round
And downward an illimitable profound.
Thus, then, the All that is is limited
In no one region of its onward paths,
For then 'tmust have forever its beyond.
And a beyond 'tis seen can never be
For aught, unless still further on there be
A somewhat somewhere that may bound the same—
So that the thing be seen still on to where
The nature of sensation of that thing
Can follow it no longer. Now because
Confess we must there's naught beside the sum,
There's no beyond, and so it lacks all end.
It matters nothing where thou post thyself,
In whatsoever regions of the same;
Even any place a man has set him down
Still leaves about him the unbounded all
Outward in all directions; or, supposing
A moment the all of space finite to be,
If some one farthest traveller runs forth
Unto the extreme coasts and throws ahead
A flying spear, is't then thy wish to think
It goes, hurled off amain, to where 'twas sent
And shoots afar, or that some object there
Can thwart and stop it? For the one or other
Thou must admit and take. Either of which
Shuts off escape for thee, and does compel
That thou concede the all spreads everywhere,
Owning no confines. Since whether there be

Aught that may block and check it so it comes
Not where 'twas sent, nor lodges in its goal,
Or whether borne along, in either view
'Thas started not from any end. And so
I'll follow on, and whereso'er thou set
The extreme coasts, I'll query, "what becomes
Thereafter of thy spear?" 'Twill come to pass
That nowhere can a world's-end be, and that
The chance for further flight prolongs forever
The flight itself. Besides, were all the space
Of the totality and sum shut in
With fixed coasts, and bounded everywhere,
Then would the abundance of world's matter flow
Together by solid weight from everywhere
Still downward to the bottom of the world,
Nor aught could happen under cope of sky,
Nor could there be a sky at all or sun—
Indeed, where matter all one heap would lie,
By having settled during infinite time.
But in reality, repose is given
Unto no bodies 'mongst the elements,
Because there is no bottom whereunto
They might, as 'twere, together flow, and where
They might take up their undisturbed abodes.
In endless motion everything goes on
Forevermore; out of all regions, even
Out of the pit below, from forth the vast,
Are hurtled bodies evermore supplied.
The nature of room, the space of the abyss
Is such that even the flashing thunderbolts
Can neither speed upon their courses through,
Gliding across eternal tracts of time,
Nor, further, bring to pass, as on they run,
That they may bate their journeying one whit:
Such huge abundance spreads for things around—
Room off to every quarter, without end.
Lastly, before our very eyes is seen
Thing to bound thing: air hedges hill from hill,
And mountain walls hedge air; land ends the sea,
And sea in turn all lands; but for the All
Truly is nothing which outside may bound.
That, too, the sum of things itself may not
Have power to fix a measure of its own,

Great nature guards, she who compels the void
To bound all body, as body all the void,
Thus rendering by these alternates the whole
An infinite; or else the one or other,
Being unbounded by the other, spreads,
Even by its single nature, ne'ertheless
Immeasurably forth....
Nor sea, nor earth, nor shining vaults of sky,
Nor breed of mortals, nor holy limbs of gods
Could keep their place least portion of an hour:
For, driven apart from out its meetings fit,
The stock of stuff, dissolved, would be borne
Along the illimitable inane afar,
Or rather, in fact, would ne'er have once combined
And given a birth to aught, since, scattered wide,
It could not be united. For of truth
Neither by counsel did the primal germs
'Stablish themselves, as by keen act of mind,
Each in its proper place; nor did they make,
Forsooth, a compact how each germ should move;
But since, being many and changed in many modes
Along the All, they're driven abroad and vexed
By blow on blow, even from all time of old,
They thus at last, after attempting all
The kinds of motion and conjoining, come
Into those great arrangements out of which
This sum of things established is create,
By which, moreover, through the mighty years,
It is preserved, when once it has been thrown
Into the proper motions, bringing to pass
That ever the streams refresh the greedy main
With river-waves abounding, and that earth,
Lapped in warm exhalations of the sun,
Renews her broods, and that the lusty race
Of breathing creatures bears and blooms, and that
The gliding fires of ether are alive—
What still the primal germs nowise could do,
Unless from out the infinite of space
Could come supply of matter, whence in season
They're wont whatever losses to repair.
For as the nature of breathing creatures wastes,
Losing its body, when deprived of food:
So all things have to be dissolved as soon

As matter, diverted by what means soever
From off its course, shall fail to be on hand.
Nor can the blows from outward still conserve,
On every side, whatever sum of a world
Has been united in a whole. They can
Indeed, by frequent beating, check a part,
Till others arriving may fulfil the sum;
But meanwhile often are they forced to spring
Rebounding back, and, as they spring, to yield,
Unto those elements whence a world derives,
Room and a time for flight, permitting them
To be from off the massy union borne
Free and afar. Wherefore, again, again:
Needs must there come a many for supply;
And also, that the blows themselves shall be
Unfailing ever, must there ever be
An infinite force of matter all sides round.
And in these problems, shrink, my Memmius, far
From yielding faith to that notorious talk:
That all things inward to the centre press;
And thus the nature of the world stands firm
With never blows from outward, nor can be
Nowhere disparted—since all height and depth
Have always inward to the centre pressed
(If thou art ready to believe that aught
Itself can rest upon itself); or that
The ponderous bodies which be under earth
Do all press upwards and do come to rest
Upon the earth, in some way upside down,
Like to those images of things we see
At present through the waters. They contend,
With like procedure, that all breathing things
Head downward roam about, and yet cannot
Tumble from earth to realms of sky below,
No more than these our bodies wing away
Spontaneously to vaults of sky above;
That, when those creatures look upon the sun,
We view the constellations of the night;
And that with us the seasons of the sky
They thus alternately divide, and thus
Do pass the night coequal to our days,
But a vain error has given these dreams to fools,
Which they've embraced with reasoning perverse

For centre none can be where world is still
Boundless, nor yet, if now a centre were,
Could aught take there a fixed position more
Than for some other cause 'tmight be dislodged.
For all of room and space we call the void
Must both through centre and non-centre yield
Alike to weights where'er their motions tend.
Nor is there any place, where, when they've come,
Bodies can be at standstill in the void,
Deprived of force of weight; nor yet may void
Furnish support to any,—nay, it must,
True to its bent of nature, still give way.
Thus in such manner not at all can things
Be held in union, as if overcome
By craving for a centre.
But besides,
Seeing they feign that not all bodies press
To centre inward, rather only those
Of earth and water (liquid of the sea,
And the big billows from the mountain slopes,
And whatsoever are encased, as 'twere,
In earthen body), contrariwise, they teach
How the thin air, and with it the hot fire,
Is borne asunder from the centre, and how,
For this all ether quivers with bright stars,
And the sun's flame along the blue is fed
(Because the heat, from out the centre flying,
All gathers there), and how, again, the boughs
Upon the tree-tops could not sprout their leaves,
Unless, little by little, from out the earth
For each were nutriment...
Lest, after the manner of the winged flames,
The ramparts of the world should flee away,
Dissolved amain throughout the mighty void,
And lest all else should likewise follow after,
Aye, lest the thundering vaults of heaven should burst
And splinter upward, and the earth forthwith
Withdraw from under our feet, and all its bulk,
Among its mingled wrecks and those of heaven,
With slipping asunder of the primal seeds,
Should pass, along the immeasurable inane,
Away forever, and, that instant, naught
Of wrack and remnant would be left, beside

The desolate space, and germs invisible.
For on whatever side thou deemest first
The primal bodies lacking, lo, that side
Will be for things the very door of death:
Wherethrough the throng of matter all will dash,
Out and abroad.
These points, if thou wilt ponder,
Then, with but paltry trouble led along...
For one thing after other will grow clear,
Nor shall the blind night rob thee of the road,
To hinder thy gaze on nature's Farthest-forth.
Thus things for things shall kindle torches new.

BOOK II

PROEM

'Tis sweet, when, down the mighty main, the winds
Roll up its waste of waters, from the land
To watch another's labouring anguish far,
Not that we joyously delight that man
Should thus be smitten, but because 'tis sweet
To mark what evils we ourselves be spared;
'Tis sweet, again, to view the mighty strife
Of armies embattled yonder o'er the plains,
Ourselves no sharers in the peril; but naught
There is more goodly than to hold the high
Serene plateaus, well fortressed by the wise,
Whence thou may'st look below on other men
And see them ev'rywhere wand'ring, all dispersed
In their lone seeking for the road of life;
Rivals in genius, or emulous in rank,
Pressing through days and nights with hugest toil
For summits of power and mastery of the world.
O wretched minds of men! O blinded hearts!
In how great perils, in what darks of life
Are spent the human years, however brief!—
O not to see that nature for herself
Barks after nothing, save that pain keep off,
Disjoined from the body, and that mind enjoy
Delightsome feeling, far from care and fear!
Therefore we see that our corporeal life
Needs little, altogether, and only such
As takes the pain away, and can besides
Strew underneath some number of delights.
More grateful 'tis at times (for nature craves
No artifice nor luxury), if forsooth
There be no golden images of boys
Along the halls, with right hands holding out
The lamps ablaze, the lights for evening feasts,
And if the house doth glitter not with gold

Nor gleam with silver, and to the lyre resound
No fretted and gilded ceilings overhead,
Yet still to lounge with friends in the soft grass
Beside a river of water, underneath
A big tree's boughs, and merrily to refresh
Our frames, with no vast outlay—most of all
If the weather is laughing and the times of the year
Besprinkle the green of the grass around with flowers.
Nor yet the quicker will hot fevers go,
If on a pictured tapestry thou toss,
Or purple robe, than if 'tis thine to lie
Upon the poor man's bedding. Wherefore, since
Treasure, nor rank, nor glory of a reign
Avail us naught for this our body, thus
Reckon them likewise nothing for the mind:
Save then perchance, when thou beholdest forth
Thy legions swarming round the Field of Mars,
Rousing a mimic warfare—either side
Strengthened with large auxiliaries and horse,
Alike equipped with arms, alike inspired;
Or save when also thou beholdest forth
Thy fleets to swarm, deploying down the sea:
For then, by such bright circumstance abashed,
Religion pales and flees thy mind; O then
The fears of death leave heart so free of care.
But if we note how all this pomp at last
Is but a drollery and a mocking sport,
And of a truth man's dread, with cares at heels,
Dreads not these sounds of arms, these savage swords
But among kings and lords of all the world
Mingles undaunted, nor is overawed
By gleam of gold nor by the splendour bright
Of purple robe, canst thou then doubt that this
Is aught, but power of thinking?—when, besides
The whole of life but labours in the dark.
For just as children tremble and fear all
In the viewless dark, so even we at times
Dread in the light so many things that be
No whit more fearsome than what children feign,
Shuddering, will be upon them in the dark.
This terror then, this darkness of the mind,
Not sunrise with its flaring spokes of light,
Nor glittering arrows of morning can disperse,

But only nature's aspect and her law.

ATOMIC MOTIONS

Now come: I will untangle for thy steps
Now by what motions the begetting bodies
Of the world-stuff beget the varied world,
And then forever resolve it when begot,
And by what force they are constrained to this,
And what the speed appointed unto them
Wherewith to travel down the vast inane:
Do thou remember to yield thee to my words.
For truly matter coheres not, crowds not tight,
Since we behold each thing to wane away,
And we observe how all flows on and off,
As 'twere, with age-old time, and from our eyes
How eld withdraws each object at the end,
Albeit the sum is seen to bide the same,
Unharmed, because these motes that leave each thing
Diminish what they part from, but endow
With increase those to which in turn they come,
Constraining these to wither in old age,
And those to flower at the prime (and yet
Biding not long among them). Thus the sum
Forever is replenished, and we live
As mortals by eternal give and take.
The nations wax, the nations wane away;
In a brief space the generations pass,
And like to runners hand the lamp of life
One unto other.
But if thou believe
That the primordial germs of things can stop,
And in their stopping give new motions birth,
Afar thou wanderest from the road of truth.
For since they wander through the void inane,
All the primordial germs of things must needs
Be borne along, either by weight their own,
Or haply by another's blow without.
For, when, in their incessancy so oft
They meet and clash, it comes to pass amain
They leap asunder, face to face: not strange—
Being most hard, and solid in their weights,

And naught opposing motion, from behind.
And that more clearly thou perceive how all
These mites of matter are darted round about,
Recall to mind how nowhere in the sum
Of All exists a bottom,—nowhere is
A realm of rest for primal bodies; since
(As amply shown and proved by reason sure)
Space has no bound nor measure, and extends
Unmetered forth in all directions round.
Since this stands certain, thus 'tis out of doubt
No rest is rendered to the primal bodies
Along the unfathomable inane; but rather,
Inveterately plied by motions mixed,
Some, at their jamming, bound aback and leave
Huge gaps between, and some from off the blow
Are hurried about with spaces small between.
And all which, brought together with slight gaps,
In more condensed union bound aback,
Linked by their own all inter-tangled shapes,—
These form the irrefragable roots of rocks
And the brute bulks of iron, and what else
Is of their kind...
The rest leap far asunder, far recoil,
Leaving huge gaps between: and these supply
For us thin air and splendour-lights of the sun.
And many besides wander the mighty void—
Cast back from unions of existing things,
Nowhere accepted in the universe,
And nowise linked in motions to the rest.
And of this fact (as I record it here)
An image, a type goes on before our eyes
Present each moment; for behold whenever
The sun's light and the rays, let in, pour down
Across dark halls of houses: thou wilt see
The many mites in many a manner mixed
Amid a void in the very light of the rays,
And battling on, as in eternal strife,
And in battalions contending without halt,
In meetings, partings, harried up and down.
From this thou mayest conjecture of what sort
The ceaseless tossing of primordial seeds
Amid the mightier void—at least so far
As small affair can for a vaster serve,

And by example put thee on the spoor
Of knowledge. For this reason too 'tis fit
Thou turn thy mind the more unto these bodies
Which here are witnessed tumbling in the light:
Namely, because such tumblings are a sign
That motions also of the primal stuff
Secret and viewless lurk beneath, behind.
For thou wilt mark here many a speck, impelled
By viewless blows, to change its little course,
And beaten backwards to return again,
Hither and thither in all directions round.
Lo, all their shifting movement is of old,
From the primeval atoms; for the same
Primordial seeds of things first move of self,
And then those bodies built of unions small
And nearest, as it were, unto the powers
Of the primeval atoms, are stirred up
By impulse of those atoms' unseen blows,
And these thereafter goad the next in size:
Thus motion ascends from the primevals on,
And stage by stage emerges to our sense,
Until those objects also move which we
Can mark in sunbeams, though it not appears
What blows do urge them.
Herein wonder not
How 'tis that, while the seeds of things are all
Moving forever, the sum yet seems to stand
Supremely still, except in cases where
A thing shows motion of its frame as whole.
For far beneath the ken of senses lies
The nature of those ultimates of the world;
And so, since those themselves thou canst not see,
Their motion also must they veil from men—
For mark, indeed, how things we can see, oft
Yet hide their motions, when afar from us
Along the distant landscape. Often thus,
Upon a hillside will the woolly flocks
Be cropping their goodly food and creeping about
Whither the summons of the grass, begemmed
With the fresh dew, is calling, and the lambs,
Well filled, are frisking, locking horns in sport:
Yet all for us seem blurred and blent afar—
A glint of white at rest on a green hill.

Again, when mighty legions, marching round,
Fill all the quarters of the plains below,
Rousing a mimic warfare, there the sheen
Shoots up the sky, and all the fields about
Glitter with brass, and from beneath, a sound
Goes forth from feet of stalwart soldiery,
And mountain walls, smote by the shouting, send
The voices onward to the stars of heaven,
And hither and thither darts the cavalry,
And of a sudden down the midmost fields
Charges with onset stout enough to rock
The solid earth: and yet some post there is
Up the high mountains, viewed from which they seem
To stand—a gleam at rest along the plains.
Now what the speed to matter's atoms given
Thou mayest in few, my Memmius, learn from this:
When first the dawn is sprinkling with new light
The lands, and all the breed of birds abroad
Flit round the trackless forests, with liquid notes
Filling the regions along the mellow air,
We see 'tis forthwith manifest to man
How suddenly the risen sun is wont
At such an hour to overspread and clothe
The whole with its own splendour; but the sun's
Warm exhalations and this serene light
Travel not down an empty void; and thus
They are compelled more slowly to advance,
Whilst, as it were, they cleave the waves of air;
Nor one by one travel these particles
Of the warm exhalations, but are all
Entangled and enmassed, whereby at once
Each is restrained by each, and from without
Checked, till compelled more slowly to advance.
But the primordial atoms with their old
Simple solidity, when forth they travel
Along the empty void, all undelayed
By aught outside them there, and they, each one
Being one unit from nature of its parts,
Are borne to that one place on which they strive
Still to lay hold, must then, beyond a doubt,
Outstrip in speed, and be more swiftly borne
Than light of sun, and over regions rush,
Of space much vaster, in the self-same time

The sun's effulgence widens round the sky.
Nor to pursue the atoms one by one,
To see the law whereby each thing goes on.
But some men, ignorant of matter, think,
Opposing this, that not without the gods,
In such adjustment to our human ways,
Can nature change the seasons of the years,
And bring to birth the grains and all of else
To which divine Delight, the guide of life,
Persuades mortality and leads it on,
That, through her artful blandishments of love,
It propagate the generations still,
Lest humankind should perish. When they feign
That gods have stablished all things but for man,
They seem in all ways mightily to lapse
From reason's truth: for ev'n if ne'er I knew
What seeds primordial are, yet would I dare
This to affirm, ev'n from deep judgment based
Upon the ways and conduct of the skies—
This to maintain by many a fact besides—
That in no wise the nature of the world
For us was builded by a power divine—
So great the faults it stands encumbered with:
The which, my Memmius, later on, for thee
We will clear up. Now as to what remains
Concerning motions we'll unfold our thought.
Now is the place, meseems, in these affairs
To prove for thee this too: nothing corporeal
Of its own force can e'er be upward borne,
Or upward go—nor let the bodies of flames
Deceive thee here: for they engendered are
With urge to upwards, taking thus increase,
Whereby grow upwards shining grains and trees,
Though all the weight within them downward bears.
Nor, when the fires will leap from under round
The roofs of houses, and swift flame laps up
Timber and beam, 'tis then to be supposed
They act of own accord, no force beneath
To urge them up. 'Tis thus that blood, discharged
From out our bodies, spurts its jets aloft
And spatters gore. And hast thou never marked
With what a force the water will disgorge
Timber and beam? The deeper, straight and down,

We push them in, and, many though we be,
The more we press with main and toil, the more
The water vomits up and flings them back,
That, more than half their length, they there emerge,
Rebounding. Yet we never doubt, meseems,
That all the weight within them downward bears
Through empty void. Well, in like manner, flames
Ought also to be able, when pressed out,
Through winds of air to rise aloft, even though
The weight within them strive to draw them down.
Hast thou not seen, sweeping so far and high,
The meteors, midnight flambeaus of the sky,
How after them they draw long trails of flame
Wherever Nature gives a thoroughfare?
How stars and constellations drop to earth,
Seest not? Nay, too, the sun from peak of heaven
Sheds round to every quarter its large heat,
And sows the new-ploughed intervales with light:
Thus also sun's heat downward tends to earth.
Athwart the rain thou seest the lightning fly;
Now here, now there, bursting from out the clouds,
The fires dash zig-zag—and that flaming power
Falls likewise down to earth.
In these affairs
We wish thee also well aware of this:
The atoms, as their own weight bears them down
Plumb through the void, at scarce determined times,
In scarce determined places, from their course
Decline a little—call it, so to speak,
Mere changed trend. For were it not their wont
Thuswise to swerve, down would they fall, each one,
Like drops of rain, through the unbottomed void;
And then collisions ne'er could be nor blows
Among the primal elements; and thus
Nature would never have created aught.
But, if perchance be any that believe
The heavier bodies, as more swiftly borne
Plumb down the void, are able from above
To strike the lighter, thus engendering blows
Able to cause those procreant motions, far
From highways of true reason they retire.
For whatsoever through the waters fall,
Or through thin air, must quicken their descent,

Each after its weight—on this account, because
Both bulk of water and the subtle air
By no means can retard each thing alike,
But give more quick before the heavier weight;
But contrariwise the empty void cannot,
On any side, at any time, to aught
Oppose resistance, but will ever yield,
True to its bent of nature. Wherefore all,
With equal speed, though equal not in weight,
Must rush, borne downward through the still inane.
Thus ne'er at all have heavier from above
Been swift to strike the lighter, gendering strokes
Which cause those divers motions, by whose means
Nature transacts her work. And so I say,
The atoms must a little swerve at times—
But only the least, lest we should seem to feign
Motions oblique, and fact refute us there.
For this we see forthwith is manifest:
Whatever the weight, it can't obliquely go,
Down on its headlong journey from above,
At least so far as thou canst mark; but who
Is there can mark by sense that naught can swerve
At all aside from off its road's straight line?
Again, if ev'r all motions are co-linked,
And from the old ever arise the new
In fixed order, and primordial seeds
Produce not by their swerving some new start
Of motion to sunder the covenants of fate,
That cause succeed not cause from everlasting,
Whence this free will for creatures o'er the lands,
Whence is it wrested from the fates,—this will
Whereby we step right forward where desire
Leads each man on, whereby the same we swerve
In motions, not as at some fixed time,
Nor at some fixed line of space, but where
The mind itself has urged? For out of doubt
In these affairs 'tis each man's will itself
That gives the start, and hence throughout our limbs
Incipient motions are diffused. Again,
Dost thou not see, when, at a point of time,
The bars are opened, how the eager strength
Of horses cannot forward break as soon
As pants their mind to do? For it behooves

That all the stock of matter, through the frame,
Be roused, in order that, through every joint,
Aroused, it press and follow mind's desire;
So thus thou seest initial motion's gendered
From out the heart, aye, verily, proceeds
First from the spirit's will, whence at the last
'Tis given forth through joints and body entire.
Quite otherwise it is, when forth we move,
Impelled by a blow of another's mighty powers
And mighty urge; for then 'tis clear enough
All matter of our total body goes,
Hurried along, against our own desire—
Until the will has pulled upon the reins
And checked it back, throughout our members all;
At whose arbitrament indeed sometimes
The stock of matter's forced to change its path,
Throughout our members and throughout our joints,
And, after being forward cast, to be
Reined up, whereat it settles back again.
So seest thou not, how, though external force
Drive men before, and often make them move,
Onward against desire, and headlong snatched,
Yet is there something in these breasts of ours
Strong to combat, strong to withstand the same?—
Wherefore no less within the primal seeds
Thou must admit, besides all blows and weight,
Some other cause of motion, whence derives
This power in us inborn, of some free act.—
Since naught from nothing can become, we see.
For weight prevents all things should come to pass
Through blows, as 'twere, by some external force;
But that man's mind itself in all it does
Hath not a fixed necessity within,
Nor is not, like a conquered thing, compelled
To bear and suffer,—this state comes to man
From that slight swervement of the elements
In no fixed line of space, in no fixed time.
Nor ever was the stock of stuff more crammed,
Nor ever, again, sundered by bigger gaps:
For naught gives increase and naught takes away;
On which account, just as they move to-day,
The elemental bodies moved of old
And shall the same hereafter evermore.

And what was wont to be begot of old
Shall be begotten under selfsame terms
And grow and thrive in power, so far as given
To each by Nature's changeless, old decrees.
The sum of things there is no power can change,
For naught exists outside, to which can flee
Out of the world matter of any kind,
Nor forth from which a fresh supply can spring,
Break in upon the founded world, and change
Whole nature of things, and turn their motions about.

ATOMIC FORMS AND THEIR COMBINATIONS

Now come, and next hereafter apprehend
What sorts, how vastly different in form,
How varied in multitudinous shapes they are—
These old beginnings of the universe;
Not in the sense that only few are furnished
With one like form, but rather not at all
In general have they likeness each with each,
No marvel: since the stock of them's so great
That there's no end (as I have taught) nor sum,
They must indeed not one and all be marked
By equal outline and by shape the same.

Moreover, humankind, and the mute flocks
Of scaly creatures swimming in the streams,
And joyous herds around, and all the wild,
And all the breeds of birds—both those that teem
In gladsome regions of the water-haunts,
About the river-banks and springs and pools,
And those that throng, flitting from tree to tree,
Through trackless woods—Go, take which one thou wilt,
In any kind: thou wilt discover still
Each from the other still unlike in shape.
Nor in no other wise could offspring know
Mother, nor mother offspring—which we see
They yet can do, distinguished one from other,
No less than human beings, by clear signs.
Thus oft before fair temples of the gods,
Beside the incense-burning altars slain,
Drops down the yearling calf, from out its breast

Breathing warm streams of blood; the orphaned mother,
Ranging meanwhile green woodland pastures round,
Knows well the footprints, pressed by cloven hoofs,
With eyes regarding every spot about,
For sight somewhere of youngling gone from her;
And, stopping short, filleth the leafy lanes
With her complaints; and oft she seeks again
Within the stall, pierced by her yearning still.
Nor tender willows, nor dew-quickened grass,
Nor the loved streams that glide along low banks,
Can lure her mind and turn the sudden pain;
Nor other shapes of calves that graze thereby
Distract her mind or lighten pain the least—
So keen her search for something known and hers.
Moreover, tender kids with bleating throats
Do know their horned dams, and butting lambs
The flocks of sheep, and thus they patter on,
Unfailingly each to its proper teat,
As nature intends. Lastly, with any grain,
Thou'lt see that no one kernel in one kind
Is so far like another, that there still
Is not in shapes some difference running through.
By a like law we see how earth is pied
With shells and conchs, where, with soft waves, the sea
Beats on the thirsty sands of curving shores.
Wherefore again, again, since seeds of things
Exist by nature, nor were wrought with hands
After a fixed pattern of one other,
They needs must flitter to and fro with shapes
In types dissimilar to one another.
Easy enough by thought of mind to solve
Why fires of lightning more can penetrate
Than these of ours from pitch-pine born on earth.
For thou canst say lightning's celestial fire,
So subtle, is formed of figures finer far,
And passes thus through holes which this our fire,
Born from the wood, created from the pine,
Cannot. Again, light passes through the horn
On the lantern's side, while rain is dashed away.
And why?—unless those bodies of light should be
Finer than those of water's genial showers.
We see how quickly through a colander
The wines will flow; how, on the other hand,

The sluggish olive-oil delays: no doubt,
Because 'tis wrought of elements more large,
Or else more crook'd and intertangled. Thus
It comes that the primordials cannot be
So suddenly sundered one from other, and seep,
One through each several hole of anything.
And note, besides, that liquor of honey or milk
Yields in the mouth agreeable taste to tongue,
Whilst nauseous wormwood, pungent centaury,
With their foul flavour set the lips awry;
Thus simple 'tis to see that whatsoever
Can touch the senses pleasingly are made
Of smooth and rounded elements, whilst those
Which seem the bitter and the sharp, are held
Entwined by elements more crook'd, and so
Are wont to tear their ways into our senses,
And rend our body as they enter in.
In short all good to sense, all bad to touch,
Being up-built of figures so unlike,
Are mutually at strife—lest thou suppose
That the shrill rasping of a squeaking saw
Consists of elements as smooth as song
Which, waked by nimble fingers, on the strings
The sweet musicians fashion; or suppose
That same-shaped atoms through men's nostrils pierce
When foul cadavers burn, as when the stage
Is with Cilician saffron sprinkled fresh,
And the altar near exhales Panchaean scent;
Or hold as of like seed the goodly hues
Of things which feast our eyes, as those which sting
Against the smarting pupil and draw tears,
Or show, with gruesome aspect, grim and vile.
For never a shape which charms our sense was made
Without some elemental smoothness; whilst
Whate'er is harsh and irksome has been framed
Still with some roughness in its elements.
Some, too, there are which justly are supposed
To be nor smooth nor altogether hooked,
With bended barbs, but slightly angled-out,
To tickle rather than to wound the sense—
And of which sort is the salt tartar of wine
And flavours of the gummed elecampane.
Again, that glowing fire and icy rime

Are fanged with teeth unlike whereby to sting
Our body's sense, the touch of each gives proof.
For touch—by sacred majesties of Gods!—
Touch is indeed the body's only sense—
Be't that something in-from-outward works,
Be't that something in the body born
Wounds, or delighteth as it passes out
Along the procreant paths of Aphrodite;
Or be't the seeds by some collision whirl
Disordered in the body and confound
By tumult and confusion all the sense—
As thou mayst find, if haply with the hand
Thyself thou strike thy body's any part.
On which account, the elemental forms
Must differ widely, as enabled thus
To cause diverse sensations.
And, again,
What seems to us the hardened and condensed
Must be of atoms among themselves more hooked,
Be held compacted deep within, as 'twere
By branch-like atoms—of which sort the chief
Are diamond stones, despisers of all blows,
And stalwart flint and strength of solid iron,
And brazen bars, which, budging hard in locks,
Do grate and scream. But what are liquid, formed
Of fluid body, they indeed must be
Of elements more smooth and round—because
Their globules severally will not cohere:
To suck the poppy-seeds from palm of hand
Is quite as easy as drinking water down,
And they, once struck, roll like unto the same.
But that thou seest among the things that flow
Some bitter, as the brine of ocean is,
Is not the least a marvel...
For since 'tis fluid, smooth its atoms are
And round, with painful rough ones mixed therein;
Yet need not these be held together hooked:
In fact, though rough, they're globular besides,
Able at once to roll, and rasp the sense.
And that the more thou mayst believe me here,
That with smooth elements are mixed the rough
(Whence Neptune's salt astringent body comes),
There is a means to separate the twain,

And thereupon dividedly to see
How the sweet water, after filtering through
So often underground, flows freshened forth
Into some hollow; for it leaves above
The primal germs of nauseating brine,
Since cling the rough more readily in earth.
Lastly, whatso thou markest to disperse
Upon the instant—smoke, and cloud, and flame—
Must not (even though not all of smooth and round)
Be yet co-linked with atoms intertwined,
That thus they can, without together cleaving,
So pierce our body and so bore the rocks.
Whatever we see...
Given to senses, that thou must perceive
They're not from linked but pointed elements.
The which now having taught, I will go on
To bind thereto a fact to this allied
And drawing from this its proof: these primal germs
Vary, yet only with finite tale of shapes.
For were these shapes quite infinite, some seeds
Would have a body of infinite increase.
For in one seed, in one small frame of any,
The shapes can't vary from one another much.
Assume, we'll say, that of three minim parts
Consist the primal bodies, or add a few:
When, now, by placing all these parts of one
At top and bottom, changing lefts and rights,
Thou hast with every kind of shift found out
What the aspect of shape of its whole body
Each new arrangement gives, for what remains,
If thou percase wouldst vary its old shapes,
New parts must then be added; follows next,
If thou percase wouldst vary still its shapes,
That by like logic each arrangement still
Requires its increment of other parts.
Ergo, an augmentation of its frame
Follows upon each novelty of forms.
Wherefore, it cannot be thou'lt undertake
That seeds have infinite differences in form,
Lest thus thou forcest some indeed to be
Of an immeasurable immensity—
Which I have taught above cannot be proved.

And now for thee barbaric robes, and gleam
Of Meliboean purple, touched with dye
Of the Thessalian shell...
The peacock's golden generations, stained
With spotted gaieties, would lie o'erthrown
By some new colour of new things more bright;
The odour of myrrh and savours of honey despised;
The swan's old lyric, and Apollo's hymns,
Once modulated on the many chords,
Would likewise sink o'ermastered and be mute:
For, lo, a somewhat, finer than the rest,
Would be arising evermore. So, too,
Into some baser part might all retire,
Even as we said to better might they come:
For, lo, a somewhat, loathlier than the rest
To nostrils, ears, and eyes, and taste of tongue,
Would then, by reasoning reversed, be there.
Since 'tis not so, but unto things are given
Their fixed limitations which do bound
Their sum on either side, 'tmust be confessed
That matter, too, by finite tale of shapes
Does differ. Again, from earth's midsummer heats
Unto the icy hoar-frosts of the year
The forward path is fixed, and by like law
O'ertravelled backwards at the dawn of spring.
For each degree of hot, and each of cold,
And the half-warm, all filling up the sum
In due progression, lie, my Memmius, there
Betwixt the two extremes: the things create
Must differ, therefore, by a finite change,
Since at each end marked off they ever are
By fixed point—on one side plagued by flames
And on the other by congealing frosts.
The which now having taught, I will go on
To bind thereto a fact to this allied
And drawing from this its proof: those primal germs
Which have been fashioned all of one like shape
Are infinite in tale; for, since the forms
Themselves are finite in divergences,
Then those which are alike will have to be
Infinite, else the sum of stuff remains
A finite—what I've proved is not the fact,
Showing in verse how corpuscles of stuff,

From everlasting and to-day the same,
Uphold the sum of things, all sides around
By old succession of unending blows.
For though thou view'st some beasts to be more rare,
And mark'st in them a less prolific stock,
Yet in another region, in lands remote,
That kind abounding may make up the count;
Even as we mark among the four-foot kind
Snake-handed elephants, whose thousands wall
With ivory ramparts India about,
That her interiors cannot entered be—
So big her count of brutes of which we see
Such few examples. Or suppose, besides,
We feign some thing, one of its kind and sole
With body born, to which is nothing like
In all the lands: yet now unless shall be
An infinite count of matter out of which
Thus to conceive and bring it forth to life,
It cannot be created and—what's more—
It cannot take its food and get increase.
Yea, if through all the world in finite tale
Be tossed the procreant bodies of one thing,
Whence, then, and where in what mode, by what power,
Shall they to meeting come together there,
In such vast ocean of matter and tumult strange?—
No means they have of joining into one.
But, just as, after mighty ship-wrecks piled,
The mighty main is wont to scatter wide
The rowers' banks, the ribs, the yards, the prow,
The masts and swimming oars, so that afar
Along all shores of lands are seen afloat
The carven fragments of the rended poop,
Giving a lesson to mortality
To shun the ambush of the faithless main,
The violence and the guile, and trust it not
At any hour, however much may smile
The crafty enticements of the placid deep:
Exactly thus, if once thou holdest true
That certain seeds are finite in their tale,
The various tides of matter, then, must needs
Scatter them flung throughout the ages all,
So that not ever can they join, as driven
Together into union, nor remain

In union, nor with increment can grow—
But facts in proof are manifest for each:
Things can be both begotten and increase.
'Tis therefore manifest that primal germs,
Are infinite in any class thou wilt—
From whence is furnished matter for all things.
Nor can those motions that bring death prevail
Forever, nor eternally entomb
The welfare of the world; nor, further, can
Those motions that give birth to things and growth
Keep them forever when created there.
Thus the long war, from everlasting waged,
With equal strife among the elements
Goes on and on. Now here, now there, prevail
The vital forces of the world—or fall.
Mixed with the funeral is the wildered wail
Of infants coming to the shores of light:
No night a day, no dawn a night hath followed
That heard not, mingling with the small birth-cries,
The wild laments, companions old of death
And the black rites.
This, too, in these affairs
'Tis fit thou hold well sealed, and keep consigned
With no forgetting brain: nothing there is
Whose nature is apparent out of hand
That of one kind of elements consists—
Nothing there is that's not of mixed seed.
And whatsoe'er possesses in itself
More largely many powers and properties
Shows thus that here within itself there are
The largest number of kinds and differing shapes
Of elements. And, chief of all, the earth
Hath in herself first bodies whence the springs,
Rolling chill waters, renew forevermore
The unmeasured main; hath whence the fires arise—
For burns in many a spot her flamed crust,
Whilst the impetuous Aetna raves indeed
From more profounder fires—and she, again,
Hath in herself the seed whence she can raise
The shining grains and gladsome trees for men;
Whence, also, rivers, fronds, and gladsome pastures
Can she supply for mountain-roaming beasts.
Wherefore great mother of gods, and mother of beasts,

And parent of man hath she alone been named.
Her hymned the old and learned bards of Greece
Seated in chariot o'er the realms of air
To drive her team of lions, teaching thus
That the great earth hangs poised and cannot lie
Resting on other earth. Unto her car
They've yoked the wild beasts, since a progeny,
However savage, must be tamed and chid
By care of parents. They have girt about
With turret-crown the summit of her head,
Since, fortressed in her goodly strongholds high,
'Tis she sustains the cities; now, adorned
With that same token, to-day is carried forth,
With solemn awe through many a mighty land,
The image of that mother, the divine.
Her the wide nations, after antique rite,
Do name Idaean Mother, giving her
Escort of Phrygian bands, since first, they say,
From out those regions 'twas that grain began
Through all the world. To her do they assign
The Galli, the emasculate, since thus
They wish to show that men who violate
The majesty of the mother and have proved
Ingrate to parents are to be adjudged
Unfit to give unto the shores of light
A living progeny. The Galli come:
And hollow cymbals, tight-skinned tambourines
Resound around to bangings of their hands;
The fierce horns threaten with a raucous bray;
The tubed pipe excites their maddened minds
In Phrygian measures; they bear before them knives,
Wild emblems of their frenzy, which have power
The rabble's ingrate heads and impious hearts
To panic with terror of the goddess' might.
And so, when through the mighty cities borne,
She blesses man with salutations mute,
They strew the highway of her journeyings
With coin of brass and silver, gifting her
With alms and largesse, and shower her and shade
With flowers of roses falling like the snow
Upon the Mother and her companion-bands.
Here is an armed troop, the which by Greeks
Are called the Phrygian Curetes. Since

Haply among themselves they use to play
In games of arms and leap in measure round
With bloody mirth and by their nodding shake
The terrorizing crests upon their heads,
This is the armed troop that represents
The arm'd Dictaean Curetes, who, in Crete,
As runs the story, whilom did out-drown
That infant cry of Zeus, what time their band,
Young boys, in a swift dance around the boy,
To measured step beat with the brass on brass,
That Saturn might not get him for his jaws,
And give its mother an eternal wound
Along her heart. And 'tis on this account
That armed they escort the mighty Mother,
Or else because they signify by this
That she, the goddess, teaches men to be
Eager with armed valour to defend
Their motherland, and ready to stand forth,
The guard and glory of their parents' years.
A tale, however beautifully wrought,
That's wide of reason by a long remove:
For all the gods must of themselves enjoy
Immortal aeons and supreme repose,
Withdrawn from our affairs, detached, afar:
Immune from peril and immune from pain,
Themselves abounding in riches of their own,
Needing not us, they are not touched by wrath
They are not taken by service or by gift.
Truly is earth insensate for all time;
But, by obtaining germs of many things,
In many a way she brings the many forth
Into the light of sun. And here, whoso
Decides to call the ocean Neptune, or
The grain-crop Ceres, and prefers to abuse
The name of Bacchus rather than pronounce
The liquor's proper designation, him
Let us permit to go on calling earth
Mother of Gods, if only he will spare
To taint his soul with foul religion.
So, too, the wooly flocks, and horned kine,
And brood of battle-eager horses, grazing
Often together along one grassy plain,
Under the cope of one blue sky, and slaking

From out one stream of water each its thirst,
All live their lives with face and form unlike,
Keeping the parents' nature, parents' habits,
Which, kind by kind, through ages they repeat.
So great in any sort of herb thou wilt,
So great again in any river of earth
Are the distinct diversities of matter.
Hence, further, every creature—any one
From out them all—compounded is the same
Of bones, blood, veins, heat, moisture, flesh, and thews—
All differing vastly in their forms, and built
Of elements dissimilar in shape.
Again, all things by fire consumed ablaze,
Within their frame lay up, if naught besides,
At least those atoms whence derives their power
To throw forth fire and send out light from under,
To shoot the sparks and scatter embers wide.
If, with like reasoning of mind, all else
Thou traverse through, thou wilt discover thus
That in their frame the seeds of many things
They hide, and divers shapes of seeds contain.
Further, thou markest much, to which are given
Along together colour and flavour and smell,
Among which, chief, are most burnt offerings.
Thus must they be of divers shapes composed.
A smell of scorching enters in our frame
Where the bright colour from the dye goes not;
And colour in one way, flavour in quite another
Works inward to our senses—so mayst see
They differ too in elemental shapes.
Thus unlike forms into one mass combine,
And things exist by intermixed seed.
But still 'tmust not be thought that in all ways
All things can be conjoined; for then wouldst view
Portents begot about thee every side:
Hulks of mankind half brute astarting up,
At times big branches sprouting from man's trunk,
Limbs of a sea-beast to a land-beast knit,
And nature along the all-producing earth
Feeding those dire Chimaeras breathing flame
From hideous jaws—Of which 'tis simple fact
That none have been begot; because we see
All are from fixed seed and fixed dam

Engendered and so function as to keep
Throughout their growth their own ancestral type.
This happens surely by a fixed law:
For from all food-stuff, when once eaten down,
Go sundered atoms, suited to each creature,
Throughout their bodies, and, conjoining there,
Produce the proper motions; but we see
How, contrariwise, nature upon the ground
Throws off those foreign to their frame; and many
With viewless bodies from their bodies fly,
By blows impelled—those impotent to join
To any part, or, when inside, to accord
And to take on the vital motions there.
But think not, haply, living forms alone
Are bound by these laws: they distinguished all.

For just as all things of creation are,
In their whole nature, each to each unlike,
So must their atoms be in shape unlike—
Not since few only are fashioned of like form,
But since they all, as general rule, are not
The same as all. Nay, here in these our verses,
Elements many, common to many words,
Thou seest, though yet 'tis needful to confess
The words and verses differ, each from each,
Compounded out of different elements—
Not since few only, as common letters, run
Through all the words, or no two words are made,
One and the other, from all like elements,
But since they all, as general rule, are not
The same as all. Thus, too, in other things,
Whilst many germs common to many things
There are, yet they, combined among themselves,
Can form new wholes to others quite unlike.
Thus fairly one may say that humankind,
The grains, the gladsome trees, are all made up
Of different atoms. Further, since the seeds
Are different, difference must there also be
In intervening spaces, thoroughfares,
Connections, weights, blows, clashings, motions, all
Which not alone distinguish living forms,
But sunder earth's whole ocean from the lands,
And hold all heaven from the lands away.

ABSENCE OF SECONDARY QUALITIES

Now come, this wisdom by my sweet toil sought
Look thou perceive, lest haply thou shouldst guess
That the white objects shining to thine eyes
Are gendered of white atoms, or the black
Of a black seed; or yet believe that aught
That's steeped in any hue should take its dye
From bits of matter tinct with hue the same.
For matter's bodies own no hue the least—
Or like to objects or, again, unlike.
But, if percase it seem to thee that mind
Itself can dart no influence of its own
Into these bodies, wide thou wand'rest off.
For since the blind-born, who have ne'er surveyed
The light of sun, yet recognise by touch
Things that from birth had ne'er a hue for them,
'Tis thine to know that bodies can be brought
No less unto the ken of our minds too,
Though yet those bodies with no dye be smeared.
Again, ourselves whatever in the dark
We touch, the same we do not find to be
Tinctured with any colour.
Now that here
I win the argument, I next will teach
Now, every colour changes, none except,
And every...
Which the primordials ought nowise to do.
Since an immutable somewhat must remain,
Lest all things utterly be brought to naught.
For change of anything from out its bounds
Means instant death of that which was before.
Wherefore be mindful not to stain with colour
The seeds of things, lest things return for thee
All utterly to naught.
But now, if seeds
Receive no property of colour, and yet
Be still endowed with variable forms
From which all kinds of colours they beget
And vary (by reason that ever it matters much
With what seeds, and in what positions joined,
And what the motions that they give and get),
Forthwith most easily thou mayst devise

Why what was black of hue an hour ago
Can of a sudden like the marble gleam,—
As ocean, when the high winds have upheaved
Its level plains, is changed to hoary waves
Of marble whiteness: for, thou mayst declare,
That, when the thing we often see as black
Is in its matter then commixed anew,
Some atoms rearranged, and some withdrawn,
And added some, 'tis seen forthwith to turn
Glowing and white. But if of azure seeds
Consist the level waters of the deep,
They could in nowise whiten: for however
Thou shakest azure seeds, the same can never
Pass into marble hue. But, if the seeds—
Which thus produce the ocean's one pure sheen—
Be now with one hue, now another dyed,
As oft from alien forms and divers shapes
A cube's produced all uniform in shape,
'Twould be but natural, even as in the cube
We see the forms to be dissimilar,
That thus we'd see in brightness of the deep
(Or in whatever one pure sheen thou wilt)
Colours diverse and all dissimilar.
Besides, the unlike shapes don't thwart the least
The whole in being externally a cube;
But differing hues of things do block and keep
The whole from being of one resultant hue.
Then, too, the reason which entices us
At times to attribute colours to the seeds
Falls quite to pieces, since white things are not
Create from white things, nor are black from black,
But evermore they are create from things
Of divers colours. Verily, the white
Will rise more readily, is sooner born
Out of no colour, than of black or aught
Which stands in hostile opposition thus.
Besides, since colours cannot be, sans light,
And the primordials come not forth to light,
'Tis thine to know they are not clothed with colour—
Truly, what kind of colour could there be
In the viewless dark? Nay, in the light itself
A colour changes, gleaming variedly,
When smote by vertical or slanting ray.

Thus in the sunlight shows the down of doves
That circles, garlanding, the nape and throat:
Now it is ruddy with a bright gold-bronze,
Now, by a strange sensation it becomes
Green-emerald blended with the coral-red.
The peacock's tail, filled with the copious light,
Changes its colours likewise, when it turns.
Wherefore, since by some blow of light begot,
Without such blow these colours can't become.
And since the pupil of the eye receives
Within itself one kind of blow, when said
To feel a white hue, then another kind,
When feeling a black or any other hue,
And since it matters nothing with what hue
The things thou touchest be perchance endowed,
But rather with what sort of shape equipped,
'Tis thine to know the atoms need not colour,
But render forth sensations, as of touch,
That vary with their varied forms.
Besides,
Since special shapes have not a special colour,
And all formations of the primal germs
Can be of any sheen thou wilt, why, then,
Are not those objects which are of them made
Suffused, each kind with colours of every kind?
For then 'twere meet that ravens, as they fly,
Should dartle from white pinions a white sheen,
Or swans turn black from seed of black, or be
Of any single varied dye thou wilt.
Again, the more an object's rent to bits,
The more thou see its colour fade away
Little by little till 'tis quite extinct;
As happens when the gaudy linen's picked
Shred after shred away: the purple there,
Phoenician red, most brilliant of all dyes,
Is lost asunder, ravelled thread by thread;
Hence canst perceive the fragments die away
From out their colour, long ere they depart
Back to the old primordials of things.
And, last, since thou concedest not all bodies
Send out a voice or smell, it happens thus
That not to all thou givest sounds and smells.
So, too, since we behold not all with eyes,

'Tis thine to know some things there are as much
Orphaned of colour, as others without smell,
And reft of sound; and those the mind alert
No less can apprehend than it can mark
The things that lack some other qualities.
But think not haply that the primal bodies
Remain despoiled alone of colour: so,
Are they from warmth dissevered and from cold
And from hot exhalations; and they move,
Both sterile of sound and dry of juice; and throw
Not any odour from their proper bodies.
Just as, when undertaking to prepare
A liquid balm of myrrh and marjoram,
And flower of nard, which to our nostrils breathes
Odour of nectar, first of all behooves
Thou seek, as far as find thou may and can,
The inodorous olive-oil (which never sends
One whiff of scent to nostrils), that it may
The least debauch and ruin with sharp tang
The odorous essence with its body mixed
And in it seethed. And on the same account
The primal germs of things must not be thought
To furnish colour in begetting things,
Nor sound, since pow'rless they to send forth aught
From out themselves, nor any flavour, too,
Nor cold, nor exhalation hot or warm.
The rest; yet since these things are mortal all—
The pliant mortal, with a body soft;
The brittle mortal, with a crumbling frame;
The hollow with a porous-all must be
Disjoined from the primal elements,
If still we wish under the world to lay
Immortal ground-works, whereupon may rest
The sum of weal and safety, lest for thee
All things return to nothing utterly.
Now, too: whate'er we see possessing sense
Must yet confessedly be stablished all
From elements insensate. And those signs,
So clear to all and witnessed out of hand,
Do not refute this dictum nor oppose;
But rather themselves do lead us by the hand,
Compelling belief that living things are born
Of elements insensate, as I say.

Sooth, we may see from out the stinking dung
Live worms spring up, when, after soaking rains,
The drenched earth rots; and all things change the same:
Lo, change the rivers, the fronds, the gladsome pastures
Into the cattle, the cattle their nature change
Into our bodies, and from our body, oft
Grow strong the powers and bodies of wild beasts
And mighty-winged birds. Thus nature changes
All foods to living frames, and procreates
From them the senses of live creatures all,
In manner about as she uncoils in flames
Dry logs of wood and turns them all to fire.
And seest not, therefore, how it matters much
After what order are set the primal germs,
And with what other germs they all are mixed,
And what the motions that they give and get?
But now, what is't that strikes thy sceptic mind,
Constraining thee to sundry arguments
Against belief that from insensate germs
The sensible is gendered?—Verily,
'Tis this: that liquids, earth, and wood, though mixed,
Are yet unable to gender vital sense.
And, therefore, 'twill be well in these affairs
This to remember: that I have not said
Senses are born, under conditions all,
From all things absolutely which create
Objects that feel; but much it matters here
Firstly, how small the seeds which thus compose
The feeling thing, then, with what shapes endowed,
And lastly what they in positions be,
In motions, in arrangements. Of which facts
Naught we perceive in logs of wood and clods;
And yet even these, when sodden by the rains,
Give birth to wormy grubs, because the bodies
Of matter, from their old arrangements stirred
By the new factor, then combine anew
In such a way as genders living things.
Next, they who deem that feeling objects can
From feeling objects be create, and these,
In turn, from others that are wont to feel
When soft they make them; for all sense is linked
With flesh, and thews, and veins—and such, we see,
Are fashioned soft and of a mortal frame.

Yet be't that these can last forever on:
They'll have the sense that's proper to a part,
Or else be judged to have a sense the same
As that within live creatures as a whole.
But of themselves those parts can never feel,
For all the sense in every member back
To something else refers—a severed hand,
Or any other member of our frame,
Itself alone cannot support sensation.
It thus remains they must resemble, then,
Live creatures as a whole, to have the power
Of feeling sensation concordant in each part
With the vital sense; and so they're bound to feel
The things we feel exactly as do we.
If such the case, how, then, can they be named
The primal germs of things, and how avoid
The highways of destruction?—since they be
Mere living things and living things be all
One and the same with mortal. Grant they could,
Yet by their meetings and their unions all,
Naught would result, indeed, besides a throng
And hurly-burly all of living things—
Precisely as men, and cattle, and wild beasts,
By mere conglomeration each with each
Can still beget not anything of new.
But if by chance they lose, inside a body,
Their own sense and another sense take on,
What, then, avails it to assign them that
Which is withdrawn thereafter? And besides,
To touch on proof that we pronounced before,
Just as we see the eggs of feathered fowls
To change to living chicks, and swarming worms
To bubble forth when from the soaking rains
The earth is sodden, sure, sensations all
Can out of non-sensations be begot.
But if one say that sense can so far rise
From non-sense by mutation, or because
Brought forth as by a certain sort of birth,
'Twill serve to render plain to him and prove
There is no birth, unless there be before
Some formed union of the elements,
Nor any change, unless they be unite.

In first place, senses can't in body be
Before its living nature's been begot,—
Since all its stuff, in faith, is held dispersed
About through rivers, air, and earth, and all
That is from earth created, nor has met
In combination, and, in proper mode,
Conjoined into those vital motions which
Kindle the all-perceiving senses—they
That keep and guard each living thing soever.
Again, a blow beyond its nature's strength
Shatters forthwith each living thing soe'er,
And on it goes confounding all the sense
Of body and mind. For of the primal germs
Are loosed their old arrangements, and, throughout,
The vital motions blocked,—until the stuff,
Shaken profoundly through the frame entire,
Undoes the vital knots of soul from body
And throws that soul, to outward wide-dispersed,
Through all the pores. For what may we surmise
A blow inflicted can achieve besides
Shaking asunder and loosening all apart?
It happens also, when less sharp the blow,
The vital motions which are left are wont
Oft to win out—win out, and stop and still
The uncouth tumults gendered by the blow,
And call each part to its own courses back,
And shake away the motion of death which now
Begins its own dominion in the body,
And kindle anew the senses almost gone.
For by what other means could they the more
Collect their powers of thought and turn again
From very doorways of destruction
Back unto life, rather than pass whereto
They be already well-nigh sped and so
Pass quite away?
Again, since pain is there
Where bodies of matter, by some force stirred up,
Through vitals and through joints, within their seats
Quiver and quake inside, but soft delight,
When they remove unto their place again:
'Tis thine to know the primal germs can be
Assaulted by no pain, nor from themselves
Take no delight; because indeed they are

Not made of any bodies of first things,
Under whose strange new motions they might ache
Or pluck the fruit of any dear new sweet.
And so they must be furnished with no sense.
Once more, if thus, that every living thing
May have sensation, needful 'tis to assign
Sense also to its elements, what then
Of those fixed elements from which mankind
Hath been, by their peculiar virtue, formed?
Of verity, they'll laugh aloud, like men,
Shaken asunder by a spasm of mirth,
Or sprinkle with dewy tear-drops cheeks and chins,
And have the cunning hardihood to say
Much on the composition of the world,
And in their turn inquire what elements
They have themselves,—since, thus the same in kind
As a whole mortal creature, even they
Must also be from other elements,
And then those others from others evermore—
So that thou darest nowhere make a stop.
Oho, I'll follow thee until thou grant
The seed (which here thou say'st speaks, laughs, and thinks)
Is yet derived out of other seeds
Which in their turn are doing just the same.
But if we see what raving nonsense this,
And that a man may laugh, though not, forsooth,
Compounded out of laughing elements,
And think and utter reason with learn'd speech,
Though not himself compounded, for a fact,
Of sapient seeds and eloquent, why, then,
Cannot those things which we perceive to have
Their own sensation be composed as well
Of intermixed seeds quite void of sense?

INFINITE WORLDS

Once more, we all from seed celestial spring,
To all is that same father, from whom earth,
The fostering mother, as she takes the drops
Of liquid moisture, pregnant bears her broods—
The shining grains, and gladsome shrubs and trees,
And bears the human race and of the wild

The generations all, the while she yields
The foods wherewith all feed their frames and lead
The genial life and propagate their kind;
Wherefore she owneth that maternal name,
By old desert. What was before from earth,
The same in earth sinks back, and what was sent
From shores of ether, that, returning home,
The vaults of sky receive. Nor thus doth death
So far annihilate things that she destroys
The bodies of matter; but she dissipates
Their combinations, and conjoins anew
One element with others; and contrives
That all things vary forms and change their colours
And get sensations and straight give them o'er.
And thus may'st know it matters with what others
And in what structure the primordial germs
Are held together, and what motions they
Among themselves do give and get; nor think
That aught we see hither and thither afloat
Upon the crest of things, and now a birth
And straightway now a ruin, inheres at rest
Deep in the eternal atoms of the world.

Why, even in these our very verses here
It matters much with what and in what order
Each element is set: the same denote
Sky, and the ocean, lands, and streams, and sun;
The same, the grains, and trees, and living things.
And if not all alike, at least the most—
But what distinctions by positions wrought!
And thus no less in things themselves, when once
Around are changed the intervals between,
The paths of matter, its connections, weights,
Blows, clashings, motions, order, structure, shapes,
The things themselves must likewise changed be.

Now to true reason give thy mind for us.
Since here strange truth is putting forth its might
To hit thee in thine ears, a new aspect
Of things to show its front. Yet naught there is
So easy that it standeth not at first
More hard to credit than it after is;
And naught soe'er that's great to such degree,

Nor wonderful so far, but all mankind
Little by little abandon their surprise.
Look upward yonder at the bright clear sky
And what it holds—the stars that wander o'er,
The moon, the radiance of the splendour-sun:
Yet all, if now they first for mortals were,
If unforeseen now first asudden shown,
What might there be more wonderful to tell,
What that the nations would before have dared
Less to believe might be?—I fancy, naught—
So strange had been the marvel of that sight.
The which o'erwearied to behold, to-day
None deigns look upward to those lucent realms.
Then, spew not reason from thy mind away,
Beside thyself because the matter's new,
But rather with keen judgment nicely weigh;
And if to thee it then appeareth true,
Render thy hands, or, if 'tis false at last,
Gird thee to combat. For my mind-of-man
Now seeks the nature of the vast Beyond
There on the other side, that boundless sum
Which lies without the ramparts of the world,
Toward which the spirit longs to peer afar,
Toward which indeed the swift elan of thought
Flies unencumbered forth.
Firstly, we find,
Off to all regions round, on either side,
Above, beneath, throughout the universe
End is there none—as I have taught, as too
The very thing of itself declares aloud,
And as from nature of the unbottomed deep
Shines clearly forth. Nor can we once suppose
In any way 'tis likely, (seeing that space
To all sides stretches infinite and free,
And seeds, innumerable in number, in sum
Bottomless, there in many a manner fly,
Bestirred in everlasting motion there),
That only this one earth and sky of ours
Hath been create and that those bodies of stuff,
So many, perform no work outside the same;
Seeing, moreover, this world too hath been
By nature fashioned, even as seeds of things
By innate motion chanced to clash and cling—

After they'd been in many a manner driven
Together at random, without design, in vain—
And as at last those seeds together dwelt,
Which, when together of a sudden thrown,
Should alway furnish the commencements fit
Of mighty things—the earth, the sea, the sky,
And race of living creatures. Thus, I say,
Again, again, 'tmust be confessed there are
Such congregations of matter otherwhere,
Like this our world which vasty ether holds
In huge embrace.

Besides, when matter abundant
Is ready there, when space on hand, nor object
Nor any cause retards, no marvel 'tis
That things are carried on and made complete,
Perforce. And now, if store of seeds there is
So great that not whole life-times of the living
Can count the tale...
And if their force and nature abide the same,
Able to throw the seeds of things together
Into their places, even as here are thrown
The seeds together in this world of ours,
'Tmust be confessed in other realms there are
Still other worlds, still other breeds of men,
And other generations of the wild.
Hence too it happens in the sum there is
No one thing single of its kind in birth,
And single and sole in growth, but rather it is
One member of some generated race,
Among full many others of like kind.
First, cast thy mind abroad upon the living:
Thou'lt find the race of mountain-ranging wild
Even thus to be, and thus the scions of men
To be begot, and lastly the mute flocks
Of scaled fish, and winged frames of birds.
Wherefore confess we must on grounds the same
That earth, sun, moon, and ocean, and all else,
Exist not sole and single—rather in number
Exceeding number. Since that deeply set
Old boundary stone of life remains for them
No less, and theirs a body of mortal birth
No less, than every kind which here on earth

Is so abundant in its members found.
Which well perceived if thou hold in mind,
Then Nature, delivered from every haughty lord,
And forthwith free, is seen to do all things
Herself and through herself of own accord,
Rid of all gods. For—by their holy hearts
Which pass in long tranquillity of peace
Untroubled ages and a serene life!—
Who hath the power (I ask), who hath the power
To rule the sum of the immeasurable,
To hold with steady hand the giant reins
Of the unfathomed deep? Who hath the power
At once to roll a multitude of skies,
At once to heat with fires ethereal all
The fruitful lands of multitudes of worlds,
To be at all times in all places near,
To stablish darkness by his clouds, to shake
The serene spaces of the sky with sound,
And hurl his lightnings,—ha, and whelm how oft
In ruins his own temples, and to rave,
Retiring to the wildernesses, there
At practice with that thunderbolt of his,
Which yet how often shoots the guilty by,
And slays the honourable blameless ones!

Ere since the birth-time of the world, ere since
The risen first-born day of sea, earth, sun,
Have many germs been added from outside,
Have many seeds been added round about,
Which the great All, the while it flung them on,
Brought hither, that from them the sea and lands
Could grow more big, and that the house of heaven
Might get more room and raise its lofty roofs
Far over earth, and air arise around.
For bodies all, from out all regions, are
Divided by blows, each to its proper thing,
And all retire to their own proper kinds:
The moist to moist retires; earth gets increase
From earthy body; and fires, as on a forge,
Beat out new fire; and ether forges ether;
Till nature, author and ender of the world,
Hath led all things to extreme bound of growth:
As haps when that which hath been poured inside

The vital veins of life is now no more
Than that which ebbs within them and runs off.
This is the point where life for each thing ends;
This is the point where nature with her powers
Curbs all increase. For whatsoe'er thou seest
Grow big with glad increase, and step by step
Climb upward to ripe age, these to themselves
Take in more bodies than they send from selves,
Whilst still the food is easily infused
Through all the veins, and whilst the things are not
So far expanded that they cast away
Such numerous atoms as to cause a waste
Greater than nutriment whereby they wax.
For 'tmust be granted, truly, that from things
Many a body ebbeth and runs off;
But yet still more must come, until the things
Have touched development's top pinnacle;
Then old age breaks their powers and ripe strength
And falls away into a worser part.
For ever the ampler and more wide a thing,
As soon as ever its augmentation ends,
It scatters abroad forthwith to all sides round
More bodies, sending them from out itself.
Nor easily now is food disseminate
Through all its veins; nor is that food enough
To equal with a new supply on hand
Those plenteous exhalations it gives off.
Thus, fairly, all things perish, when with ebbing
They're made less dense and when from blows without
They are laid low; since food at last will fail
Extremest eld, and bodies from outside
Cease not with thumping to undo a thing
And overmaster by infesting blows.

Thus, too, the ramparts of the mighty world
On all sides round shall taken be by storm,
And tumble to wrack and shivered fragments down.
For food it is must keep things whole, renewing;
'Tis food must prop and give support to all,—
But to no purpose, since nor veins suffice
To hold enough, nor nature ministers
As much as needful. And even now 'tis thus:
Its age is broken and the earth, outworn

With many parturitions, scarce creates
The little lives—she who created erst
All generations and gave forth at birth
Enormous bodies of wild beasts of old.
For never, I fancy, did a golden cord
From off the firmament above let down
The mortal generations to the fields;
Nor sea, nor breakers pounding on the rocks
Created them; but earth it was who bore—
The same to-day who feeds them from herself.
Besides, herself of own accord, she first
The shining grains and vineyards of all joy
Created for mortality; herself
Gave the sweet fruitage and the pastures glad,
Which now to-day yet scarcely wax in size,
Even when aided by our toiling arms.
We break the ox, and wear away the strength
Of sturdy farm-hands; iron tools to-day
Barely avail for tilling of the fields,
So niggardly they grudge our harvestings,
So much increase our labour. Now to-day
The aged ploughman, shaking of his head,
Sighs o'er and o'er that labours of his hands
Have fallen out in vain, and, as he thinks
How present times are not as times of old,
Often he praises the fortunes of his sire,
And crackles, prating, how the ancient race,
Fulfilled with piety, supported life
With simple comfort in a narrow plot,
Since, man for man, the measure of each field
Was smaller far i' the old days. And, again,
The gloomy planter of the withered vine
Rails at the season's change and wearies heaven,
Nor grasps that all of things by sure degrees
Are wasting away and going to the tomb,
Outworn by venerable length of life.

BOOK III

PROEM

O thou who first uplifted in such dark
So clear a torch aloft, who first shed light
Upon the profitable ends of man,
O thee I follow, glory of the Greeks,
And set my footsteps squarely planted now
Even in the impress and the marks of thine—
Less like one eager to dispute the palm,
More as one craving out of very love
That I may copy thee!—for how should swallow
Contend with swans or what compare could be
In a race between young kids with tumbling legs
And the strong might of the horse? Our father thou,
And finder-out of truth, and thou to us
Suppliest a father's precepts; and from out
Those scriven leaves of thine, renowned soul
(Like bees that sip of all in flowery wolds),
We feed upon thy golden sayings all—
Golden, and ever worthiest endless life.
For soon as ever thy planning thought that sprang
From god-like mind begins its loud proclaim
Of nature's courses, terrors of the brain
Asunder flee, the ramparts of the world
Dispart away, and through the void entire
I see the movements of the universe.
Rises to vision the majesty of gods,
And their abodes of everlasting calm
Which neither wind may shake nor rain-cloud splash,
Nor snow, congealed by sharp frosts, may harm
With its white downfall: ever, unclouded sky
O'er roofs, and laughs with far-diffused light.
And nature gives to them their all, nor aught
May ever pluck their peace of mind away.
But nowhere to my vision rise no more
The vaults of Acheron, though the broad earth
Bars me no more from gazing down o'er all
Which under our feet is going on below

Along the void. O, here in these affairs
Some new divine delight and trembling awe
Takes hold through me, that thus by power of thine
Nature, so plain and manifest at last,
Hath been on every side laid bare to man!

And since I've taught already of what sort
The seeds of all things are, and how, distinct
In divers forms, they flit of own accord,
Stirred with a motion everlasting on,
And in what mode things be from them create,
Now, after such matters, should my verse, meseems,
Make clear the nature of the mind and soul,
And drive that dread of Acheron without,
Headlong, which so confounds our human life
Unto its deeps, pouring o'er all that is
The black of death, nor leaves not anything
To prosper—a liquid and unsullied joy.
For as to what men sometimes will affirm:
That more than Tartarus (the realm of death)
They fear diseases and a life of shame,
And know the substance of the soul is blood,
Or rather wind (if haply thus their whim),
And so need naught of this our science, then
Thou well may'st note from what's to follow now
That more for glory do they braggart forth
Than for belief. For mark these very same:
Exiles from country, fugitives afar
From sight of men, with charges foul attaint,
Abased with every wretchedness, they yet
Live, and where'er the wretches come, they yet
Make the ancestral sacrifices there,
Butcher the black sheep, and to gods below
Offer the honours, and in bitter case
Turn much more keenly to religion.
Wherefore, it's surer testing of a man
In doubtful perils—mark him as he is
Amid adversities; for then alone
Are the true voices conjured from his breast,
The mask off-stripped, reality behind.
And greed, again, and the blind lust of honours
Which force poor wretches past the bounds of law,
And, oft allies and ministers of crime,

To push through nights and days with hugest toil
To rise untrammelled to the peaks of power—
These wounds of life in no mean part are kept
Festering and open by this fright of death.
For ever we see fierce Want and foul Disgrace
Dislodged afar from secure life and sweet,
Like huddling Shapes before the doors of death.
And whilst, from these, men wish to scape afar,
Driven by false terror, and afar remove,
With civic blood a fortune they amass,
They double their riches, greedy, heapers-up
Of corpse on corpse they have a cruel laugh
For the sad burial of a brother-born,
And hatred and fear of tables of their kin.
Likewise, through this same terror, envy oft
Makes them to peak because before their eyes
That man is lordly, that man gazed upon
Who walks begirt with honour glorious,
Whilst they in filth and darkness roll around;
Some perish away for statues and a name,
And oft to that degree, from fright of death,
Will hate of living and beholding light
Take hold on humankind that they inflict
Their own destruction with a gloomy heart—
Forgetful that this fear is font of cares,
This fear the plague upon their sense of shame,
And this that breaks the ties of comradry
And oversets all reverence and faith,
Mid direst slaughter. For long ere to-day
Often were traitors to country and dear parents
Through quest to shun the realms of Acheron.
For just as children tremble and fear all
In the viewless dark, so even we at times
Dread in the light so many things that be
No whit more fearsome than what children feign,
Shuddering, will be upon them in the dark.
This terror, then, this darkness of the mind,
Not sunrise with its flaring spokes of light,
Nor glittering arrows of morning sun disperse,
But only nature's aspect and her law.

NATURE AND COMPOSITION OF THE MIND

First, then, I say, the mind which oft we call
The intellect, wherein is seated life's
Counsel and regimen, is part no less
Of man than hand and foot and eyes are parts
Of one whole breathing creature. [But some hold]
That sense of mind is in no fixed part seated,
But is of body some one vital state,—
Named "harmony" by Greeks, because thereby
We live with sense, though intellect be not
In any part: as oft the body is said
To have good health (when health, however, 's not
One part of him who has it), so they place
The sense of mind in no fixed part of man.
Mightily, diversly, meseems they err.
Often the body palpable and seen
Sickens, while yet in some invisible part
We feel a pleasure; oft the other way,
A miserable in mind feels pleasure still
Throughout his body—quite the same as when
A foot may pain without a pain in head.
Besides, when these our limbs are given o'er
To gentle sleep and lies the burdened frame
At random void of sense, a something else
Is yet within us, which upon that time
Bestirs itself in many a wise, receiving
All motions of joy and phantom cares of heart.
Now, for to see that in man's members dwells
Also the soul, and body ne'er is wont
To feel sensation by a "harmony"
Take this in chief: the fact that life remains
Oft in our limbs, when much of body's gone;
Yet that same life, when particles of heat,
Though few, have scattered been, and through the mouth
Air has been given forth abroad, forthwith
Forever deserts the veins, and leaves the bones.
Thus mayst thou know that not all particles
Perform like parts, nor in like manner all
Are props of weal and safety: rather those—
The seeds of wind and exhalations warm—
Take care that in our members life remains.

Therefore a vital heat and wind there is
Within the very body, which at death
Deserts our frames. And so, since nature of mind
And even of soul is found to be, as 'twere,
A part of man, give over "harmony"—
Name to musicians brought from Helicon,—
Unless themselves they filched it otherwise,
To serve for what was lacking name till then.
Whate'er it be, they're welcome to it—thou,
Hearken my other maxims.

Mind and soul,
I say, are held conjoined one with other,
And form one single nature of themselves;
But chief and regnant through the frame entire
Is still that counsel which we call the mind,
And that cleaves seated in the midmost breast.
Here leap dismay and terror; round these haunts
Be blandishments of joys; and therefore here
The intellect, the mind. The rest of soul,
Throughout the body scattered, but obeys—
Moved by the nod and motion of the mind.
This, for itself, sole through itself, hath thought;
This for itself hath mirth, even when the thing
That moves it, moves nor soul nor body at all.
And as, when head or eye in us is smit
By assailing pain, we are not tortured then
Through all the body, so the mind alone
Is sometimes smitten, or livens with a joy,
Whilst yet the soul's remainder through the limbs
And through the frame is stirred by nothing new.
But when the mind is moved by shock more fierce,
We mark the whole soul suffering all at once
Along man's members: sweats and pallors spread
Over the body, and the tongue is broken,
And fails the voice away, and ring the ears,
Mists blind the eyeballs, and the joints collapse,—
Aye, men drop dead from terror of the mind.
Hence, whoso will can readily remark
That soul conjoined is with mind, and, when
'Tis strook by influence of the mind, forthwith
In turn it hits and drives the body too.

And this same argument establisheth
That nature of mind and soul corporeal is:
For when 'tis seen to drive the members on,
To snatch from sleep the body, and to change
The countenance, and the whole state of man
To rule and turn,—what yet could never be
Sans contact, and sans body contact fails—
Must we not grant that mind and soul consist
Of a corporeal nature?—And besides
Thou markst that likewise with this body of ours
Suffers the mind and with our body feels.
If the dire speed of spear that cleaves the bones
And bares the inner thews hits not the life,
Yet follows a fainting and a foul collapse,
And, on the ground, dazed tumult in the mind,
And whiles a wavering will to rise afoot.
So nature of mind must be corporeal, since
From stroke and spear corporeal 'tis in throes.

Now, of what body, what components formed
Is this same mind I will go on to tell.
First, I aver, 'tis superfine, composed
Of tiniest particles—that such the fact
Thou canst perceive, if thou attend, from this:
Nothing is seen to happen with such speed
As what the mind proposes and begins;
Therefore the same bestirs itself more swiftly
Than aught whose nature's palpable to eyes.
But what's so agile must of seeds consist
Most round, most tiny, that they may be moved,
When hit by impulse slight. So water moves,
In waves along, at impulse just the least—
Being create of little shapes that roll;
But, contrariwise, the quality of honey
More stable is, its liquids more inert,
More tardy its flow; for all its stock of matter
Cleaves more together, since, indeed, 'tis made
Of atoms not so smooth, so fine, and round.
For the light breeze that hovers yet can blow
High heaps of poppy-seed away for thee
Downward from off the top; but, contrariwise,
A pile of stones or spiny ears of wheat
It can't at all. Thus, in so far as bodies

Are small and smooth, is their mobility;
But, contrariwise, the heavier and more rough,
The more immovable they prove. Now, then,
Since nature of mind is movable so much,
Consist it must of seeds exceeding small
And smooth and round. Which fact once known to thee,
Good friend, will serve thee opportune in else.
This also shows the nature of the same,
How nice its texture, in how small a space
'Twould go, if once compacted as a pellet:
When death's unvexed repose gets hold on man
And mind and soul retire, thou markest there
From the whole body nothing ta'en in form,
Nothing in weight. Death grants ye everything,
But vital sense and exhalation hot.
Thus soul entire must be of smallmost seeds,
Twined through the veins, the vitals, and the thews,
Seeing that, when 'tis from whole body gone,
The outward figuration of the limbs
Is unimpaired and weight fails not a whit.
Just so, when vanished the bouquet of wine,
Or when an unguent's perfume delicate
Into the winds away departs, or when
From any body savour's gone, yet still
The thing itself seems minished naught to eyes,
Thereby, nor aught abstracted from its weight—
No marvel, because seeds many and minute
Produce the savours and the redolence
In the whole body of the things. And so,
Again, again, nature of mind and soul
'Tis thine to know created is of seeds
The tiniest ever, since at flying-forth
It beareth nothing of the weight away.

Yet fancy not its nature simple so.
For an impalpable aura, mixed with heat,
Deserts the dying, and heat draws off the air;
And heat there's none, unless commixed with air:
For, since the nature of all heat is rare,
Athrough it many seeds of air must move.
Thus nature of mind is triple; yet those all
Suffice not for creating sense—since mind
Accepteth not that aught of these can cause

Sense-bearing motions, and much less the thoughts
A man revolves in mind. So unto these
Must added be a somewhat, and a fourth;
That somewhat's altogether void of name;
Than which existeth naught more mobile, naught
More an impalpable, of elements
More small and smooth and round. That first transmits
Sense-bearing motions through the frame, for that
Is roused the first, composed of little shapes;
Thence heat and viewless force of wind take up
The motions, and thence air, and thence all things
Are put in motion; the blood is strook, and then
The vitals all begin to feel, and last
To bones and marrow the sensation comes—
Pleasure or torment. Nor will pain for naught
Enter so far, nor a sharp ill seep through,
But all things be perturbed to that degree
That room for life will fail, and parts of soul
Will scatter through the body's every pore.
Yet as a rule, almost upon the skin
These motion all are stopped, and this is why
We have the power to retain our life.

Now in my eagerness to tell thee how
They are commixed, through what unions fit
They function so, my country's pauper-speech
Constrains me sadly. As I can, however,
I'll touch some points and pass. In such a wise
Course these primordials 'mongst one another
With inter-motions that no one can be
From other sundered, nor its agency
Perform, if once divided by a space;
Like many powers in one body they work.
As in the flesh of any creature still
Is odour and savour and a certain warmth,
And yet from all of these one bulk of body
Is made complete, so, viewless force of wind
And warmth and air, commingled, do create
One nature, by that mobile energy
Assisted which from out itself to them
Imparts initial motion, whereby first
Sense-bearing motion along the vitals springs.
For lurks this essence far and deep and under,

Nor in our body is aught more shut from view,
And 'tis the very soul of all the soul.
And as within our members and whole frame
The energy of mind and power of soul
Is mixed and latent, since create it is
Of bodies small and few, so lurks this fourth,
This essence void of name, composed of small,
And seems the very soul of all the soul,
And holds dominion o'er the body all.
And by like reason wind and air and heat
Must function so, commingled through the frame,
And now the one subside and now another
In interchange of dominance, that thus
From all of them one nature be produced,
Lest heat and wind apart, and air apart,
Make sense to perish, by disseverment.
There is indeed in mind that heat it gets
When seething in rage, and flashes from the eyes
More swiftly fire; there is, again, that wind,
Much, and so cold, companion of all dread,
Which rouses the shudder in the shaken frame;
There is no less that state of air composed,
Making the tranquil breast, the serene face.
But more of hot have they whose restive hearts,
Whose minds of passion quickly seethe in rage—
Of which kind chief are fierce abounding lions,
Who often with roaring burst the breast o'erwrought,
Unable to hold the surging wrath within;
But the cold mind of stags has more of wind,
And speedier through their inwards rouses up
The icy currents which make their members quake.
But more the oxen live by tranquil air,
Nor e'er doth smoky torch of wrath applied,
O'erspreading with shadows of a darkling murk,
Rouse them too far; nor will they stiffen stark,
Pierced through by icy javelins of fear;
But have their place half-way between the two—
Stags and fierce lions. Thus the race of men:
Though training make them equally refined,
It leaves those pristine vestiges behind
Of each mind's nature. Nor may we suppose
Evil can e'er be rooted up so far
That one man's not more given to fits of wrath,

Another's not more quickly touched by fear,
A third not more long-suffering than he should.
And needs must differ in many things besides
The varied natures and resulting habits
Of humankind—of which not now can I
Expound the hidden causes, nor find names
Enough for all the divers shapes of those
Primordials whence this variation springs.
But this meseems I'm able to declare:
Those vestiges of natures left behind
Which reason cannot quite expel from us
Are still so slight that naught prevents a man
From living a life even worthy of the gods.

So then this soul is kept by all the body,
Itself the body's guard, and source of weal:
For they with common roots cleave each to each,
Nor can be torn asunder without death.
Not easy 'tis from lumps of frankincense
To tear their fragrance forth, without its nature
Perishing likewise: so, not easy 'tis
From all the body nature of mind and soul
To draw away, without the whole dissolved.
With seeds so intertwined even from birth,
They're dowered conjointly with a partner-life;
No energy of body or mind, apart,
Each of itself without the other's power,
Can have sensation; but our sense, enkindled
Along the vitals, to flame is blown by both
With mutual motions. Besides the body alone
Is nor begot nor grows, nor after death
Seen to endure. For not as water at times
Gives off the alien heat, nor is thereby
Itself destroyed, but unimpaired remains—
Not thus, I say, can the deserted frame
Bear the dissevering of its joined soul,
But, rent and ruined, moulders all away.
Thus the joint contact of the body and soul
Learns from their earliest age the vital motions,
Even when still buried in the mother's womb;
So no dissevering can hap to them,
Without their bane and ill. And thence mayst see
That, as conjoined is their source of weal,

Conjoined also must their nature be.

If one, moreover, denies that body feel,
And holds that soul, through all the body mixed,
Takes on this motion which we title "sense,"
He battles in vain indubitable facts:
For who'll explain what body's feeling is,
Except by what the public fact itself
Has given and taught us?"But when soul is parted,
Body's without all sense." True!—loses what
Was even in its life-time not its own;
And much beside it loses, when soul's driven
Forth from that life-time. Or, to say that eyes
Themselves can see no thing, but through the same
The mind looks forth, as out of opened doors,
Is—a hard saying; since the feel in eyes
Says the reverse. For this itself draws on
And forces into the pupils of our eyes
Our consciousness. And note the case when often
We lack the power to see refulgent things,
Because our eyes are hampered by their light—
With a mere doorway this would happen not;
For, since it is our very selves that see,
No open portals undertake the toil.
Besides, if eyes of ours but act as doors,
Methinks that, were our sight removed, the mind
Ought then still better to behold a thing—
When even the door-posts have been cleared away.

Herein in these affairs nowise take up
What honoured sage, Democritus, lays down—
That proposition, that primordials
Of body and mind, each super-posed on each,
Vary alternately and interweave
The fabric of our members. For not only
Are the soul-elements smaller far than those
Which this our body and inward parts compose,
But also are they in their number less,
And scattered sparsely through our frame. And thus
This canst thou guarantee: soul's primal germs
Maintain between them intervals as large
At least as are the smallest bodies, which,
When thrown against us, in our body rouse

Sense-bearing motions. Hence it comes that we
Sometimes don't feel alighting on our frames
The clinging dust, or chalk that settles soft;
Nor mists of night, nor spider's gossamer
We feel against us, when, upon our road,
Its net entangles us, nor on our head
The dropping of its withered garmentings;
Nor bird-feathers, nor vegetable down,
Flying about, so light they barely fall;
Nor feel the steps of every crawling thing,
Nor each of all those footprints on our skin
Of midges and the like. To that degree
Must many primal germs be stirred in us
Ere once the seeds of soul that through our frame
Are intermingled 'gin to feel that those
Primordials of the body have been strook,
And ere, in pounding with such gaps between,
They clash, combine and leap apart in turn.

But mind is more the keeper of the gates,
Hath more dominion over life than soul.
For without intellect and mind there's not
One part of soul can rest within our frame
Least part of time; companioning, it goes
With mind into the winds away, and leaves
The icy members in the cold of death.
But he whose mind and intellect abide
Himself abides in life. However much
The trunk be mangled, with the limbs lopped off,
The soul withdrawn and taken from the limbs,
Still lives the trunk and draws the vital air.
Even when deprived of all but all the soul,
Yet will it linger on and cleave to life,—
Just as the power of vision still is strong,
If but the pupil shall abide unharmed,
Even when the eye around it's sorely rent—
Provided only thou destroyest not
Wholly the ball, but, cutting round the pupil,
Leavest that pupil by itself behind—
For more would ruin sight. But if that centre,
That tiny part of eye, be eaten through,
Forthwith the vision fails and darkness comes,
Though in all else the unblemished ball be clear.

'Tis by like compact that the soul and mind
Are each to other bound forevermore.

THE SOUL IS MORTAL

Now come: that thou mayst able be to know
That minds and the light souls of all that live
Have mortal birth and death, I will go on
Verses to build meet for thy rule of life,
Sought after long, discovered with sweet toil.
But under one name I'd have thee yoke them both;
And when, for instance, I shall speak of soul,
Teaching the same to be but mortal, think
Thereby I'm speaking also of the mind—
Since both are one, a substance inter-joined.
First, then, since I have taught how soul exists
A subtle fabric, of particles minute,
Made up from atoms smaller much than those
Of water's liquid damp, or fog, or smoke,
So in mobility it far excels,
More prone to move, though strook by lighter cause
Even moved by images of smoke or fog—
As where we view, when in our sleeps we're lulled,
The altars exhaling steam and smoke aloft—
For, beyond doubt, these apparitions come
To us from outward. Now, then, since thou seest,
Their liquids depart, their waters flow away,
When jars are shivered, and since fog and smoke
Depart into the winds away, believe
The soul no less is shed abroad and dies
More quickly far, more quickly is dissolved
Back to its primal bodies, when withdrawn
From out man's members it has gone away.
For, sure, if body (container of the same
Like as a jar), when shivered from some cause,
And rarefied by loss of blood from veins,
Cannot for longer hold the soul, how then
Thinkst thou it can be held by any air—
A stuff much rarer than our bodies be?

Besides we feel that mind to being comes
Along with body, with body grows and ages.

For just as children totter round about
With frames infirm and tender, so there follows
A weakling wisdom in their minds; and then,
Where years have ripened into robust powers,
Counsel is also greater, more increased
The power of mind; thereafter, where already
The body's shattered by master-powers of eld,
And fallen the frame with its enfeebled powers,
Thought hobbles, tongue wanders, and the mind gives way;
All fails, all's lacking at the selfsame time.
Therefore it suits that even the soul's dissolved,
Like smoke, into the lofty winds of air;
Since we behold the same to being come
Along with body and grow, and, as I've taught,
Crumble and crack, therewith outworn by eld.

Then, too, we see, that, just as body takes
Monstrous diseases and the dreadful pain,
So mind its bitter cares, the grief, the fear;
Wherefore it tallies that the mind no less
Partaker is of death; for pain and disease
Are both artificers of death,—as well
We've learned by the passing of many a man ere now.
Nay, too, in diseases of body, often the mind
Wanders afield; for 'tis beside itself,
And crazed it speaks, or many a time it sinks,
With eyelids closing and a drooping nod,
In heavy drowse, on to eternal sleep;
From whence nor hears it any voices more,
Nor able is to know the faces here
Of those about him standing with wet cheeks
Who vainly call him back to light and life.
Wherefore mind too, confess we must, dissolves,
Seeing, indeed, contagions of disease
Enter into the same. Again, O why,
When the strong wine has entered into man,
And its diffused fire gone round the veins,
Why follows then a heaviness of limbs,
A tangle of the legs as round he reels,
A stuttering tongue, an intellect besoaked,
Eyes all aswim, and hiccups, shouts, and brawls,
And whatso else is of that ilk?—Why this?—
If not that violent and impetuous wine

Is wont to confound the soul within the body?
But whatso can confounded be and balked,
Gives proof, that if a hardier cause got in,
'Twould hap that it would perish then, bereaved
Of any life thereafter. And, moreover,
Often will some one in a sudden fit,
As if by stroke of lightning, tumble down
Before our eyes, and sputter foam, and grunt,
Blither, and twist about with sinews taut,
Gasp up in starts, and weary out his limbs
With tossing round. No marvel, since distract
Through frame by violence of disease.

Confounds, he foams, as if to vomit soul,
As on the salt sea boil the billows round
Under the master might of winds. And now
A groan's forced out, because his limbs are griped,
But, in the main, because the seeds of voice
Are driven forth and carried in a mass
Outwards by mouth, where they are wont to go,
And have a builded highway. He becomes
Mere fool, since energy of mind and soul
Confounded is, and, as I've shown, to-riven,
Asunder thrown, and torn to pieces all
By the same venom. But, again, where cause
Of that disease has faced about, and back
Retreats sharp poison of corrupted frame
Into its shadowy lairs, the man at first
Arises reeling, and gradually comes back
To all his senses and recovers soul.
Thus, since within the body itself of man
The mind and soul are by such great diseases
Shaken, so miserably in labour distraught,
Why, then, believe that in the open air,
Without a body, they can pass their life,
Immortal, battling with the master winds?
And, since we mark the mind itself is cured,
Like the sick body, and restored can be
By medicine, this is forewarning too
That mortal lives the mind. For proper it is
That whosoe'er begins and undertakes
To alter the mind, or meditates to change
Any another nature soever, should add

New parts, or readjust the order given,
Or from the sum remove at least a bit.
But what's immortal willeth for itself
Its parts be nor increased, nor rearranged,
Nor any bit soever flow away:
For change of anything from out its bounds
Means instant death of that which was before.
Ergo, the mind, whether in sickness fallen,
Or by the medicine restored, gives signs,
As I have taught, of its mortality.
So surely will a fact of truth make head
'Gainst errors' theories all, and so shut off
All refuge from the adversary, and rout
Error by two-edged confutation.

And since the mind is of a man one part,
Which in one fixed place remains, like ears,
And eyes, and every sense which pilots life;
And just as hand, or eye, or nose, apart,
Severed from us, can neither feel nor be,
But in the least of time is left to rot,
Thus mind alone can never be, without
The body and the man himself, which seems,
As 'twere the vessel of the same—or aught
Whate'er thou'lt feign as yet more closely joined:
Since body cleaves to mind by surest bonds.

Again, the body's and the mind's live powers
Only in union prosper and enjoy;
For neither can nature of mind, alone of self
Sans body, give the vital motions forth;
Nor, then, can body, wanting soul, endure
And use the senses. Verily, as the eye,
Alone, up-rended from its roots, apart
From all the body, can peer about at naught,
So soul and mind it seems are nothing able,
When by themselves. No marvel, because, commixed
Through veins and inwards, and through bones and thews,
Their elements primordial are confined
By all the body, and own no power free
To bound around through interspaces big,
Thus, shut within these confines, they take on
Motions of sense, which, after death, thrown out

Beyond the body to the winds of air,
Take on they cannot—and on this account,
Because no more in such a way confined.
For air will be a body, be alive,
If in that air the soul can keep itself,
And in that air enclose those motions all
Which in the thews and in the body itself
A while ago 'twas making. So for this,
Again, again, I say confess we must,
That, when the body's wrappings are unwound,
And when the vital breath is forced without,
The soul, the senses of the mind dissolve,—
Since for the twain the cause and ground of life
Is in the fact of their conjoined estate.

Once more, since body's unable to sustain
Division from the soul, without decay
And obscene stench, how canst thou doubt but that
The soul, uprisen from the body's deeps,
Has filtered away, wide-drifted like a smoke,
Or that the changed body crumbling fell
With ruin so entire, because, indeed,
Its deep foundations have been moved from place,
The soul out-filtering even through the frame,
And through the body's every winding way
And orifice? And so by many means
Thou'rt free to learn that nature of the soul
Hath passed in fragments out along the frame,
And that 'twas shivered in the very body
Ere ever it slipped abroad and swam away
Into the winds of air. For never a man
Dying appears to feel the soul go forth
As one sure whole from all his body at once,
Nor first come up the throat and into mouth;
But feels it failing in a certain spot,
Even as he knows the senses too dissolve
Each in its own location in the frame.
But were this mind of ours immortal mind,
Dying 'twould scarce bewail a dissolution,
But rather the going, the leaving of its coat,
Like to a snake. Wherefore, when once the body
Hath passed away, admit we must that soul,
Shivered in all that body, perished too.

Nay, even when moving in the bounds of life,
Often the soul, now tottering from some cause,
Craves to go out, and from the frame entire
Loosened to be; the countenance becomes
Flaccid, as if the supreme hour were there;
And flabbily collapse the members all
Against the bloodless trunk—the kind of case
We see when we remark in common phrase,
"That man's quite gone," or "fainted dead away";
And where there's now a bustle of alarm,
And all are eager to get some hold upon
The man's last link of life. For then the mind
And all the power of soul are shook so sore,
And these so totter along with all the frame,
That any cause a little stronger might
Dissolve them altogether.—Why, then, doubt
That soul, when once without the body thrust,
There in the open, an enfeebled thing,
Its wrappings stripped away, cannot endure
Not only through no everlasting age,
But even, indeed, through not the least of time?

Then, too, why never is the intellect,
The counselling mind, begotten in the head,
The feet, the hands, instead of cleaving still
To one sole seat, to one fixed haunt, the breast,
If not that fixed places be assigned
For each thing's birth, where each, when 'tis create,
Is able to endure, and that our frames
Have such complex adjustments that no shift
In order of our members may appear?
To that degree effect succeeds to cause,
Nor is the flame once wont to be create
In flowing streams, nor cold begot in fire.

Besides, if nature of soul immortal be,
And able to feel, when from our frame disjoined,
The same, I fancy, must be thought to be
Endowed with senses five,—nor is there way
But this whereby to image to ourselves
How under-souls may roam in Acheron.
Thus painters and the elder race of bards
Have pictured souls with senses so endowed.

But neither eyes, nor nose, nor hand, alone
Apart from body can exist for soul,
Nor tongue nor ears apart. And hence indeed
Alone by self they can nor feel nor be.

And since we mark the vital sense to be
In the whole body, all one living thing,
If of a sudden a force with rapid stroke
Should slice it down the middle and cleave in twain,
Beyond a doubt likewise the soul itself,
Divided, dissevered, asunder will be flung
Along with body. But what severed is
And into sundry parts divides, indeed
Admits it owns no everlasting nature.
We hear how chariots of war, areek
With hurly slaughter, lop with flashing scythes
The limbs away so suddenly that there,
Fallen from the trunk, they quiver on the earth,
The while the mind and powers of the man
Can feel no pain, for swiftness of his hurt,
And sheer abandon in the zest of battle:
With the remainder of his frame he seeks
Anew the battle and the slaughter, nor marks
How the swift wheels and scythes of ravin have dragged
Off with the horses his left arm and shield;
Nor other how his right has dropped away,
Mounting again and on. A third attempts
With leg dismembered to arise and stand,
Whilst, on the ground hard by, the dying foot
Twitches its spreading toes. And even the head,
When from the warm and living trunk lopped off,
Keeps on the ground the vital countenance
And open eyes, until 't has rendered up
All remnants of the soul. Nay, once again:
If, when a serpent's darting forth its tongue,
And lashing its tail, thou gettest chance to hew
With axe its length of trunk to many parts,
Thou'lt see each severed fragment writhing round
With its fresh wound, and spattering up the sod,
And there the fore-part seeking with the jaws
After the hinder, with bite to stop the pain.
So shall we say that these be souls entire
In all those fractions?—but from that 'twould follow

One creature'd have in body many souls.
Therefore, the soul, which was indeed but one,
Has been divided with the body too:
Each is but mortal, since alike is each
Hewn into many parts. Again, how often
We view our fellow going by degrees,
And losing limb by limb the vital sense;
First nails and fingers of the feet turn blue,
Next die the feet and legs, then o'er the rest
Slow crawl the certain footsteps of cold death.
And since this nature of the soul is torn,
Nor mounts away, as at one time, entire,
We needs must hold it mortal. But perchance
If thou supposest that the soul itself
Can inward draw along the frame, and bring
Its parts together to one place, and so
From all the members draw the sense away,
Why, then, that place in which such stock of soul
Collected is, should greater seem in sense.
But since such place is nowhere, for a fact,
As said before, 'tis rent and scattered forth,
And so goes under. Or again, if now
I please to grant the false, and say that soul
Can thus be lumped within the frames of those
Who leave the sunshine, dying bit by bit,
Still must the soul as mortal be confessed;
Nor aught it matters whether to wrack it go,
Dispersed in the winds, or, gathered in a mass
From all its parts, sink down to brutish death,
Since more and more in every region sense
Fails the whole man, and less and less of life
In every region lingers.

And besides,
If soul immortal is, and winds its way
Into the body at the birth of man,
Why can we not remember something, then,
Of life-time spent before? why keep we not
Some footprints of the things we did of, old?
But if so changed hath been the power of mind,
That every recollection of things done
Is fallen away, at no o'erlong remove
Is that, I trow, from what we mean by death.

Wherefore 'tis sure that what hath been before
Hath died, and what now is is now create.

Moreover, if after the body hath been built
Our mind's live powers are wont to be put in,
Just at the moment that we come to birth,
And cross the sills of life, 'twould scarcely fit
For them to live as if they seemed to grow
Along with limbs and frame, even in the blood,
But rather as in a cavern all alone.
(Yet all the body duly throngs with sense.)
But public fact declares against all this:
For soul is so entwined through the veins,
The flesh, the thews, the bones, that even the teeth
Share in sensation, as proven by dull ache,
By twinge from icy water, or grating crunch
Upon a stone that got in mouth with bread.
Wherefore, again, again, souls must be thought
Nor void of birth, nor free from law of death;
Nor, if, from outward, in they wound their way,
Could they be thought as able so to cleave
To these our frames, nor, since so interwove,
Appears it that they're able to go forth
Unhurt and whole and loose themselves unscathed
From all the thews, articulations, bones.
But, if perchance thou thinkest that the soul,
From outward winding in its way, is wont
To seep and soak along these members ours,
Then all the more 'twill perish, being thus
With body fused—for what will seep and soak
Will be dissolved and will therefore die.
For just as food, dispersed through all the pores
Of body, and passed through limbs and all the frame,
Perishes, supplying from itself the stuff
For other nature, thus the soul and mind,
Though whole and new into a body going,
Are yet, by seeping in, dissolved away,
Whilst, as through pores, to all the frame there pass
Those particles from which created is
This nature of mind, now ruler of our body,
Born from that soul which perished, when divided
Along the frame. Wherefore it seems that soul
Hath both a natal and funeral hour.

Besides are seeds of soul there left behind
In the breathless body, or not? If there they are,
It cannot justly be immortal deemed,
Since, shorn of some parts lost, 'thas gone away:
But if, borne off with members uncorrupt,
'Thas fled so absolutely all away
It leaves not one remainder of itself
Behind in body, whence do cadavers, then,
From out their putrid flesh exhale the worms,
And whence does such a mass of living things,
Boneless and bloodless, o'er the bloated frame
Bubble and swarm? But if perchance thou thinkest
That souls from outward into worms can wind,
And each into a separate body come,
And reckonest not why many thousand souls
Collect where only one has gone away,
Here is a point, in sooth, that seems to need
Inquiry and a putting to the test:
Whether the souls go on a hunt for seeds
Of worms wherewith to build their dwelling places,
Or enter bodies ready-made, as 'twere.
But why themselves they thus should do and toil
'Tis hard to say, since, being free of body,
They flit around, harassed by no disease,
Nor cold nor famine; for the body labours
By more of kinship to these flaws of life,
And mind by contact with that body suffers
So many ills. But grant it be for them
However useful to construct a body
To which to enter in, 'tis plain they can't.
Then, souls for self no frames nor bodies make,
Nor is there how they once might enter in
To bodies ready-made—for they cannot
Be nicely interwoven with the same,
And there'll be formed no interplay of sense
Common to each.

Again, why is't there goes
Impetuous rage with lion's breed morose,
And cunning with foxes, and to deer why given
The ancestral fear and tendency to flee,
And why in short do all the rest of traits

Engender from the very start of life
In the members and mentality, if not
Because one certain power of mind that came
From its own seed and breed waxes the same
Along with all the body? But were mind
Immortal, were it wont to change its bodies,
How topsy-turvy would earth's creatures act!
The Hyrcan hound would flee the onset oft
Of antlered stag, the scurrying hawk would quake
Along the winds of air at the coming dove,
And men would dote, and savage beasts be wise;
For false the reasoning of those that say
Immortal mind is changed by change of body—
For what is changed dissolves, and therefore dies.
For parts are re-disposed and leave their order;
Wherefore they must be also capable
Of dissolution through the frame at last,
That they along with body perish all.
But should some say that always souls of men
Go into human bodies, I will ask:
How can a wise become a dullard soul?
And why is never a child's a prudent soul?
And the mare's filly why not trained so well
As sturdy strength of steed? We may be sure
They'll take their refuge in the thought that mind
Becomes a weakling in a weakling frame.
Yet be this so, 'tis needful to confess
The soul but mortal, since, so altered now
Throughout the frame, it loses the life and sense
It had before. Or how can mind wax strong
Coequally with body and attain
The craved flower of life, unless it be
The body's colleague in its origins?
Or what's the purport of its going forth
From aged limbs?—fears it, perhaps, to stay,
Pent in a crumbled body? Or lest its house,
Outworn by venerable length of days,
May topple down upon it? But indeed
For an immortal perils are there none.

Again, at parturitions of the wild
And at the rites of Love, that souls should stand
Ready hard by seems ludicrous enough—

Immortals waiting for their mortal limbs
In numbers innumerable, contending madly
Which shall be first and chief to enter in!—
Unless perchance among the souls there be
Such treaties stablished that the first to come
Flying along, shall enter in the first,
And that they make no rivalries of strength!

Again, in ether can't exist a tree,
Nor clouds in ocean deeps, nor in the fields
Can fishes live, nor blood in timber be,
Nor sap in boulders: fixed and arranged
Where everything may grow and have its place.
Thus nature of mind cannot arise alone
Without the body, nor exist afar
From thews and blood. But if 'twere possible,
Much rather might this very power of mind
Be in the head, the shoulders or the heels,
And, born in any part soever, yet
In the same man, in the same vessel abide.
But since within this body even of ours
Stands fixed and appears arranged sure
Where soul and mind can each exist and grow,
Deny we must the more that they can have
Duration and birth, wholly outside the frame.
For, verily, the mortal to conjoin
With the eternal, and to feign they feel
Together, and can function each with each,
Is but to dote: for what can be conceived
Of more unlike, discrepant, ill-assorted,
Than something mortal in a union joined
With an immortal and a secular
To bear the outrageous tempests?

Then, again,
Whatever abides eternal must indeed
Either repel all strokes, because 'tis made
Of solid body, and permit no entrance
Of aught with power to sunder from within
The parts compact—as are those seeds of stuff
Whose nature we've exhibited before;
Or else be able to endure through time
For this: because they are from blows exempt,

As is the void, the which abides untouched,
Unsmit by any stroke; or else because
There is no room around, whereto things can,
As 'twere, depart in dissolution all,—
Even as the sum of sums eternal is,
Without or place beyond whereto things may
Asunder fly, or bodies which can smite,
And thus dissolve them by the blows of might.

But if perchance the soul's to be adjudged
Immortal, mainly on ground 'tis kept secure
In vital forces—either because there come
Never at all things hostile to its weal,
Or else because what come somehow retire,
Repelled or ere we feel the harm they work,

For, lo, besides that, when the frame's diseased,
Soul sickens too, there cometh, many a time,
That which torments it with the things to be,
Keeps it in dread, and wearies it with cares;
And even when evil acts are of the past,
Still gnaw the old transgressions bitterly.
Add, too, that frenzy, peculiar to the mind,
And that oblivion of the things that were;
Add its submergence in the murky waves
Of drowse and torpor.

FOLLY OF THE FEAR OF DEATH

Therefore death to us
Is nothing, nor concerns us in the least,
Since nature of mind is mortal evermore.
And just as in the ages gone before
We felt no touch of ill, when all sides round
To battle came the Carthaginian host,
And the times, shaken by tumultuous war,
Under the aery coasts of arching heaven
Shuddered and trembled, and all humankind
Doubted to which the empery should fall
By land and sea, thus when we are no more,
When comes that sundering of our body and soul

Through which we're fashioned to a single state,
Verily naught to us, us then no more,
Can come to pass, naught move our senses then—
No, not if earth confounded were with sea,
And sea with heaven. But if indeed do feel
The nature of mind and energy of soul,
After their severance from this body of ours,
Yet nothing 'tis to us who in the bonds
And wedlock of the soul and body live,
Through which we're fashioned to a single state.
And, even if time collected after death
The matter of our frames and set it all
Again in place as now, and if again
To us the light of life were given, O yet
That process too would not concern us aught,
When once the self-succession of our sense
Has been asunder broken. And now and here,
Little enough we're busied with the selves
We were aforetime, nor, concerning them,
Suffer a sore distress. For shouldst thou gaze
Backwards across all yesterdays of time
The immeasurable, thinking how manifold
The motions of matter are, then couldst thou well
Credit this too: often these very seeds
(From which we are to-day) of old were set
In the same order as they are to-day—
Yet this we can't to consciousness recall
Through the remembering mind. For there hath been
An interposed pause of life, and wide
Have all the motions wandered everywhere
From these our senses. For if woe and ail
Perchance are toward, then the man to whom
The bane can happen must himself be there
At that same time. But death precludeth this,
Forbidding life to him on whom might crowd
Such irk and care; and granted 'tis to know:
Nothing for us there is to dread in death,
No wretchedness for him who is no more,
The same estate as if ne'er born before,
When death immortal hath ta'en the mortal life.
Hence, where thou seest a man to grieve because
When dead he rots with body laid away,
Or perishes in flames or jaws of beasts,

Know well: he rings not true, and that beneath
Still works an unseen sting upon his heart,
However he deny that he believes.
His shall be aught of feeling after death.
For he, I fancy, grants not what he says,
Nor what that presupposes, and he fails
To pluck himself with all his roots from life
And cast that self away, quite unawares
Feigning that some remainder's left behind.
For when in life one pictures to oneself
His body dead by beasts and vultures torn,
He pities his state, dividing not himself
Therefrom, removing not the self enough
From the body flung away, imagining
Himself that body, and projecting there
His own sense, as he stands beside it: hence
He grieves that he is mortal born, nor marks
That in true death there is no second self
Alive and able to sorrow for self destroyed,
Or stand lamenting that the self lies there
Mangled or burning. For if it an evil is
Dead to be jerked about by jaw and fang
Of the wild brutes, I see not why 'twere not
Bitter to lie on fires and roast in flames,
Or suffocate in honey, and, reclined
On the smooth oblong of an icy slab,
Grow stiff in cold, or sink with load of earth
Down-crushing from above.

"Thee now no more
The joyful house and best of wives shall welcome,
Nor little sons run up to snatch their kisses
And touch with silent happiness thy heart.
Thou shalt not speed in undertakings more,
Nor be the warder of thine own no more.
Poor wretch," they say, "one hostile hour hath ta'en
Wretchedly from thee all life's many guerdons,"
But add not, "yet no longer unto thee
Remains a remnant of desire for them"
If this they only well perceived with mind
And followed up with maxims, they would free
Their state of man from anguish and from fear.
"O even as here thou art, aslumber in death,

So shalt thou slumber down the rest of time,
Released from every harrying pang. But we,
We have bewept thee with insatiate woe,
Standing beside whilst on the awful pyre
Thou wert made ashes; and no day shall take
For us the eternal sorrow from the breast."
But ask the mourner what's the bitterness
That man should waste in an eternal grief,
If, after all, the thing's but sleep and rest?
For when the soul and frame together are sunk
In slumber, no one then demands his self
Or being. Well, this sleep may be forever,
Without desire of any selfhood more,
For all it matters unto us asleep.
Yet not at all do those primordial germs
Roam round our members, at that time, afar
From their own motions that produce our senses—
Since, when he's startled from his sleep, a man
Collects his senses. Death is, then, to us
Much less—if there can be a less than that
Which is itself a nothing: for there comes
Hard upon death a scattering more great
Of the throng of matter, and no man wakes up
On whom once falls the icy pause of life.

This too, O often from the soul men say,
Along their couches holding of the cups,
With faces shaded by fresh wreaths awry:
"Brief is this fruit of joy to paltry man,
Soon, soon departed, and thereafter, no,
It may not be recalled."—As if, forsooth,
It were their prime of evils in great death
To parch, poor tongues, with thirst and arid drought,
Or chafe for any lack.

Once more, if Nature
Should of a sudden send a voice abroad,
And her own self inveigh against us so:
"Mortal, what hast thou of such grave concern
That thou indulgest in too sickly plaints?
Why this bemoaning and beweeping death?
For if thy life aforetime and behind
To thee was grateful, and not all thy good

Was heaped as in sieve to flow away
And perish unavailingly, why not,
Even like a banqueter, depart the halls,
Laden with life? why not with mind content
Take now, thou fool, thy unafflicted rest?
But if whatever thou enjoyed hath been
Lavished and lost, and life is now offence,
Why seekest more to add—which in its turn
Will perish foully and fall out in vain?
O why not rather make an end of life,
Of labour? For all I may devise or find
To pleasure thee is nothing: all things are
The same forever. Though not yet thy body
Wrinkles with years, nor yet the frame exhausts
Outworn, still things abide the same, even if
Thou goest on to conquer all of time
With length of days, yea, if thou never diest"—
What were our answer, but that Nature here
Urges just suit and in her words lays down
True cause of action? Yet should one complain,
Riper in years and elder, and lament,
Poor devil, his death more sorely than is fit,
Then would she not, with greater right, on him
Cry out, inveighing with a voice more shrill:
"Off with thy tears, and choke thy whines, buffoon!
Thou wrinklest—after thou hast had the sum
Of the guerdons of life; yet, since thou cravest ever
What's not at hand, contemning present good,
That life has slipped away, unperfected
And unavailing unto thee. And now,
Or ere thou guessed it, death beside thy head
Stands—and before thou canst be going home
Sated and laden with the goodly feast.
But now yield all that's alien to thine age,—
Up, with good grace! make room for sons: thou must."
Justly, I fancy, would she reason thus,
Justly inveigh and gird: since ever the old
Outcrowded by the new gives way, and ever
The one thing from the others is repaired.
Nor no man is consigned to the abyss
Of Tartarus, the black. For stuff must be,
That thus the after-generations grow,—
Though these, their life completed, follow thee;

And thus like thee are generations all—
Already fallen, or some time to fall.
So one thing from another rises ever;
And in fee-simple life is given to none,
But unto all mere usufruct.

Look back:
Nothing to us was all fore-passed eld
Of time the eternal, ere we had a birth.
And Nature holds this like a mirror up
Of time-to-be when we are dead and gone.
And what is there so horrible appears?
Now what is there so sad about it all?
Is't not serener far than any sleep?

And, verily, those tortures said to be
In Acheron, the deep, they all are ours
Here in this life. No Tantalus, benumbed
With baseless terror, as the fables tell,
Fears the huge boulder hanging in the air:
But, rather, in life an empty dread of Gods
Urges mortality, and each one fears
Such fall of fortune as may chance to him.
Nor eat the vultures into Tityus
Prostrate in Acheron, nor can they find,
Forsooth, throughout eternal ages, aught
To pry around for in that mighty breast.
However hugely he extend his bulk—
Who hath for outspread limbs not acres nine,
But the whole earth—he shall not able be
To bear eternal pain nor furnish food
From his own frame forever. But for us
A Tityus is he whom vultures rend
Prostrate in love, whom anxious anguish eats,
Whom troubles of any unappeased desires
Asunder rip. We have before our eyes
Here in this life also a Sisyphus
In him who seeketh of the populace
The rods, the axes fell, and evermore
Retires a beaten and a gloomy man.
For to seek after power—an empty name,
Nor given at all—and ever in the search
To endure a world of toil, O this it is

To shove with shoulder up the hill a stone
Which yet comes rolling back from off the top,
And headlong makes for levels of the plain.
Then to be always feeding an ingrate mind,
Filling with good things, satisfying never—
As do the seasons of the year for us,
When they return and bring their progenies
And varied charms, and we are never filled
With the fruits of life—O this, I fancy, 'tis
To pour, like those young virgins in the tale,
Waters into a sieve, unfilled forever.

Cerberus and Furies, and that Lack of Light
Tartarus, out-belching from his mouth the surge
Of horrible heat—the which are nowhere, nor
Indeed can be: but in this life is fear
Of retributions just and expiations
For evil acts: the dungeon and the leap
From that dread rock of infamy, the stripes,
The executioners, the oaken rack,
The iron plates, bitumen, and the torch.
And even though these are absent, yet the mind,
With a fore-fearing conscience, plies its goads
And burns beneath the lash, nor sees meanwhile
What terminus of ills, what end of pine
Can ever be, and feareth lest the same
But grow more heavy after death. Of truth,
The life of fools is Acheron on earth.
This also to thy very self sometimes
Repeat thou mayst: "Lo, even good Ancus left
The sunshine with his eyes, in divers things
A better man than thou, O worthless hind;
And many other kings and lords of rule
Thereafter have gone under, once who swayed
O'er mighty peoples. And he also, he—
Who whilom paved a highway down the sea,
And gave his legionaries thoroughfare
Along the deep, and taught them how to cross
The pools of brine afoot, and did contemn,
Trampling upon it with his cavalry,
The bellowings of ocean—poured his soul
From dying body, as his light was ta'en.
And Scipio's son, the thunderbolt of war,

Horror of Carthage, gave his bones to earth,
Like to the lowliest villein in the house.
Add finders-out of sciences and arts;
Add comrades of the Heliconian dames,
Among whom Homer, sceptered o'er them all,
Now lies in slumber sunken with the rest.
Then, too, Democritus, when ripened eld
Admonished him his memory waned away,
Of own accord offered his head to death.
Even Epicurus went, his light of life
Run out, the man in genius who o'er-topped
The human race, extinguishing all others,
As sun, in ether arisen, all the stars.
Wilt thou, then, dally, thou complain to go?—
For whom already life's as good as dead,
Whilst yet thou livest and lookest?—who in sleep
Wastest thy life—time's major part, and snorest
Even when awake, and ceasest not to see
The stuff of dreams, and bearest a mind beset
By baseless terror, nor discoverest oft
What's wrong with thee, when, like a sotted wretch,
Thou'rt jostled along by many crowding cares,
And wanderest reeling round, with mind aswim."

If men, in that same way as on the mind
They feel the load that wearies with its weight,
Could also know the causes whence it comes,
And why so great the heap of ill on heart,
O not in this sort would they live their life,
As now so much we see them, knowing not
What 'tis they want, and seeking ever and ever
A change of place, as if to drop the burden.
The man who sickens of his home goes out,
Forth from his splendid halls, and straight—returns,
Feeling i'faith no better off abroad.
He races, driving his Gallic ponies along,
Down to his villa, madly,—as in haste
To hurry help to a house afire.—At once
He yawns, as soon as foot has touched the threshold,
Or drowsily goes off in sleep and seeks
Forgetfulness, or maybe bustles about
And makes for town again. In such a way
Each human flees himself—a self in sooth,

As happens, he by no means can escape;
And willy-nilly he cleaves to it and loathes,
Sick, sick, and guessing not the cause of ail.
Yet should he see but that, O chiefly then,
Leaving all else, he'd study to divine
The nature of things, since here is in debate
Eternal time and not the single hour,
Mortal's estate in whatsoever remains
After great death.

And too, when all is said,
What evil lust of life is this so great
Subdues us to live, so dreadfully distraught
In perils and alarms? one fixed end
Of life abideth for mortality;
Death's not to shun, and we must go to meet.
Besides we're busied with the same devices,
Ever and ever, and we are at them ever,
And there's no new delight that may be forged
By living on. But whilst the thing we long for
Is lacking, that seems good above all else;
Thereafter, when we've touched it, something else
We long for; ever one equal thirst of life
Grips us agape. And doubtful 'tis what fortune
The future times may carry, or what be
That chance may bring, or what the issue next
Awaiting us. Nor by prolonging life
Take we the least away from death's own time,
Nor can we pluck one moment off, whereby
To minish the aeons of our state of death.
Therefore, O man, by living on, fulfil
As many generations as thou may:
Eternal death shall there be waiting still;
And he who died with light of yesterday
Shall be no briefer time in death's No-more
Than he who perished months or years before.

BOOK IV

PROEM

I wander afield, thriving in sturdy thought,
Through unpathed haunts of the Pierides,
Trodden by step of none before. I joy
To come on undefiled fountains there,
To drain them deep; I joy to pluck new flowers,
To seek for this my head a signal crown
From regions where the Muses never yet
Have garlanded the temples of a man:
First, since I teach concerning mighty things,
And go right on to loose from round the mind
The tightened coils of dread religion;
Next, since, concerning themes so dark, I frame
Song so pellucid, touching all throughout
Even with the Muses' charm—which, as 'twould seem,
Is not without a reasonable ground:
For as physicians, when they seek to give
Young boys the nauseous wormwood, first do touch
The brim around the cup with the sweet juice
And yellow of the honey, in order that
The thoughtless age of boyhood be cajoled
As far as the lips, and meanwhile swallow down
The wormwood's bitter draught, and, though befooled,
Be yet not merely duped, but rather thus
Grow strong again with recreated health:
So now I too (since this my doctrine seems
In general somewhat woeful unto those
Who've had it not in hand, and since the crowd
Starts back from it in horror) have desired
To expound our doctrine unto thee in song
Soft-speaking and Pierian, and, as 'twere,
To touch it with sweet honey of the Muse—
If by such method haply I might hold
The mind of thee upon these lines of ours,
Till thou dost learn the nature of all things

And understandest their utility.

EXISTENCE AND CHARACTER OF THE IMAGES

But since I've taught already of what sort
The seeds of all things are, and how distinct
In divers forms they flit of own accord,
Stirred with a motion everlasting on,
And in what mode things be from them create,
And since I've taught what the mind's nature is,
And of what things 'tis with the body knit
And thrives in strength, and by what mode uptorn
That mind returns to its primordials,
Now will I undertake an argument—
One for these matters of supreme concern—
That there exist those somewhats which we call
The images of things: these, like to films
Scaled off the utmost outside of the things,
Flit hither and thither through the atmosphere,
And the same terrify our intellects,
Coming upon us waking or in sleep,
When oft we peer at wonderful strange shapes
And images of people lorn of light,
Which oft have horribly roused us when we lay
In slumber—that haply nevermore may we
Suppose that souls get loose from Acheron,
Or shades go floating in among the living,
Or aught of us is left behind at death,
When body and mind, destroyed together, each
Back to its own primordials goes away.

And thus I say that effigies of things,
And tenuous shapes from off the things are sent,
From off the utmost outside of the things,
Which are like films or may be named a rind,
Because the image bears like look and form
With whatso body has shed it fluttering forth—
A fact thou mayst, however dull thy wits,
Well learn from this: mainly, because we see
Even 'mongst visible objects many be
That send forth bodies, loosely some diffused—
Like smoke from oaken logs and heat from fires—

And some more interwoven and condensed—
As when the locusts in the summertime
Put off their glossy tunics, or when calves
At birth drop membranes from their body's surface,
Or when, again, the slippery serpent doffs
Its vestments 'mongst the thorns—for oft we see
The breres augmented with their flying spoils:
Since such takes place, 'tis likewise certain too
That tenuous images from things are sent,
From off the utmost outside of the things.
For why those kinds should drop and part from things,
Rather than others tenuous and thin,
No power has man to open mouth to tell;
Especially, since on outsides of things
Are bodies many and minute which could,
In the same order which they had before,
And with the figure of their form preserved,
Be thrown abroad, and much more swiftly too,
Being less subject to impediments,
As few in number and placed along the front.
For truly many things we see discharge
Their stuff at large, not only from their cores
Deep-set within, as we have said above,
But from their surfaces at times no less—
Their very colours too. And commonly
The awnings, saffron, red and dusky blue,
Stretched overhead in mighty theatres,
Upon their poles and cross-beams fluttering,
Have such an action quite; for there they dye
And make to undulate with their every hue
The circled throng below, and all the stage,
And rich attire in the patrician seats.
And ever the more the theatre's dark walls
Around them shut, the more all things within
Laugh in the bright suffusion of strange glints,
The daylight being withdrawn. And therefore, since
The canvas hangings thus discharge their dye
From off their surface, things in general must
Likewise their tenuous effigies discharge,
Because in either case they are off-thrown
From off the surface. So there are indeed
Such certain prints and vestiges of forms
Which flit around, of subtlest texture made,

Invisible, when separate, each and one.
Again, all odour, smoke, and heat, and such
Streams out of things diffusedly, because,
Whilst coming from the deeps of body forth
And rising out, along their bending path
They're torn asunder, nor have gateways straight
Wherethrough to mass themselves and struggle abroad.
But contrariwise, when such a tenuous film
Of outside colour is thrown off, there's naught
Can rend it, since 'tis placed along the front
Ready to hand. Lastly those images
Which to our eyes in mirrors do appear,
In water, or in any shining surface,
Must be, since furnished with like look of things,
Fashioned from images of things sent out.
There are, then, tenuous effigies of forms,
Like unto them, which no one can divine
When taken singly, which do yet give back,
When by continued and recurrent discharge
Expelled, a picture from the mirrors' plane.
Nor otherwise, it seems, can they be kept
So well conserved that thus be given back
Figures so like each object.

Now then, learn
How tenuous is the nature of an image.
And in the first place, since primordials be
So far beneath our senses, and much less
E'en than those objects which begin to grow
Too small for eyes to note, learn now in few
How nice are the beginnings of all things—
That this, too, I may yet confirm in proof:
First, living creatures are sometimes so small
That even their third part can nowise be seen;
Judge, then, the size of any inward organ—
What of their sphered heart, their eyes, their limbs,
The skeleton?—How tiny thus they are!
And what besides of those first particles
Whence soul and mind must fashioned be?—Seest not
How nice and how minute? Besides, whatever
Exhales from out its body a sharp smell—
The nauseous absinth, or the panacea,
Strong southernwood, or bitter centaury—

If never so lightly with thy [fingers] twain
Perchance [thou touch] a one of them

Then why not rather know that images
Flit hither and thither, many, in many modes,
Bodiless and invisible?

But lest
Haply thou holdest that those images
Which come from objects are the sole that flit,
Others indeed there be of own accord
Begot, self-formed in earth's aery skies,
Which, moulded to innumerable shapes,
Are borne aloft, and, fluid as they are,
Cease not to change appearance and to turn
Into new outlines of all sorts of forms;
As we behold the clouds grow thick on high
And smirch the serene vision of the world,
Stroking the air with motions. For oft are seen
The giants' faces flying far along
And trailing a spread of shadow; and at times
The mighty mountains and mountain-sundered rocks
Going before and crossing on the sun,
Whereafter a monstrous beast dragging amain
And leading in the other thunderheads.
Now [hear] how easy and how swift they be
Engendered, and perpetually flow off
From things and gliding pass away....

For ever every outside streams away
From off all objects, since discharge they may;
And when this outside reaches other things,
As chiefly glass, it passes through; but where
It reaches the rough rocks or stuff of wood,
There 'tis so rent that it cannot give back
An image. But when gleaming objects dense,
As chiefly mirrors, have been set before it,
Nothing of this sort happens. For it can't
Go, as through glass, nor yet be rent—its safety,
By virtue of that smoothness, being sure.
'Tis therefore that from them the images
Stream back to us; and howso suddenly
Thou place, at any instant, anything

Before a mirror, there an image shows;
Proving that ever from a body's surface
Flow off thin textures and thin shapes of things.
Thus many images in little time
Are gendered; so their origin is named
Rightly a speedy. And even as the sun
Must send below, in little time, to earth
So many beams to keep all things so full
Of light incessant; thus, on grounds the same,
From things there must be borne, in many modes,
To every quarter round, upon the moment,
The many images of things; because
Unto whatever face of things we turn
The mirror, things of form and hue the same
Respond. Besides, though but a moment since
Serenest was the weather of the sky,
So fiercely sudden is it foully thick
That ye might think that round about all murk
Had parted forth from Acheron and filled
The mighty vaults of sky—so grievously,
As gathers thus the storm-clouds' gruesome night,
Do faces of black horror hang on high—
Of which how small a part an image is
There's none to tell or reckon out in words.

Now come; with what swift motion they are borne,
These images, and what the speed assigned
To them across the breezes swimming on—
So that o'er lengths of space a little hour
Alone is wasted, toward whatever region
Each with its divers impulse tends—I'll tell
In verses sweeter than they many are;
Even as the swan's slight note is better far
Than that dispersed clamour of the cranes
Among the southwind's aery clouds. And first,
One oft may see that objects which are light
And made of tiny bodies are the swift;
In which class is the sun's light and his heat,
Since made from small primordial elements
Which, as it were, are forward knocked along
And through the interspaces of the air
To pass delay not, urged by blows behind;
For light by light is instantly supplied

And gleam by following gleam is spurred and driven.
Thus likewise must the images have power
Through unimaginable space to speed
Within a point of time,—first, since a cause
Exceeding small there is, which at their back
Far forward drives them and propels, where, too,
They're carried with such winged lightness on;
And, secondly, since furnished, when sent off,
With texture of such rareness that they can
Through objects whatsoever penetrate
And ooze, as 'twere, through intervening air.
Besides, if those fine particles of things
Which from so deep within are sent abroad,
As light and heat of sun, are seen to glide
And spread themselves through all the space of heaven
Upon one instant of the day, and fly
O'er sea and lands and flood the heaven, what then
Of those which on the outside stand prepared,
When they're hurled off with not a thing to check
Their going out? Dost thou not see indeed
How swifter and how farther must they go
And speed through manifold the length of space
In time the same that from the sun the rays
O'erspread the heaven? This also seems to be
Example chief and true with what swift speed
The images of things are borne about:
That soon as ever under open skies
Is spread the shining water, all at once,
If stars be out in heaven, upgleam from earth,
Serene and radiant in the water there,
The constellations of the universe—
Now seest thou not in what a point of time
An image from the shores of ether falls
Unto the shores of earth? Wherefore, again,
And yet again, 'tis needful to confess
With wondrous...

THE SENSES AND MENTAL PICTURES

Bodies that strike the eyes, awaking sight.
From certain things flow odours evermore,
As cold from rivers, heat from sun, and spray

From waves of ocean, eater-out of walls
Around the coasts. Nor ever cease to flit
The varied voices, sounds athrough the air.
Then too there comes into the mouth at times
The wet of a salt taste, when by the sea
We roam about; and so, whene'er we watch
The wormword being mixed, its bitter stings.
To such degree from all things is each thing
Borne streamingly along, and sent about
To every region round; and nature grants
Nor rest nor respite of the onward flow,
Since 'tis incessantly we feeling have,
And all the time are suffered to descry
And smell all things at hand, and hear them sound.
Besides, since shape examined by our hands
Within the dark is known to be the same
As that by eyes perceived within the light
And lustrous day, both touch and sight must be
By one like cause aroused. So, if we test
A square and get its stimulus on us
Within the dark, within the light what square
Can fall upon our sight, except a square
That images the things? Wherefore it seems
The source of seeing is in images,
Nor without these can anything be viewed.

Now these same films I name are borne about
And tossed and scattered into regions all.
But since we do perceive alone through eyes,
It follows hence that whitherso we turn
Our sight, all things do strike against it there
With form and hue. And just how far from us
Each thing may be away, the image yields
To us the power to see and chance to tell:
For when 'tis sent, at once it shoves ahead
And drives along the air that's in the space
Betwixt it and our eyes. And thus this air
All glides athrough our eyeballs, and, as 'twere,
Brushes athrough our pupils and thuswise
Passes across. Therefore it comes we see
How far from us each thing may be away,
And the more air there be that's driven before,
And too the longer be the brushing breeze

Against our eyes, the farther off removed
Each thing is seen to be: forsooth, this work
With mightily swift order all goes on,
So that upon one instant we may see
What kind the object and how far away.

Nor over-marvellous must this be deemed
In these affairs that, though the films which strike
Upon the eyes cannot be singly seen,
The things themselves may be perceived. For thus
When the wind beats upon us stroke by stroke
And when the sharp cold streams, 'tis not our wont
To feel each private particle of wind
Or of that cold, but rather all at once;
And so we see how blows affect our body,
As if one thing were beating on the same
And giving us the feel of its own body
Outside of us. Again, whene'er we thump
With finger-tip upon a stone, we touch
But the rock's surface and the outer hue,
Nor feel that hue by contact—rather feel
The very hardness deep within the rock.

Now come, and why beyond a looking-glass
An image may be seen, perceive. For seen
It soothly is, removed far within.
'Tis the same sort as objects peered upon
Outside in their true shape, whene'er a door
Yields through itself an open peering-place,
And lets us see so many things outside
Beyond the house. Also that sight is made
By a twofold twin air: for first is seen
The air inside the door-posts; next the doors,
The twain to left and right; and afterwards
A light beyond comes brushing through our eyes,
Then other air, then objects peered upon
Outside in their true shape. And thus, when first
The image of the glass projects itself,
As to our gaze it comes, it shoves ahead
And drives along the air that's in the space
Betwixt it and our eyes, and brings to pass
That we perceive the air ere yet the glass.
But when we've also seen the glass itself,

Forthwith that image which from us is borne
Reaches the glass, and there thrown back again
Comes back unto our eyes, and driving rolls
Ahead of itself another air, that then
'Tis this we see before itself, and thus
It looks so far removed behind the glass.
Wherefore again, again, there's naught for wonder
In those which render from the mirror's plane
A vision back, since each thing comes to pass
By means of the two airs. Now, in the glass
The right part of our members is observed
Upon the left, because, when comes the image
Hitting against the level of the glass,
'Tis not returned unshifted; but forced off
Backwards in line direct and not oblique,—
Exactly as whoso his plaster-mask
Should dash, before 'twere dry, on post or beam,
And it should straightway keep, at clinging there,
Its shape, reversed, facing him who threw,
And so remould the features it gives back:
It comes that now the right eye is the left,
The left the right. An image too may be
From mirror into mirror handed on,
Until of idol-films even five or six
Have thus been gendered. For whatever things
Shall hide back yonder in the house, the same,
However far removed in twisting ways,
May still be all brought forth through bending paths
And by these several mirrors seen to be
Within the house, since nature so compels
All things to be borne backward and spring off
At equal angles from all other things.
To such degree the image gleams across
From mirror unto mirror; where 'twas left
It comes to be the right, and then again
Returns and changes round unto the left.
Again, those little sides of mirrors curved
Proportionate to the bulge of our own flank
Send back to us their idols with the right
Upon the right; and this is so because
Either the image is passed on along
From mirror unto mirror, and thereafter,
When twice dashed off, flies back unto ourselves;

Or else the image wheels itself around,
When once unto the mirror it has come,
Since the curved surface teaches it to turn
To usward. Further, thou might'st well believe
That these film-idols step along with us
And set their feet in unison with ours
And imitate our carriage, since from that
Part of a mirror whence thou hast withdrawn
Straightway no images can be returned.

Further, our eye-balls tend to flee the bright
And shun to gaze thereon; the sun even blinds,
If thou goest on to strain them unto him,
Because his strength is mighty, and the films
Heavily downward from on high are borne
Through the pure ether and the viewless winds,
And strike the eyes, disordering their joints.
So piecing lustre often burns the eyes,
Because it holdeth many seeds of fire
Which, working into eyes, engender pain.
Again, whatever jaundiced people view
Becomes wan-yellow, since from out their bodies
Flow many seeds wan-yellow forth to meet
The films of things, and many too are mixed
Within their eye, which by contagion paint
All things with sallowness. Again, we view
From dark recesses things that stand in light,
Because, when first has entered and possessed
The open eyes this nearer darkling air,
Swiftly the shining air and luminous
Followeth in, which purges then the eyes
And scatters asunder of that other air
The sable shadows, for in large degrees
This air is nimbler, nicer, and more strong.
And soon as ever 'thas filled and oped with light
The pathways of the eyeballs, which before
Black air had blocked, there follow straightaway
Those films of things out-standing in the light,
Provoking vision—what we cannot do
From out the light with objects in the dark,
Because that denser darkling air behind
Followeth in, and fills each aperture
And thus blockades the pathways of the eyes

That there no images of any things
Can be thrown in and agitate the eyes.

And when from far away we do behold
The squared towers of a city, oft
Rounded they seem,—on this account because
Each distant angle is perceived obtuse,
Or rather it is not perceived at all;
And perishes its blow nor to our gaze
Arrives its stroke, since through such length of air
Are borne along the idols that the air
Makes blunt the idol of the angle's point
By numerous collidings. When thuswise
The angles of the tower each and all
Have quite escaped the sense, the stones appear
As rubbed and rounded on a turner's wheel—
Yet not like objects near and truly round,
But with a semblance to them, shadowily.
Likewise, our shadow in the sun appears
To move along and follow our own steps
And imitate our carriage—if thou thinkest
Air that is thus bereft of light can walk,
Following the gait and motion of mankind.
For what we use to name a shadow, sure
Is naught but air deprived of light. No marvel:
Because the earth from spot to spot is reft
Progressively of light of sun, whenever
In moving round we get within its way,
While any spot of earth by us abandoned
Is filled with light again, on this account
It comes to pass that what was body's shadow
Seems still the same to follow after us
In one straight course. Since, evermore pour in
New lights of rays, and perish then the old,
Just like the wool that's drawn into the flame.
Therefore the earth is easily spoiled of light
And easily refilled and from herself
Washeth the black shadows quite away.

And yet in this we don't at all concede
That eyes be cheated. For their task it is
To note in whatsoever place be light,
In what be shadow: whether or no the gleams

Be still the same, and whether the shadow which
Just now was here is that one passing thither,
Or whether the facts be what we said above,
'Tis after all the reasoning of mind
That must decide; nor can our eyeballs know
The nature of reality. And so
Attach thou not this fault of mind to eyes,
Nor lightly think our senses everywhere
Are tottering. The ship in which we sail
Is borne along, although it seems to stand;
The ship that bides in roadstead is supposed
There to be passing by. And hills and fields
Seem fleeing fast astern, past which we urge
The ship and fly under the bellying sails.
The stars, each one, do seem to pause, affixed
To the ethereal caverns, though they all
Forever are in motion, rising out
And thence revisiting their far descents
When they have measured with their bodies bright
The span of heaven. And likewise sun and moon
Seem biding in a roadstead,—objects which,
As plain fact proves, are really borne along.
Between two mountains far away aloft
From midst the whirl of waters open lies
A gaping exit for the fleet, and yet
They seem conjoined in a single isle.
When boys themselves have stopped their spinning round,
The halls still seem to whirl and posts to reel,
Until they now must almost think the roofs
Threaten to ruin down upon their heads.
And now, when nature begins to lift on high
The sun's red splendour and the tremulous fires,
And raise him o'er the mountain-tops, those mountains—
O'er which he seemeth then to thee to be,
His glowing self hard by atingeing them
With his own fire—are yet away from us
Scarcely two thousand arrow-shots, indeed
Oft scarce five hundred courses of a dart;
Although between those mountains and the sun
Lie the huge plains of ocean spread beneath
The vasty shores of ether, and intervene
A thousand lands, possessed by many a folk
And generations of wild beasts. Again,

A pool of water of but a finger's depth,
Which lies between the stones along the pave,
Offers a vision downward into earth
As far, as from the earth o'erspread on high
The gulfs of heaven; that thus thou seemest to view
Clouds down below and heavenly bodies plunged
Wondrously in heaven under earth.
Then too, when in the middle of the stream
Sticks fast our dashing horse, and down we gaze
Into the river's rapid waves, some force
Seems then to bear the body of the horse,
Though standing still, reversely from his course,
And swiftly push up-stream. And wheresoe'er
We cast our eyes across, all objects seem
Thus to be onward borne and flow along
In the same way as we. A portico,
Albeit it stands well propped from end to end
On equal columns, parallel and big,
Contracts by stages in a narrow cone,
When from one end the long, long whole is seen,—
Until, conjoining ceiling with the floor,
And the whole right side with the left, it draws
Together to a cone's nigh-viewless point.
To sailors on the main the sun he seems
From out the waves to rise, and in the waves
To set and bury his light—because indeed
They gaze on naught but water and the sky.
Again, to gazers ignorant of the sea,
Vessels in port seem, as with broken poops,
To lean upon the water, quite agog;
For any portion of the oars that's raised
Above the briny spray is straight, and straight
The rudders from above. But other parts,
Those sunk, immersed below the water-line,
Seem broken all and bended and inclined
Sloping to upwards, and turned back to float
Almost atop the water. And when the winds
Carry the scattered drifts along the sky
In the night-time, then seem to glide along
The radiant constellations 'gainst the clouds
And there on high to take far other course
From that whereon in truth they're borne. And then,
If haply our hand be set beneath one eye

And press below thereon, then to our gaze
Each object which we gaze on seems to be,
By some sensation twain—then twain the lights
Of lampions burgeoning in flowers of flame,
And twain the furniture in all the house,
Two-fold the visages of fellow-men,
And twain their bodies. And again, when sleep
Has bound our members down in slumber soft
And all the body lies in deep repose,
Yet then we seem to self to be awake
And move our members; and in night's blind gloom
We think to mark the daylight and the sun;
And, shut within a room, yet still we seem
To change our skies, our oceans, rivers, hills,
To cross the plains afoot, and hear new sounds,
Though still the austere silence of the night
Abides around us, and to speak replies,
Though voiceless. Other cases of the sort
Wondrously many do we see, which all
Seek, so to say, to injure faith in sense—
In vain, because the largest part of these
Deceives through mere opinions of the mind,
Which we do add ourselves, feigning to see
What by the senses are not seen at all.
For naught is harder than to separate
Plain facts from dubious, which the mind forthwith
Adds by itself.

Again, if one suppose
That naught is known, he knows not whether this
Itself is able to be known, since he
Confesses naught to know. Therefore with him
I waive discussion—who has set his head
Even where his feet should be. But let me grant
That this he knows,—I question: whence he knows
What 'tis to know and not-to-know in turn,
And what created concept of the truth,
And what device has proved the dubious
To differ from the certain?—since in things
He's heretofore seen naught of true. Thou'lt find
That from the senses first hath been create
Concept of truth, nor can the senses be
Rebutted. For criterion must be found

Worthy of greater trust, which shall defeat
Through own authority the false by true;
What, then, than these our senses must there be
Worthy a greater trust? Shall reason, sprung
From some false sense, prevail to contradict
Those senses, sprung as reason wholly is
From out the senses?—For lest these be true,
All reason also then is falsified.
Or shall the ears have power to blame the eyes,
Or yet the touch the ears? Again, shall taste
Accuse this touch or shall the nose confute
Or eyes defeat it? Methinks not so it is:
For unto each has been divided off
Its function quite apart, its power to each;
And thus we're still constrained to perceive
The soft, the cold, the hot apart, apart
All divers hues and whatso things there be
Conjoined with hues. Likewise the tasting tongue
Has its own power apart, and smells apart
And sounds apart are known. And thus it is
That no one sense can e'er convict another.
Nor shall one sense have power to blame itself,
Because it always must be deemed the same,
Worthy of equal trust. And therefore what
At any time unto these senses showed,
The same is true. And if the reason be
Unable to unravel us the cause
Why objects, which at hand were square, afar
Seemed rounded, yet it more availeth us,
Lacking the reason, to pretend a cause
For each configuration, than to let
From out our hands escape the obvious things
And injure primal faith in sense, and wreck
All those foundations upon which do rest
Our life and safety. For not only reason
Would topple down; but even our very life
Would straightaway collapse, unless we dared
To trust our senses and to keep away
From headlong heights and places to be shunned
Of a like peril, and to seek with speed
Their opposites! Again, as in a building,
If the first plumb-line be askew, and if
The square deceiving swerve from lines exact,

And if the level waver but the least
In any part, the whole construction then
Must turn out faulty—shelving and askew,
Leaning to back and front, incongruous,
That now some portions seem about to fall,
And falls the whole ere long—betrayed indeed
By first deceiving estimates: so too
Thy calculations in affairs of life
Must be askew and false, if sprung for thee
From senses false. So all that troop of words
Marshalled against the senses is quite vain.

And now remains to demonstrate with ease
How other senses each their things perceive.
Firstly, a sound and every voice is heard,
When, getting into ears, they strike the sense
With their own body. For confess we must
Even voice and sound to be corporeal,
Because they're able on the sense to strike.
Besides voice often scrapes against the throat,
And screams in going out do make more rough
The wind-pipe—naturally enough, methinks,
When, through the narrow exit rising up
In larger throng, these primal germs of voice
Have thus begun to issue forth. In sooth,
Also the door of the mouth is scraped against
[By air blown outward] from distended [cheeks].
And thus no doubt there is, that voice and words
Consist of elements corporeal,
With power to pain. Nor art thou unaware
Likewise how much of body's ta'en away,
How much from very thews and powers of men
May be withdrawn by steady talk, prolonged
Even from the rising splendour of the morn
To shadows of black evening,—above all
If 't be outpoured with most exceeding shouts.
Therefore the voice must be corporeal,
Since the long talker loses from his frame
A part.
Moreover, roughness in the sound
Comes from the roughness in the primal germs,
As a smooth sound from smooth ones is create;
Nor have these elements a form the same

When the trump rumbles with a hollow roar,
As when barbaric Berecynthian pipe
Buzzes with raucous boomings, or when swans
By night from icy shores of Helicon
With wailing voices raise their liquid dirge.

Thus, when from deep within our frame we force
These voices, and at mouth expel them forth,
The mobile tongue, artificer of words,
Makes them articulate, and too the lips
By their formations share in shaping them.
Hence when the space is short from starting-point
To where that voice arrives, the very words
Must too be plainly heard, distinctly marked.
For then the voice conserves its own formation,
Conserves its shape. But if the space between
Be longer than is fit, the words must be
Through the much air confounded, and the voice
Disordered in its flight across the winds—
And so it haps, that thou canst sound perceive,
Yet not determine what the words may mean;
To such degree confounded and encumbered
The voice approaches us. Again, one word,
Sent from the crier's mouth, may rouse all ears
Among the populace. And thus one voice
Scatters asunder into many voices,
Since it divides itself for separate ears,
Imprinting form of word and a clear tone.
But whatso part of voices fails to hit
The ears themselves perishes, borne beyond,
Idly diffused among the winds. A part,
Beating on solid porticoes, tossed back
Returns a sound; and sometimes mocks the ear
With a mere phantom of a word. When this
Thou well hast noted, thou canst render count
Unto thyself and others why it is
Along the lonely places that the rocks
Give back like shapes of words in order like,
When search we after comrades wandering
Among the shady mountains, and aloud
Call unto them, the scattered. I have seen
Spots that gave back even voices six or seven
For one thrown forth—for so the very hills,

Dashing them back against the hills, kept on
With their reverberations. And these spots
The neighbouring country-side doth feign to be
Haunts of the goat-foot satyrs and the nymphs;
And tells ye there be fauns, by whose night noise
And antic revels yonder they declare
The voiceless silences are broken oft,
And tones of strings are made and wailings sweet
Which the pipe, beat by players' finger-tips,
Pours out; and far and wide the farmer-race
Begins to hear, when, shaking the garmentings
Of pine upon his half-beast head, god-Pan
With puckered lip oft runneth o'er and o'er
The open reeds,—lest flute should cease to pour
The woodland music! Other prodigies
And wonders of this ilk they love to tell,
Lest they be thought to dwell in lonely spots
And even by gods deserted. This is why
They boast of marvels in their story-tellings;
Or by some other reason are led on—
Greedy, as all mankind hath ever been,
To prattle fables into ears.

Again,
One need not wonder how it comes about
That through those places (through which eyes cannot
View objects manifest) sounds yet may pass
And assail the ears. For often we observe
People conversing, though the doors be closed;
No marvel either, since all voice unharmed
Can wind through bended apertures of things,
While idol-films decline to—for they're rent,
Unless along straight apertures they swim,
Like those in glass, through which all images
Do fly across. And yet this voice itself,
In passing through shut chambers of a house,
Is dulled, and in a jumble enters ears,
And sound we seem to hear far more than words.
Moreover, a voice is into all directions
Divided up, since off from one another
New voices are engendered, when one voice
Hath once leapt forth, outstarting into many—
As oft a spark of fire is wont to sprinkle

Itself into its several fires. And so,
Voices do fill those places hid behind,
Which all are in a hubbub round about,
Astir with sound. But idol-films do tend,
As once sent forth, in straight directions all;
Wherefore one can inside a wall see naught,
Yet catch the voices from beyond the same.

Nor tongue and palate, whereby we flavour feel,
Present more problems for more work of thought.
Firstly, we feel a flavour in the mouth,
When forth we squeeze it, in chewing up our food,—
As any one perchance begins to squeeze
With hand and dry a sponge with water soaked.
Next, all which forth we squeeze is spread about
Along the pores and intertwined paths
Of the loose-textured tongue. And so, when smooth
The bodies of the oozy flavour, then
Delightfully they touch, delightfully
They treat all spots, around the wet and trickling
Enclosures of the tongue. And contrariwise,
They sting and pain the sense with their assault,
According as with roughness they're supplied.
Next, only up to palate is the pleasure
Coming from flavour; for in truth when down
'Thas plunged along the throat, no pleasure is,
Whilst into all the frame it spreads around;
Nor aught it matters with what food is fed
The body, if only what thou take thou canst
Distribute well digested to the frame
And keep the stomach in a moist career.
Now, how it is we see some food for some,
Others for others....
I will unfold, or wherefore what to some
Is foul and bitter, yet the same to others
Can seem delectable to eat,—why here
So great the distance and the difference is
That what is food to one to some becomes
Fierce poison, as a certain snake there is
Which, touched by spittle of a man, will waste
And end itself by gnawing up its coil.
Again, fierce poison is the hellebore
To us, but puts the fat on goats and quails.

That thou mayst know by what devices this
Is brought about, in chief thou must recall
What we have said before, that seeds are kept
Commixed in things in divers modes. Again,
As all the breathing creatures which take food
Are outwardly unlike, and outer cut
And contour of their members bounds them round,
Each differing kind by kind, they thus consist
Of seeds of varying shape. And furthermore,
Since seeds do differ, divers too must be
The interstices and paths (which we do call
The apertures) in all the members, even
In mouth and palate too. Thus some must be
More small or yet more large, three-cornered some
And others squared, and many others round,
And certain of them many-angled too
In many modes. For, as the combination
And motion of their divers shapes demand,
The shapes of apertures must be diverse
And paths must vary according to their walls
That bound them. Hence when what is sweet to some,
Becomes to others bitter, for him to whom
'Tis sweet, the smoothest particles must needs
Have entered caressingly the palate's pores.
And, contrariwise, with those to whom that sweet
Is sour within the mouth, beyond a doubt
The rough and barbed particles have got
Into the narrows of the apertures.
Now easy it is from these affairs to know
Whatever...
Indeed, where one from o'er-abundant bile
Is stricken with fever, or in other wise
Feels the roused violence of some malady,
There the whole frame is now upset, and there
All the positions of the seeds are changed,—
So that the bodies which before were fit
To cause the savour, now are fit no more,
And now more apt are others which be able
To get within the pores and gender sour.
Both sorts, in sooth, are intermixed in honey—
What oft we've proved above to thee before.
Now come, and I will indicate what wise
Impact of odour on the nostrils touches.

And first, 'tis needful there be many things
From whence the streaming flow of varied odours
May roll along, and we're constrained to think
They stream and dart and sprinkle themselves about
Impartially. But for some breathing creatures
One odour is more apt, to others another—
Because of differing forms of seeds and pores.
Thus on and on along the zephyrs bees
Are led by odour of honey, vultures too
By carcasses. Again, the forward power
Of scent in dogs doth lead the hunter on
Whithersoever the splay-foot of wild beast
Hath hastened its career; and the white goose,
The saviour of the Roman citadel,
Forescents afar the odour of mankind.
Thus, diversly to divers ones is given
Peculiar smell that leadeth each along
To his own food or makes him start aback
From loathsome poison, and in this wise are
The generations of the wild preserved.

Yet is this pungence not alone in odours
Or in the class of flavours; but, likewise,
The look of things and hues agree not all
So well with senses unto all, but that
Some unto some will be, to gaze upon,
More keen and painful. Lo, the raving lions,
They dare not face and gaze upon the cock
Who's wont with wings to flap away the night
From off the stage, and call the beaming morn
With clarion voice—and lions straightway thus
Bethink themselves of flight, because, ye see,
Within the body of the cocks there be
Some certain seeds, which, into lions' eyes
Injected, bore into the pupils deep
And yield such piercing pain they can't hold out
Against the cocks, however fierce they be—
Whilst yet these seeds can't hurt our gaze the least,
Either because they do not penetrate,
Or since they have free exit from the eyes
As soon as penetrating, so that thus
They cannot hurt our eyes in any part
By there remaining.

To speak once more of odour;
Whatever assail the nostrils, some can travel
A longer way than others. None of them,
However, 's borne so far as sound or voice—
While I omit all mention of such things
As hit the eyesight and assail the vision.
For slowly on a wandering course it comes
And perishes sooner, by degrees absorbed
Easily into all the winds of air;—
And first, because from deep inside the thing
It is discharged with labour (for the fact
That every object, when 'tis shivered, ground,
Or crumbled by the fire, will smell the stronger
Is sign that odours flow and part away
From inner regions of the things). And next,
Thou mayest see that odour is create
Of larger primal germs than voice, because
It enters not through stony walls, wherethrough
Unfailingly the voice and sound are borne;
Wherefore, besides, thou wilt observe 'tis not
So easy to trace out in whatso place
The smelling object is. For, dallying on
Along the winds, the particles cool off,
And then the scurrying messengers of things
Arrive our senses, when no longer hot.
So dogs oft wander astray, and hunt the scent.

Now mark, and hear what objects move the mind,
And learn, in few, whence unto intellect
Do come what come. And first I tell thee this:
That many images of objects rove
In many modes to every region round—
So thin that easily the one with other,
When once they meet, uniteth in mid-air,
Like gossamer or gold-leaf. For, indeed,
Far thinner are they in their fabric than
Those images which take a hold on eyes
And smite the vision, since through body's pores
They penetrate, and inwardly stir up
The subtle nature of mind and smite the sense.
Thus, Centaurs and the limbs of Scyllas, thus
The Cerberus-visages of dogs we see,

And images of people gone before—
Dead men whose bones earth bosomed long ago;
Because the images of every kind
Are everywhere about us borne—in part
Those which are gendered in the very air
Of own accord, in part those others which
From divers things do part away, and those
Which are compounded, made from out their shapes.
For soothly from no living Centaur is
That phantom gendered, since no breed of beast
Like him was ever; but, when images
Of horse and man by chance have come together,
They easily cohere, as aforesaid,
At once, through subtle nature and fabric thin.
In the same fashion others of this ilk
Created are. And when they're quickly borne
In their exceeding lightness, easily
(As earlier I showed) one subtle image,
Compounded, moves by its one blow the mind,
Itself so subtle and so strangely quick.

That these things come to pass as I record,
From this thou easily canst understand:
So far as one is unto other like,
Seeing with mind as well as with the eyes
Must come to pass in fashion not unlike.
Well, now, since I have shown that I perceive
Haply a lion through those idol-films
Such as assail my eyes, 'tis thine to know
Also the mind is in like manner moved,
And sees, nor more nor less than eyes do see
(Except that it perceives more subtle films)
The lion and aught else through idol-films.
And when the sleep has overset our frame,
The mind's intelligence is now awake,
Still for no other reason, save that these—
The self-same films as when we are awake—
Assail our minds, to such degree indeed
That we do seem to see for sure the man
Whom, void of life, now death and earth have gained
Dominion over. And nature forces this
To come to pass because the body's senses
Are resting, thwarted through the members all,

Unable now to conquer false with true;
And memory lies prone and languishes
In slumber, nor protests that he, the man
Whom the mind feigns to see alive, long since
Hath been the gain of death and dissolution.

And further, 'tis no marvel idols move
And toss their arms and other members round
In rhythmic time—and often in men's sleeps
It haps an image this is seen to do;
In sooth, when perishes the former image,
And other is gendered of another pose,
That former seemeth to have changed its gestures.
Of course the change must be conceived as speedy;
So great the swiftness and so great the store
Of idol-things, and (in an instant brief
As mind can mark) so great, again, the store
Of separate idol-parts to bring supplies.

It happens also that there is supplied
Sometimes an image not of kind the same;
But what before was woman, now at hand
Is seen to stand there, altered into male;
Or other visage, other age succeeds;
But slumber and oblivion take care
That we shall feel no wonder at the thing.

And much in these affairs demands inquiry,
And much, illumination—if we crave
With plainness to exhibit facts. And first,
Why doth the mind of one to whom the whim
To think has come behold forthwith that thing?
Or do the idols watch upon our will,
And doth an image unto us occur,
Directly we desire—if heart prefer
The sea, the land, or after all the sky?
Assemblies of the citizens, parades,
Banquets, and battles, these and all doth she,
Nature, create and furnish at our word?—
Maugre the fact that in same place and spot
Another's mind is meditating things
All far unlike. And what, again, of this:
When we in sleep behold the idols step,

In measure, forward, moving supple limbs,
Whilst forth they put each supple arm in turn
With speedy motion, and with eyeing heads
Repeat the movement, as the foot keeps time?
Forsooth, the idols they are steeped in art,
And wander to and fro well taught indeed,—
Thus to be able in the time of night
To make such games! Or will the truth be this:
Because in one least moment that we mark—
That is, the uttering of a single sound—
There lurk yet many moments, which the reason
Discovers to exist, therefore it comes
That, in a moment how so brief ye will,
The divers idols are hard by, and ready
Each in its place diverse? So great the swiftness,
So great, again, the store of idol-things,
And so, when perishes the former image,
And other is gendered of another pose,
The former seemeth to have changed its gestures.
And since they be so tenuous, mind can mark
Sharply alone the ones it strains to see;
And thus the rest do perish one and all,
Save those for which the mind prepares itself.
Further, it doth prepare itself indeed,
And hopes to see what follows after each—
Hence this result. For hast thou not observed
How eyes, essaying to perceive the fine,
Will strain in preparation, otherwise
Unable sharply to perceive at all?
Yet know thou canst that, even in objects plain,
If thou attendest not, 'tis just the same
As if 'twere all the time removed and far.
What marvel, then, that mind doth lose the rest,
Save those to which 'thas given up itself?
So 'tis that we conjecture from small signs
Things wide and weighty, and involve ourselves
In snarls of self-deceit.

SOME VITAL FUNCTIONS

In these affairs
We crave that thou wilt passionately flee
The one offence, and anxiously wilt shun
The error of presuming the clear lights
Of eyes created were that we might see;
Or thighs and knees, aprop upon the feet,
Thuswise can bended be, that we might step
With goodly strides ahead; or forearms joined
Unto the sturdy uppers, or serving hands
On either side were given, that we might do
Life's own demands. All such interpretation
Is aft-for-fore with inverse reasoning,
Since naught is born in body so that we
May use the same, but birth engenders use:
No seeing ere the lights of eyes were born,
No speaking ere the tongue created was;
But origin of tongue came long before
Discourse of words, and ears created were
Much earlier than any sound was heard;
And all the members, so meseems, were there
Before they got their use: and therefore, they
Could not be gendered for the sake of use.
But contrariwise, contending in the fight
With hand to hand, and rending of the joints,
And fouling of the limbs with gore, was there,
O long before the gleaming spears ere flew;
And nature prompted man to shun a wound,
Before the left arm by the aid of art
Opposed the shielding targe. And, verily,
Yielding the weary body to repose,
Far ancienter than cushions of soft beds,
And quenching thirst is earlier than cups.
These objects, therefore, which for use and life
Have been devised, can be conceived as found
For sake of using. But apart from such
Are all which first were born and afterwards
Gave knowledge of their own utility—
Chief in which sort we note the senses, limbs:
Wherefore, again, 'tis quite beyond thy power
To hold that these could thus have been create

For office of utility.
Likewise,
'Tis nothing strange that all the breathing creatures
Seek, even by nature of their frame, their food.
Yes, since I've taught thee that from off the things
Stream and depart innumerable bodies
In modes innumerable too; but most
Must be the bodies streaming from the living—
Which bodies, vexed by motion evermore,
Are through the mouth exhaled innumerable,
When weary creatures pant, or through the sweat
Squeezed forth innumerable from deep within.
Thus body rarefies, so undermined
In all its nature, and pain attends its state.
And so the food is taken to underprop
The tottering joints, and by its interfusion
To re-create their powers, and there stop up
The longing, open-mouthed through limbs and veins,
For eating. And the moist no less departs
Into all regions that demand the moist;
And many heaped-up particles of hot,
Which cause such burnings in these bellies of ours,
The liquid on arriving dissipates
And quenches like a fire, that parching heat
No longer now can scorch the frame. And so,
Thou seest how panting thirst is washed away
From off our body, how the hunger-pang
It, too, appeased.
Now, how it comes that we,
Whene'er we wish, can step with strides ahead,
And how 'tis given to move our limbs about,
And what device is wont to push ahead
This the big load of our corporeal frame,
I'll say to thee—do thou attend what's said.
I say that first some idol-films of walking
Into our mind do fall and smite the mind,
As said before. Thereafter will arises;
For no one starts to do a thing, before
The intellect previsions what it wills;
And what it there pre-visioneth depends
On what that image is. When, therefore, mind
Doth so bestir itself that it doth will
To go and step along, it strikes at once

That energy of soul that's sown about
In all the body through the limbs and frame—
And this is easy of performance, since
The soul is close conjoined with the mind.
Next, soul in turn strikes body, and by degrees
Thus the whole mass is pushed along and moved.
Then too the body rarefies, and air,
Forsooth as ever of such nimbleness,
Comes on and penetrates aboundingly
Through opened pores, and thus is sprinkled round
Unto all smallest places in our frame.
Thus then by these twain factors, severally,
Body is borne like ship with oars and wind.
Nor yet in these affairs is aught for wonder
That particles so fine can whirl around
So great a body and turn this weight of ours;
For wind, so tenuous with its subtle body,
Yet pushes, driving on the mighty ship
Of mighty bulk; one hand directs the same,
Whatever its momentum, and one helm
Whirls it around, whither ye please; and loads,
Many and huge, are moved and hoisted high
By enginery of pulley-blocks and wheels,
With but light strain.
Now, by what modes this sleep
Pours through our members waters of repose
And frees the breast from cares of mind, I'll tell
In verses sweeter than they many are;
Even as the swan's slight note is better far
Than that dispersed clamour of the cranes
Among the southwind's aery clouds. Do thou
Give me sharp ears and a sagacious mind,—
That thou mayst not deny the things to be
Whereof I'm speaking, nor depart away
With bosom scorning these the spoken truths,
Thyself at fault unable to perceive.
Sleep chiefly comes when energy of soul
Hath now been scattered through the frame, and part
Expelled abroad and gone away, and part
Crammed back and settling deep within the frame—
Whereafter then our loosened members droop.
For doubt is none that by the work of soul
Exist in us this sense, and when by slumber

That sense is thwarted, we are bound to think
The soul confounded and expelled abroad—
Yet not entirely, else the frame would lie
Drenched in the everlasting cold of death.
In sooth, where no one part of soul remained
Lurking among the members, even as fire
Lurks buried under many ashes, whence
Could sense amain rekindled be in members,
As flame can rise anew from unseen fire?

By what devices this strange state and new
May be occasioned, and by what the soul
Can be confounded and the frame grow faint,
I will untangle: see to it, thou, that I
Pour forth my words not unto empty winds.
In first place, body on its outer parts—
Since these are touched by neighbouring aery gusts—
Must there be thumped and strook by blows of air
Repeatedly. And therefore almost all
Are covered either with hides, or else with shells,
Or with the horny callus, or with bark.
Yet this same air lashes their inner parts,
When creatures draw a breath or blow it out.
Wherefore, since body thus is flogged alike
Upon the inside and the out, and blows
Come in upon us through the little pores
Even inward to our body's primal parts
And primal elements, there comes to pass
By slow degrees, along our members then,
A kind of overthrow; for then confounded
Are those arrangements of the primal germs
Of body and of mind. It comes to pass
That next a part of soul's expelled abroad,
A part retreateth in recesses hid,
A part, too, scattered all about the frame,
Cannot become united nor engage
In interchange of motion. Nature now
So hedges off approaches and the paths;
And thus the sense, its motions all deranged,
Retires down deep within; and since there's naught,
As 'twere, to prop the frame, the body weakens,
And all the members languish, and the arms
And eyelids fall, and, as ye lie abed,

Even there the houghs will sag and loose their powers.
Again, sleep follows after food, because
The food produces same result as air,
Whilst being scattered round through all the veins;
And much the heaviest is that slumber which,
Full or fatigued, thou takest; since 'tis then
That the most bodies disarrange themselves,
Bruised by labours hard. And in same wise,
This three-fold change: a forcing of the soul
Down deeper, more a casting-forth of it,
A moving more divided in its parts
And scattered more.

And to whate'er pursuit
A man most clings absorbed, or what the affairs
On which we theretofore have tarried much,
And mind hath strained upon the more, we seem
In sleep not rarely to go at the same.
The lawyers seem to plead and cite decrees,
Commanders they to fight and go at frays,
Sailors to live in combat with the winds,
And we ourselves indeed to make this book,
And still to seek the nature of the world
And set it down, when once discovered, here
In these my country's leaves. Thus all pursuits,
All arts in general seem in sleeps to mock
And master the minds of men. And whosoever
Day after day for long to games have given
Attention undivided, still they keep
(As oft we note), even when they've ceased to grasp
Those games with their own senses, open paths
Within the mind wherethrough the idol-films
Of just those games can come. And thus it is
For many a day thereafter those appear
Floating before the eyes, that even awake
They think they view the dancers moving round
Their supple limbs, and catch with both the ears
The liquid song of harp and speaking chords,
And view the same assembly on the seats,
And manifold bright glories of the stage—
So great the influence of pursuit and zest,
And of the affairs wherein 'thas been the wont
Of men to be engaged-nor only men,

But soothly all the animals. Behold,
Thou'lt see the sturdy horses, though outstretched,
Yet sweating in their sleep, and panting ever,
And straining utmost strength, as if for prize,
As if, with barriers opened now...
And hounds of huntsmen oft in soft repose
Yet toss asudden all their legs about,
And growl and bark, and with their nostrils sniff
The winds again, again, as though indeed
They'd caught the scented foot-prints of wild beasts,
And, even when wakened, often they pursue
The phantom images of stags, as though
They did perceive them fleeing on before,
Until the illusion's shaken off and dogs
Come to themselves again. And fawning breed
Of house-bred whelps do feel the sudden urge
To shake their bodies and start from off the ground,
As if beholding stranger-visages.
And ever the fiercer be the stock, the more
In sleep the same is ever bound to rage.
But flee the divers tribes of birds and vex
With sudden wings by night the groves of gods,
When in their gentle slumbers they have dreamed
Of hawks in chase, aswooping on for fight.
Again, the minds of mortals which perform
With mighty motions mighty enterprises,
Often in sleep will do and dare the same
In manner like. Kings take the towns by storm,
Succumb to capture, battle on the field,
Raise a wild cry as if their throats were cut
Even then and there. And many wrestle on
And groan with pains, and fill all regions round
With mighty cries and wild, as if then gnawed
By fangs of panther or of lion fierce.
Many amid their slumbers talk about
Their mighty enterprises, and have often
Enough become the proof of their own crimes.
Many meet death; many, as if headlong
From lofty mountains tumbling down to earth
With all their frame, are frenzied in their fright;
And after sleep, as if still mad in mind,
They scarce come to, confounded as they are
By ferment of their frame. The thirsty man,

Likewise, he sits beside delightful spring
Or river and gulpeth down with gaping throat
Nigh the whole stream. And oft the innocent young,
By sleep o'ermastered, think they lift their dress
By pail or public jordan and then void
The water filtered down their frame entire
And drench the Babylonian coverlets,
Magnificently bright. Again, those males
Into the surging channels of whose years
Now first has passed the seed (engendered
Within their members by the ripened days)
Are in their sleep confronted from without
By idol-images of some fair form—
Tidings of glorious face and lovely bloom,
Which stir and goad the regions turgid now
With seed abundant; so that, as it were
With all the matter acted duly out,
They pour the billows of a potent stream
And stain their garment.

And as said before,
That seed is roused in us when once ripe age
Has made our body strong...
As divers causes give to divers things
Impulse and irritation, so one force
In human kind rouses the human seed
To spurt from man. As soon as ever it issues,
Forced from its first abodes, it passes down
In the whole body through the limbs and frame,
Meeting in certain regions of our thews,
And stirs amain the genitals of man.
The goaded regions swell with seed, and then
Comes the delight to dart the same at what
The mad desire so yearns, and body seeks
That object, whence the mind by love is pierced.
For well-nigh each man falleth toward his wound,
And our blood spurts even toward the spot from whence
The stroke wherewith we are strook, and if indeed
The foe be close, the red jet reaches him.
Thus, one who gets a stroke from Venus' shafts—
Whether a boy with limbs effeminate
Assault him, or a woman darting love
From all her body—that one strains to get

Even to the thing whereby he's hit, and longs
To join with it and cast into its frame
The fluid drawn even from within its own.
For the mute craving doth presage delight.

THE PASSION OF LOVE

This craving 'tis that's Venus unto us:
From this, engender all the lures of love,
From this, O first hath into human hearts
Trickled that drop of joyance which ere long
Is by chill care succeeded. Since, indeed,
Though she thou lovest now be far away,
Yet idol-images of her are near
And the sweet name is floating in thy ear.
But it behooves to flee those images;
And scare afar whatever feeds thy love;
And turn elsewhere thy mind; and vent the sperm,
Within thee gathered, into sundry bodies,
Nor, with thy thoughts still busied with one love,
Keep it for one delight, and so store up
Care for thyself and pain inevitable.
For, lo, the ulcer just by nourishing
Grows to more life with deep inveteracy,
And day by day the fury swells aflame,
And the woe waxes heavier day by day—
Unless thou dost destroy even by new blows
The former wounds of love, and curest them
While yet they're fresh, by wandering freely round
After the freely-wandering Venus, or
Canst lead elsewhere the tumults of thy mind.

Nor doth that man who keeps away from love
Yet lack the fruits of Venus; rather takes
Those pleasures which are free of penalties.
For the delights of Venus, verily,
Are more unmixed for mortals sane-of-soul
Than for those sick-at-heart with love-pining.
Yea, in the very moment of possessing,
Surges the heat of lovers to and fro,
Restive, uncertain; and they cannot fix
On what to first enjoy with eyes and hands.

The parts they sought for, those they squeeze so tight,
And pain the creature's body, close their teeth
Often against her lips, and smite with kiss
Mouth into mouth,—because this same delight
Is not unmixed; and underneath are stings
Which goad a man to hurt the very thing,
Whate'er it be, from whence arise for him
Those germs of madness. But with gentle touch
Venus subdues the pangs in midst of love,
And the admixture of a fondling joy
Doth curb the bites of passion. For they hope
That by the very body whence they caught
The heats of love their flames can be put out.
But nature protests 'tis all quite otherwise;
For this same love it is the one sole thing
Of which, the more we have, the fiercer burns
The breast with fell desire. For food and drink
Are taken within our members; and, since they
Can stop up certain parts, thus, easily
Desire of water is glutted and of bread.
But, lo, from human face and lovely bloom
Naught penetrates our frame to be enjoyed
Save flimsy idol-images and vain—
A sorry hope which oft the winds disperse.
As when the thirsty man in slumber seeks
To drink, and water ne'er is granted him
Wherewith to quench the heat within his members,
But after idols of the liquids strives
And toils in vain, and thirsts even whilst he gulps
In middle of the torrent, thus in love
Venus deludes with idol-images
The lovers. Nor they cannot sate their lust
By merely gazing on the bodies, nor
They cannot with their palms and fingers rub
Aught from each tender limb, the while they stray
Uncertain over all the body. Then,
At last, with members intertwined, when they
Enjoy the flower of their age, when now
Their bodies have sweet presage of keen joys,
And Venus is about to sow the fields
Of woman, greedily their frames they lock,
And mingle the slaver of their mouths, and breathe
Into each other, pressing teeth on mouths—

Yet to no purpose, since they're powerless
To rub off aught, or penetrate and pass
With body entire into body—for oft
They seem to strive and struggle thus to do;
So eagerly they cling in Venus' bonds,
Whilst melt away their members, overcome
By violence of delight. But when at last
Lust, gathered in the thews, hath spent itself,
There come a brief pause in the raging heat—
But then a madness just the same returns
And that old fury visits them again,
When once again they seek and crave to reach
They know not what, all powerless to find
The artifice to subjugate the bane.
In such uncertain state they waste away
With unseen wound.

To which be added too,
They squander powers and with the travail wane;
Be added too, they spend their futile years
Under another's beck and call; their duties
Neglected languish and their honest name
Reeleth sick, sick; and meantime their estates
Are lost in Babylonian tapestries;
And unguents and dainty Sicyonian shoes
Laugh on her feet; and (as ye may be sure)
Big emeralds of green light are set in gold;
And rich sea-purple dress by constant wear
Grows shabby and all soaked with Venus' sweat;
And the well-earned ancestral property
Becometh head-bands, coifs, and many a time
The cloaks, or garments Alidensian
Or of the Cean isle. And banquets, set
With rarest cloth and viands, are prepared—
And games of chance, and many a drinking cup,
And unguents, crowns and garlands. All in vain,
Since from amid the well-spring of delights
Bubbles some drop of bitter to torment
Among the very flowers—when haply mind
Gnaws into self, now stricken with remorse
For slothful years and ruin in baudels,
Or else because she's left him all in doubt
By launching some sly word, which still like fire

Lives wildly, cleaving to his eager heart;
Or else because he thinks she darts her eyes
Too much about and gazes at another,—
And in her face sees traces of a laugh.

These ills are found in prospering love and true;
But in crossed love and helpless there be such
As through shut eyelids thou canst still take in—
Uncounted ills; so that 'tis better far
To watch beforehand, in the way I've shown,
And guard against enticements. For to shun
A fall into the hunting-snares of love
Is not so hard, as to get out again,
When tangled in the very nets, and burst
The stoutly-knotted cords of Aphrodite.
Yet even when there enmeshed with tangled feet,
Still canst thou scape the danger-lest indeed
Thou standest in the way of thine own good,
And overlookest first all blemishes
Of mind and body of thy much preferred,
Desirable dame. For so men do,
Eyeless with passion, and assign to them
Graces not theirs in fact. And thus we see
Creatures in many a wise crooked and ugly
The prosperous sweethearts in a high esteem;
And lovers gird each other and advise
To placate Venus, since their friends are smit
With a base passion—miserable dupes
Who seldom mark their own worst bane of all.
The black-skinned girl is "tawny like the honey";
The filthy and the fetid's "negligee";
The cat-eyed she's "a little Pallas," she;
The sinewy and wizened's "a gazelle";
The pudgy and the pigmy is "piquant,
One of the Graces sure"; the big and bulky
O she's "an Admiration, imposante";
The stuttering and tongue-tied "sweetly lisps";
The mute girl's "modest"; and the garrulous,
The spiteful spit-fire, is "a sparkling wit";
And she who scarcely lives for scrawniness
Becomes "a slender darling"; "delicate"
Is she who's nearly dead of coughing-fit;
The pursy female with protuberant breasts

She is "like Ceres when the goddess gave
Young Bacchus suck"; the pug-nosed lady-love
"A Satyress, a feminine Silenus";
The blubber-lipped is "all one luscious kiss"—
A weary while it were to tell the whole.
But let her face possess what charm ye will,
Let Venus' glory rise from all her limbs,—
Forsooth there still are others; and forsooth
We lived before without her; and forsooth
She does the same things—and we know she does—
All, as the ugly creature, and she scents,
Yes she, her wretched self with vile perfumes;
Whom even her handmaids flee and giggle at
Behind her back. But he, the lover, in tears
Because shut out, covers her threshold o'er
Often with flowers and garlands, and anoints
Her haughty door-posts with the marjoram,
And prints, poor fellow, kisses on the doors—
Admitted at last, if haply but one whiff
Got to him on approaching, he would seek
Decent excuses to go out forthwith;
And his lament, long pondered, then would fall
Down at his heels; and there he'd damn himself
For his fatuity, observing how
He had assigned to that same lady more—
Than it is proper to concede to mortals.
And these our Venuses are 'ware of this.
Wherefore the more are they at pains to hide
All the-behind-the-scenes of life from those
Whom they desire to keep in bonds of love—
In vain, since ne'ertheless thou canst by thought
Drag all the matter forth into the light
And well search out the cause of all these smiles;
And if of graceful mind she be and kind,
Do thou, in thy turn, overlook the same,
And thus allow for poor mortality.
Nor sighs the woman always with feigned love,
Who links her body round man's body locked
And holds him fast, making his kisses wet
With lips sucked into lips; for oft she acts
Even from desire, and, seeking mutual joys,
Incites him there to run love's race-course through.
Nor otherwise can cattle, birds, wild beasts,

And sheep and mares submit unto the males,
Except that their own nature is in heat,
And burns abounding and with gladness takes
Once more the Venus of the mounting males.
And seest thou not how those whom mutual pleasure
Hath bound are tortured in their common bonds?
How often in the cross-roads dogs that pant
To get apart strain eagerly asunder
With utmost might?—When all the while they're fast
In the stout links of Venus. But they'd ne'er
So pull, except they knew those mutual joys—
So powerful to cast them unto snares
And hold them bound. Wherefore again, again,
Even as I say, there is a joint delight.

And when perchance, in mingling seed with his,
The female hath o'erpowered the force of male
And by a sudden fling hath seized it fast,
Then are the offspring, more from mothers' seed,
More like their mothers; as, from fathers' seed,
They're like to fathers. But whom seest to be
Partakers of each shape, one equal blend
Of parents' features, these are generate
From fathers' body and from mothers' blood,
When mutual and harmonious heat hath dashed
Together seeds, aroused along their frames
By Venus' goads, and neither of the twain
Mastereth or is mastered. Happens too
That sometimes offspring can to being come
In likeness of their grandsires, and bring back
Often the shapes of grandsires' sires, because
Their parents in their bodies oft retain
Concealed many primal germs, commixed
In many modes, which, starting with the stock,
Sire handeth down to son, himself a sire;
Whence Venus by a variable chance
Engenders shapes, and diversely brings back
Ancestral features, voices too, and hair.
A female generation rises forth
From seed paternal, and from mother's body
Exist created males: since sex proceeds
No more from singleness of seed than faces
Or bodies or limbs of ours: for every birth

Is from a twofold seed; and what's created
Hath, of that parent which it is more like,
More than its equal share; as thou canst mark,—
Whether the breed be male or female stock.

Nor do the powers divine grudge any man
The fruits of his seed-sowing, so that never
He be called "father" by sweet children his,
And end his days in sterile love forever.
What many men suppose; and gloomily
They sprinkle the altars with abundant blood,
And make the high platforms odorous with burnt gifts,
To render big by plenteous seed their wives—
And plague in vain godheads and sacred lots.
For sterile are these men by seed too thick,
Or else by far too watery and thin.
Because the thin is powerless to cleave
Fast to the proper places, straightaway
It trickles from them, and, returned again,
Retires abortively. And then since seed
More gross and solid than will suit is spent
By some men, either it flies not forth amain
With spurt prolonged enough, or else it fails
To enter suitably the proper places,
Or, having entered, the seed is weakly mixed
With seed of the woman: harmonies of Venus
Are seen to matter vastly here; and some
Impregnate some more readily, and from some
Some women conceive more readily and become
Pregnant. And many women, sterile before
In several marriage-beds, have yet thereafter
Obtained the mates from whom they could conceive
The baby-boys, and with sweet progeny
Grow rich. And even for husbands (whose own wives,
Although of fertile wombs, have borne for them
No babies in the house) are also found
Concordant natures so that they at last
Can bulwark their old age with goodly sons.
A matter of great moment 'tis in truth,
That seeds may mingle readily with seeds
Suited for procreation, and that thick
Should mix with fluid seeds, with thick the fluid.
And in this business 'tis of some import

Upon what diet life is nourished:
For some foods thicken seeds within our members,
And others thin them out and waste away.
And in what modes the fond delight itself
Is carried on—this too importeth vastly.
For commonly 'tis thought that wives conceive
More readily in manner of wild-beasts,
After the custom of the four-foot breeds,
Because so postured, with the breasts beneath
And buttocks then upreared, the seeds can take
Their proper places. Nor is need the least
For wives to use the motions of blandishment;
For thus the woman hinders and resists
Her own conception, if too joyously
Herself she treats the Venus of the man
With haunches heaving, and with all her bosom
Now yielding like the billows of the sea—
Aye, from the ploughshare's even course and track
She throws the furrow, and from proper places
Deflects the spurt of seed. And courtesans
Are thuswise wont to move for their own ends,
To keep from pregnancy and lying in,
And all the while to render Venus more
A pleasure for the men—the which meseems
Our wives have never need of.

Sometimes too
It happens—and through no divinity
Nor arrows of Venus—that a sorry chit
Of scanty grace will be beloved by man;
For sometimes she herself by very deeds,
By her complying ways, and tidy habits,
Will easily accustom thee to pass
With her thy life-time—and, moreover, lo,
Long habitude can gender human love,
Even as an object smitten o'er and o'er
By blows, however lightly, yet at last
Is overcome and wavers. Seest thou not,
Besides, how drops of water falling down
Against the stones at last bore through the stones?

BOOK V

PROEM

O WHO can build with puissant breast a song
Worthy the majesty of these great finds?
Or who in words so strong that he can frame
The fit laudations for deserts of him
Who left us heritors of such vast prizes,
By his own breast discovered and sought out?—
There shall be none, methinks, of mortal stock.
For if must needs be named for him the name
Demanded by the now known majesty
Of these high matters, then a god was he,—
Hear me, illustrious Memmius—a god;
Who first and chief found out that plan of life
Which now is called philosophy, and who
By cunning craft, out of such mighty waves,
Out of such mighty darkness, moored life
In havens so serene, in light so clear.
Compare those old discoveries divine
Of others: lo, according to the tale,
Ceres established for mortality
The grain, and Bacchus juice of vine-born grape,
Though life might yet without these things abide,
Even as report saith now some peoples live.
But man's well-being was impossible
Without a breast all free. Wherefore the more
That man doth justly seem to us a god,
From whom sweet solaces of life, afar
Distributed o'er populous domains,
Now soothe the minds of men. But if thou thinkest
Labours of Hercules excel the same,
Much farther from true reasoning thou farest.
For what could hurt us now that mighty maw

Of Nemeaean Lion, or what the Boar
Who bristled in Arcadia? Or, again,
O what could Cretan Bull, or Hydra, pest
Of Lerna, fenced with vipers venomous?
Or what the triple-breasted power of her
The three-fold Geryon...
The sojourners in the Stymphalian fens
So dreadfully offend us, or the Steeds
Of Thracian Diomedes breathing fire
From out their nostrils off along the zones
Bistonian and Ismarian? And the Snake,
The dread fierce gazer, guardian of the golden
And gleaming apples of the Hesperides,
Coiled round the tree-trunk with tremendous bulk,
O what, again, could he inflict on us
Along the Atlantic shore and wastes of sea?—
Where neither one of us approacheth nigh
Nor no barbarian ventures. And the rest
Of all those monsters slain, even if alive,
Unconquered still, what injury could they do?
None, as I guess. For so the glutted earth
Swarms even now with savage beasts, even now
Is filled with anxious terrors through the woods
And mighty mountains and the forest deeps—
Quarters 'tis ours in general to avoid.
But lest the breast be purged, what conflicts then,
What perils, must bosom, in our own despite!
O then how great and keen the cares of lust
That split the man distraught! How great the fears!
And lo, the pride, grim greed, and wantonness—
How great the slaughters in their train! and lo,
Debaucheries and every breed of sloth!
Therefore that man who subjugated these,
And from the mind expelled, by words indeed,
Not arms, O shall it not be seemly him
To dignify by ranking with the gods?—
And all the more since he was wont to give,
Concerning the immortal gods themselves,
Many pronouncements with a tongue divine,
And to unfold by his pronouncements all
The nature of the world.

ARGUMENT OF THE BOOK AND NEW PROEM AGAINST A

TELEOLOGICAL CONCEPT

And walking now
In his own footprints, I do follow through
His reasonings, and with pronouncements teach
The covenant whereby all things are framed,
How under that covenant they must abide
Nor ever prevail to abrogate the aeons'
Inexorable decrees,—how (as we've found),
In class of mortal objects, o'er all else,
The mind exists of earth-born frame create
And impotent unscathed to abide
Across the mighty aeons, and how come
In sleep those idol-apparitions,
That so befool intelligence when we
Do seem to view a man whom life has left.
Thus far we've gone; the order of my plan
Hath brought me now unto the point where I
Must make report how, too, the universe
Consists of mortal body, born in time,
And in what modes that congregated stuff
Established itself as earth and sky,
Ocean, and stars, and sun, and ball of moon;
And then what living creatures rose from out
The old telluric places, and what ones
Were never born at all; and in what mode
The human race began to name its things
And use the varied speech from man to man;
And in what modes hath bosomed in their breasts
That awe of gods, which halloweth in all lands
Fanes, altars, groves, lakes, idols of the gods.
Also I shall untangle by what power
The steersman nature guides the sun's courses,
And the meanderings of the moon, lest we,
Percase, should fancy that of own free will
They circle their perennial courses round,
Timing their motions for increase of crops
And living creatures, or lest we should think
They roll along by any plan of gods.
For even those men who have learned full well
That godheads lead a long life free of care,
If yet meanwhile they wonder by what plan
Things can go on (and chiefly yon high things

Observed o'erhead on the ethereal coasts),
Again are hurried back unto the fears
Of old religion and adopt again
Harsh masters, deemed almighty,—wretched men,
Unwitting what can be and what cannot,
And by what law to each its scope prescribed,
Its boundary stone that clings so deep in Time.

But for the rest,—lest we delay thee here
Longer by empty promises—behold,
Before all else, the seas, the lands, the sky:
O Memmius, their threefold nature, lo,
Their bodies three, three aspects so unlike,
Three frames so vast, a single day shall give
Unto annihilation! Then shall crash
That massive form and fabric of the world
Sustained so many aeons! Nor do I
Fail to perceive how strange and marvellous
This fact must strike the intellect of man,—
Annihilation of the sky and earth
That is to be,—and with what toil of words
'Tis mine to prove the same; as happens oft
When once ye offer to man's listening ears
Something before unheard of, but may not
Subject it to the view of eyes for him
Nor put it into hand—the sight and touch,
Whereby the opened highways of belief
Lead most directly into human breast
And regions of intelligence. But yet
I will speak out. The fact itself, perchance,
Will force belief in these my words, and thou
Mayst see, in little time, tremendously
With risen commotions of the lands all things
Quaking to pieces—which afar from us
May she, the steersman Nature, guide: and may
Reason, O rather than the fact itself,
Persuade us that all things can be o'erthrown
And sink with awful-sounding breakage down!

But ere on this I take a step to utter
Oracles holier and soundlier based
Than ever the Pythian pronounced for men
From out the tripod and the Delphian laurel,

I will unfold for thee with learned words
Many a consolation, lest perchance,
Still bridled by religion, thou suppose
Lands, sun, and sky, sea, constellations, moon,
Must dure forever, as of frame divine—
And so conclude that it is just that those,
(After the manner of the Giants), should all
Pay the huge penalties for monstrous crime,
Who by their reasonings do overshake
The ramparts of the universe and wish
There to put out the splendid sun of heaven,
Branding with mortal talk immortal things—
Though these same things are even so far removed
From any touch of deity and seem
So far unworthy of numbering with the gods,
That well they may be thought to furnish rather
A goodly instance of the sort of things
That lack the living motion, living sense.
For sure 'tis quite beside the mark to think
That judgment and the nature of the mind
In any kind of body can exist—
Just as in ether can't exist a tree,
Nor clouds in the salt sea, nor in the fields
Can fishes live, nor blood in timber be,
Nor sap in boulders: fixed and arranged
Where everything may grow and have its place.
Thus nature of mind cannot arise alone
Without the body, nor have its being far
From thews and blood. Yet if 'twere possible?—
Much rather might this very power of mind
Be in the head, the shoulders, or the heels,
And, born in any part soever, yet
In the same man, in the same vessel abide
But since within this body even of ours
Stands fixed and appears arranged sure
Where soul and mind can each exist and grow,
Deny we must the more that they can dure
Outside the body and the breathing form
In rotting clods of earth, in the sun's fire,
In water, or in ether's skiey coasts.
Therefore these things no whit are furnished
With sense divine, since never can they be
With life-force quickened.

Likewise, thou canst ne'er
Believe the sacred seats of gods are here
In any regions of this mundane world;
Indeed, the nature of the gods, so subtle,
So far removed from these our senses, scarce
Is seen even by intelligence of mind.
And since they've ever eluded touch and thrust
Of human hands, they cannot reach to grasp
Aught tangible to us. For what may not
Itself be touched in turn can never touch.
Wherefore, besides, also their seats must be
Unlike these seats of ours,—even subtle too,
As meet for subtle essence—as I'll prove
Hereafter unto thee with large discourse.
Further, to say that for the sake of men
They willed to prepare this world's magnificence,
And that 'tis therefore duty and behoof
To praise the work of gods as worthy praise,
And that 'tis sacrilege for men to shake
Ever by any force from out their seats
What hath been stablished by the Forethought old
To everlasting for races of mankind,
And that 'tis sacrilege to assault by words
And overtopple all from base to beam,—
Memmius, such notions to concoct and pile,
Is verily—to dote. Our gratefulness,
O what emoluments could it confer
Upon Immortals and upon the Blessed
That they should take a step to manage aught
For sake of us? Or what new factor could,
After so long a time, inveigle them—
The hitherto reposeful—to desire
To change their former life? For rather he
Whom old things chafe seems likely to rejoice
At new; but one that in fore-passed time
Hath chanced upon no ill, through goodly years,
O what could ever enkindle in such an one
Passion for strange experiment? Or what
The evil for us, if we had ne'er been born?—
As though, forsooth, in darkling realms and woe
Our life were lying till should dawn at last
The day-spring of creation! Whosoever

Hath been begotten wills perforce to stay
In life, so long as fond delight detains;
But whoso ne'er hath tasted love of life,
And ne'er was in the count of living things,
What hurts it him that he was never born?
Whence, further, first was planted in the gods
The archetype for gendering the world
And the fore-notion of what man is like,
So that they knew and pre-conceived with mind
Just what they wished to make? Or how were known
Ever the energies of primal germs,
And what those germs, by interchange of place,
Could thus produce, if nature's self had not
Given example for creating all?
For in such wise primordials of things,
Many in many modes, astir by blows
From immemorial aeons, in motion too
By their own weights, have evermore been wont
To be so borne along and in all modes
To meet together and to try all sorts
Which, by combining one with other, they
Are powerful to create, that thus it is
No marvel now, if they have also fallen
Into arrangements such, and if they've passed
Into vibrations such, as those whereby
This sum of things is carried on to-day
By fixed renewal. But knew I never what
The seeds primordial were, yet would I dare
This to affirm, even from deep judgments based
Upon the ways and conduct of the skies—
This to maintain by many a fact besides—
That in no wise the nature of all things
For us was fashioned by a power divine—
So great the faults it stands encumbered with.
First, mark all regions which are overarched
By the prodigious reaches of the sky:
One yawning part thereof the mountain-chains
And forests of the beasts do have and hold;
And cliffs, and desert fens, and wastes of sea
(Which sunder afar the beaches of the lands)
Possess it merely; and, again, thereof
Well-nigh two-thirds intolerable heat
And a perpetual fall of frost doth rob

From mortal kind. And what is left to till,
Even that the force of nature would o'errun
With brambles, did not human force oppose,—
Long wont for livelihood to groan and sweat
Over the two-pronged mattock and to cleave
The soil in twain by pressing on the plough.

Unless, by the ploughshare turning the fruitful clods
And kneading the mould, we quicken into birth,
[The crops] spontaneously could not come up
Into the free bright air. Even then sometimes,
When things acquired by the sternest toil
Are now in leaf, are now in blossom all,
Either the skiey sun with baneful heats
Parches, or sudden rains or chilling rime
Destroys, or flaws of winds with furious whirl
Torment and twist. Beside these matters, why
Doth nature feed and foster on land and sea
The dreadful breed of savage beasts, the foes
Of the human clan? Why do the seasons bring
Distempers with them? Wherefore stalks at large
Death, so untimely? Then, again, the babe,
Like to the castaway of the raging surf,
Lies naked on the ground, speechless, in want
Of every help for life, when nature first
Hath poured him forth upon the shores of light
With birth-pangs from within the mother's womb,
And with a plaintive wail he fills the place,—
As well befitting one for whom remains
In life a journey through so many ills.
But all the flocks and herds and all wild beasts
Come forth and grow, nor need the little rattles,
Nor must be treated to the humouring nurse's
Dear, broken chatter; nor seek they divers clothes
To suit the changing skies; nor need, in fine,
Nor arms, nor lofty ramparts, wherewithal
Their own to guard—because the earth herself
And nature, artificer of the world, bring forth
Aboundingly all things for all.

THE WORLD IS NOT ETERNAL

And first,
Since body of earth and water, air's light breath,
And fiery exhalations (of which four
This sum of things is seen to be compact)
So all have birth and perishable frame,
Thus the whole nature of the world itself
Must be conceived as perishable too.
For, verily, those things of which we see
The parts and members to have birth in time
And perishable shapes, those same we mark
To be invariably born in time
And born to die. And therefore when I see
The mightiest members and the parts of this
Our world consumed and begot again,
'Tis mine to know that also sky above
And earth beneath began of old in time
And shall in time go under to disaster.

And lest in these affairs thou deemest me
To have seized upon this point by sleight to serve
My own caprice—because I have assumed
That earth and fire are mortal things indeed,
And have not doubted water and the air
Both perish too and have affirmed the same
To be again begotten and wax big—
Mark well the argument: in first place, lo,
Some certain parts of earth, grievously parched
By unremitting suns, and trampled on
By a vast throng of feet, exhale abroad
A powdery haze and flying clouds of dust,
Which the stout winds disperse in the whole air.
A part, moreover, of her sod and soil
Is summoned to inundation by the rains;
And rivers graze and gouge the banks away.
Besides, whatever takes a part its own
In fostering and increasing [aught]...

Is rendered back; and since, beyond a doubt,
Earth, the all-mother, is beheld to be
Likewise the common sepulchre of things,

Therefore thou seest her minished of her plenty,
And then again augmented with new growth.

And for the rest, that sea, and streams, and springs
Forever with new waters overflow,
And that perennially the fluids well,
Needeth no words—the mighty flux itself
Of multitudinous waters round about
Declareth this. But whatso water first
Streams up is ever straightway carried off,
And thus it comes to pass that all in all
There is no overflow; in part because
The burly winds (that over-sweep amain)
And skiey sun (that with his rays dissolves)
Do minish the level seas; in part because
The water is diffused underground
Through all the lands. The brine is filtered off,
And then the liquid stuff seeps back again
And all regathers at the river-heads,
Whence in fresh-water currents on it flows
Over the lands, adown the channels which
Were cleft erstwhile and erstwhile bore along
The liquid-footed floods.

Now, then, of air
I'll speak, which hour by hour in all its body
Is changed innumerably. For whatso'er
Streams up in dust or vapour off of things,
The same is all and always borne along
Into the mighty ocean of the air;
And did not air in turn restore to things
Bodies, and thus recruit them as they stream,
All things by this time had resolved been
And changed into air. Therefore it never
Ceases to be engendered off of things
And to return to things, since verily
In constant flux do all things stream.

Likewise,
The abounding well-spring of the liquid light,
The ethereal sun, doth flood the heaven o'er
With constant flux of radiance ever new,
And with fresh light supplies the place of light,

Upon the instant. For whatever effulgence
Hath first streamed off, no matter where it falls,
Is lost unto the sun. And this 'tis thine
To know from these examples: soon as clouds
Have first begun to under-pass the sun,
And, as it were, to rend the rays of light
In twain, at once the lower part of them
Is lost entire, and earth is overcast
Where'er the thunderheads are rolled along—
So know thou mayst that things forever need
A fresh replenishment of gleam and glow,
And each effulgence, foremost flashed forth,
Perisheth one by one. Nor otherwise
Can things be seen in sunlight, lest alway
The fountain-head of light supply new light.
Indeed your earthly beacons of the night,
The hanging lampions and the torches, bright
With darting gleams and dense with livid soot,
Do hurry in like manner to supply
With ministering heat new light amain;
Are all alive to quiver with their fires,—
Are so alive, that thus the light ne'er leaves
The spots it shines on, as if rent in twain:
So speedily is its destruction veiled
By the swift birth of flame from all the fires.
Thus, then, we must suppose that sun and moon
And stars dart forth their light from under-births
Ever and ever new, and whatso flames
First rise do perish always one by one—
Lest, haply, thou shouldst think they each endure
Inviolable.

    Again, perceivest not
How stones are also conquered by Time?—
Not how the lofty towers ruin down,
And boulders crumble?—Not how shrines of gods
And idols crack outworn?—Nor how indeed
The holy Influence hath yet no power
There to postpone the Terminals of Fate,
Or headway make 'gainst Nature's fixed decrees?
Again, behold we not the monuments
Of heroes, now in ruins, asking us,
In their turn likewise, if we don't believe

They also age with eld? Behold we not
The rended basalt ruining amain
Down from the lofty mountains, powerless
To dure and dree the mighty forces there
Of finite time?—for they would never fall
Rended asudden, if from infinite Past
They had prevailed against all engin'ries
Of the assaulting aeons, with no crash.

Again, now look at This, which round, above,
Contains the whole earth in its one embrace:
If from itself it procreates all things—
As some men tell—and takes them to itself
When once destroyed, entirely must it be
Of mortal birth and body; for whate'er
From out itself giveth to other things
Increase and food, the same perforce must be
Minished, and then recruited when it takes
Things back into itself.

Besides all this,
If there had been no origin-in-birth
Of lands and sky, and they had ever been
The everlasting, why, ere Theban war
And obsequies of Troy, have other bards
Not also chanted other high affairs?
Whither have sunk so oft so many deeds
Of heroes? Why do those deeds live no more,
Ingrafted in eternal monuments
Of glory? Verily, I guess, because
The Sum is new, and of a recent date
The nature of our universe, and had
Not long ago its own exordium.
Wherefore, even now some arts are being still
Refined, still increased: now unto ships
Is being added many a new device;
And but the other day musician-folk
Gave birth to melic sounds of organing;
And, then, this nature, this account of things
Hath been discovered latterly, and I
Myself have been discovered only now,
As first among the first, able to turn
The same into ancestral Roman speech.

Yet if, percase, thou deemest that ere this
Existed all things even the same, but that
Perished the cycles of the human race
In fiery exhalations, or cities fell
By some tremendous quaking of the world,
Or rivers in fury, after constant rains,
Had plunged forth across the lands of earth
And whelmed the towns—then, all the more must thou
Confess, defeated by the argument,
That there shall be annihilation too
Of lands and sky. For at a time when things
Were being taxed by maladies so great,
And so great perils, if some cause more fell
Had then assailed them, far and wide they would
Have gone to disaster and supreme collapse.
And by no other reasoning are we
Seen to be mortal, save that all of us
Sicken in turn with those same maladies
With which have sickened in the past those men
Whom nature hath removed from life.

Whatever abides eternal must indeed
Either repel all strokes, because 'tis made
Of solid body, and permit no entrance
Of aught with power to sunder from within
The parts compact—as are those seeds of stuff
Whose nature we've exhibited before;
Or else be able to endure through time
For this: because they are from blows exempt,
As is the void, the which abides untouched,
Unsmit by any stroke; or else because
There is no room around, whereto things can,
As 'twere, depart in dissolution all,—
Even as the sum of sums eternal is,
Without or place beyond whereto things may
Asunder fly, or bodies which can smite,
And thus dissolve them by the blows of might.
But not of solid body, as I've shown,
Exists the nature of the world, because
In things is intermingled there a void;
Nor is the world yet as the void, nor are,
Moreover, bodies lacking which, percase,
Rising from out the infinite, can fell

With fury-whirlwinds all this sum of things,
Or bring upon them other cataclysm
Of peril strange; and yonder, too, abides
The infinite space and the profound abyss—
Whereinto, lo, the ramparts of the world
Can yet be shivered. Or some other power
Can pound upon them till they perish all.
Thus is the door of doom, O nowise barred
Against the sky, against the sun and earth
And deep-sea waters, but wide open stands
And gloats upon them, monstrous and agape.
Wherefore, again, 'tis needful to confess
That these same things are born in time; for things
Which are of mortal body could indeed
Never from infinite past until to-day
Have spurned the multitudinous assaults
Of the immeasurable aeons old.

Again, since battle so fiercely one with other
The four most mighty members the world,
Aroused in an all unholy war,
Seest not that there may be for them an end
Of the long strife?—Or when the skiey sun
And all the heat have won dominion o'er
The sucked-up waters all?—And this they try
Still to accomplish, though as yet they fail,—
For so aboundingly the streams supply
New store of waters that 'tis rather they
Who menace the world with inundations vast
From forth the unplumbed chasms of the sea.
But vain—since winds (that over-sweep amain)
And skiey sun (that with his rays dissolves)
Do minish the level seas and trust their power
To dry up all, before the waters can
Arrive at the end of their endeavouring.
Breathing such vasty warfare, they contend
In balanced strife the one with other still
Concerning mighty issues,—though indeed
The fire was once the more victorious,
And once—as goes the tale—the water won
A kingdom in the fields. For fire o'ermastered
And licked up many things and burnt away,
What time the impetuous horses of the Sun

Snatched Phaethon headlong from his skiey road
Down the whole ether and over all the lands.
But the omnipotent Father in keen wrath
Then with the sudden smite of thunderbolt
Did hurl the mighty-minded hero off
Those horses to the earth. And Sol, his sire,
Meeting him as he fell, caught up in hand
The ever-blazing lampion of the world,
And drave together the pell-mell horses there
And yoked them all a-tremble, and amain,
Steering them over along their own old road,
Restored the cosmos,—as forsooth we hear
From songs of ancient poets of the Greeks—
A tale too far away from truth, meseems.
For fire can win when from the infinite
Has risen a larger throng of particles
Of fiery stuff; and then its powers succumb,
Somehow subdued again, or else at last
It shrivels in torrid atmospheres the world.
And whilom water too began to win—
As goes the story—when it overwhelmed
The lives of men with billows; and thereafter,
When all that force of water-stuff which forth
From out the infinite had risen up
Did now retire, as somehow turned aside,
The rain-storms stopped, and streams their fury checked.

FORMATION OF THE WORLD
AND ASTRONOMICAL QUESTIONS

But in what modes that conflux of first-stuff
Did found the multitudinous universe
Of earth, and sky, and the unfathomed deeps
Of ocean, and courses of the sun and moon,
I'll now in order tell. For of a truth
Neither by counsel did the primal germs
'Stablish themselves, as by keen act of mind,
Each in its proper place; nor did they make,
Forsooth, a compact how each germ should move;
But, lo, because primordials of things,
Many in many modes, astir by blows
From immemorial aeons, in motion too
By their own weights, have evermore been wont

To be so borne along and in all modes
To meet together and to try all sorts
Which, by combining one with other, they
Are powerful to create: because of this
It comes to pass that those primordials,
Diffused far and wide through mighty aeons,
The while they unions try, and motions too,
Of every kind, meet at the last amain,
And so become oft the commencements fit
Of mighty things—earth, sea, and sky, and race
Of living creatures.

In that long-ago
The wheel of the sun could nowhere be discerned
Flying far up with its abounding blaze,
Nor constellations of the mighty world,
Nor ocean, nor heaven, nor even earth nor air.
Nor aught of things like unto things of ours
Could then be seen—but only some strange storm
And a prodigious hurly-burly mass
Compounded of all kinds of primal germs,
Whose battling discords in disorder kept
Interstices, and paths, coherencies,
And weights, and blows, encounterings, and motions,
Because, by reason of their forms unlike
And varied shapes, they could not all thuswise
Remain conjoined nor harmoniously
Have interplay of movements. But from there
Portions began to fly asunder, and like
With like to join, and to block out a world,
And to divide its members and dispose
Its mightier parts—that is, to set secure
The lofty heavens from the lands, and cause
The sea to spread with waters separate,
And fires of ether separate and pure
Likewise to congregate apart.

For, lo,
First came together the earthy particles
(As being heavy and intertangled) there
In the mid-region, and all began to take
The lowest abodes; and ever the more they got
One with another intertangled, the more

They pressed from out their mass those particles
Which were to form the sea, the stars, the sun,
And moon, and ramparts of the mighty world—
For these consist of seeds more smooth and round
And of much smaller elements than earth.
And thus it was that ether, fraught with fire,
First broke away from out the earthen parts,
Athrough the innumerable pores of earth,
And raised itself aloft, and with itself
Bore lightly off the many starry fires;
And not far otherwise we often see,
And the still lakes and the perennial streams
Exhale a mist, and even as earth herself
Is seen at times to smoke, when first at dawn
The light of the sun, the many-rayed, begins
To redden into gold, over the grass
Begemmed with dew. When all of these are brought
Together overhead, the clouds on high
With now concreted body weave a cover
Beneath the heavens. And thuswise ether too,
Light and diffusive, with concreted body
On all sides spread, on all sides bent itself
Into a dome, and, far and wide diffused
On unto every region on all sides,
Thus hedged all else within its greedy clasp.
Hard upon ether came the origins
Of sun and moon, whose globes revolve in air
Midway between the earth and mightiest ether,—
For neither took them, since they weighed too little
To sink and settle, but too much to glide
Along the upmost shores; and yet they are
In such a wise midway between the twain
As ever to whirl their living bodies round,
And ever to dure as parts of the wide Whole;
In the same fashion as certain members may
In us remain at rest, whilst others move.
When, then, these substances had been withdrawn,
Amain the earth, where now extend the vast
Cerulean zones of all the level seas,
Caved in, and down along the hollows poured
The whirlpools of her brine; and day by day
The more the tides of ether and rays of sun
On every side constrained into one mass

The earth by lashing it again, again,
Upon its outer edges (so that then,
Being thus beat upon, 'twas all condensed
About its proper centre), ever the more
The salty sweat, from out its body squeezed,
Augmented ocean and the fields of foam
By seeping through its frame, and all the more
Those many particles of heat and air
Escaping, began to fly aloft, and form,
By condensation there afar from earth,
The high refulgent circuits of the heavens.
The plains began to sink, and windy slopes
Of the high mountains to increase; for rocks
Could not subside, nor all the parts of ground
Settle alike to one same level there.

Thus, then, the massy weight of earth stood firm
With now concreted body, when (as 'twere)
All of the slime of the world, heavy and gross,
Had run together and settled at the bottom,
Like lees or bilge. Then ocean, then the air,
Then ether herself, the fraught-with-fire, were all
Left with their liquid bodies pure and free,
And each more lighter than the next below;
And ether, most light and liquid of the three,
Floats on above the long aerial winds,
Nor with the brawling of the winds of air
Mingles its liquid body. It doth leave
All there—those under-realms below her heights—
There to be overset in whirlwinds wild,—
Doth leave all there to brawl in wayward gusts,
Whilst, gliding with a fixed impulse still,
Itself it bears its fires along. For, lo,
That ether can flow thus steadily on, on,
With one unaltered urge, the Pontus proves—
That sea which floweth forth with fixed tides,
Keeping one onward tenor as it glides.

And that the earth may there abide at rest
In the mid-region of the world, it needs
Must vanish bit by bit in weight and lessen,
And have another substance underneath,
Conjoined to it from its earliest age

In linked unison with the vasty world's
Realms of the air in which it roots and lives.
On this account, the earth is not a load,
Nor presses down on winds of air beneath;
Even as unto a man his members be
Without all weight—the head is not a load
Unto the neck; nor do we feel the whole
Weight of the body to centre in the feet.
But whatso weights come on us from without,
Weights laid upon us, these harass and chafe,
Though often far lighter. For to such degree
It matters always what the innate powers
Of any given thing may be. The earth
Was, then, no alien substance fetched amain,
And from no alien firmament cast down
On alien air; but was conceived, like air,
In the first origin of this the world,
As a fixed portion of the same, as now
Our members are seen to be a part of us.

Besides, the earth, when of a sudden shook
By the big thunder, doth with her motion shake
All that's above her—which she ne'er could do
By any means, were earth not bounden fast
Unto the great world's realms of air and sky:
For they cohere together with common roots,
Conjoined both, even from their earliest age,
In linked unison. Aye, seest thou not
That this most subtle energy of soul
Supports our body, though so heavy a weight,—
Because, indeed, 'tis with it so conjoined
In linked unison? What power, in sum,
Can raise with agile leap our body aloft,
Save energy of mind which steers the limbs?
Now seest thou not how powerful may be
A subtle nature, when conjoined it is
With heavy body, as air is with the earth
Conjoined, and energy of mind with us?

Now let us sing what makes the stars to move.
In first place, if the mighty sphere of heaven
Revolveth round, then needs we must aver
That on the upper and the under pole

Presses a certain air, and from without
Confines them and encloseth at each end;
And that, moreover, another air above
Streams on athwart the top of the sphere and tends
In same direction as are rolled along
The glittering stars of the eternal world;
Or that another still streams on below
To whirl the sphere from under up and on
In opposite direction—as we see
The rivers turn the wheels and water-scoops.
It may be also that the heavens do all
Remain at rest, whilst yet are borne along
The lucid constellations; either because
Swift tides of ether are by sky enclosed,
And whirl around, seeking a passage out,
And everywhere make roll the starry fires
Through the Summanian regions of the sky;
Or else because some air, streaming along
From an eternal quarter off beyond,
Whileth the driven fires, or, then, because
The fires themselves have power to creep along,
Going wherever their food invites and calls,
And feeding their flaming bodies everywhere
Throughout the sky. Yet which of these is cause
In this our world 'tis hard to say for sure;
But what can be throughout the universe,
In divers worlds on divers plan create,
This only do I show, and follow on
To assign unto the motions of the stars
Even several causes which 'tis possible
Exist throughout the universal All;
Of which yet one must be the cause even here
Which maketh motion for our constellations.
Yet to decide which one of them it be
Is not the least the business of a man
Advancing step by cautious step, as I.

Nor can the sun's wheel larger be by much
Nor its own blaze much less than either seems
Unto our senses. For from whatso spaces
Fires have the power on us to cast their beams
And blow their scorching exhalations forth
Against our members, those same distances

Take nothing by those intervals away
From bulk of flames; and to the sight the fire
Is nothing shrunken. Therefore, since the heat
And the outpoured light of skiey sun
Arrive our senses and caress our limbs,
Form too and bigness of the sun must look
Even here from earth just as they really be,
So that thou canst scarce nothing take or add.
And whether the journeying moon illuminate
The regions round with bastard beams, or throw
From off her proper body her own light,—
Whichever it be, she journeys with a form
Naught larger than the form doth seem to be
Which we with eyes of ours perceive. For all
The far removed objects of our gaze
Seem through much air confused in their look
Ere minished in their bigness. Wherefore, moon,
Since she presents bright look and clear-cut form,
May there on high by us on earth be seen
Just as she is with extreme bounds defined,
And just of the size. And lastly, whatso fires
Of ether thou from earth beholdest, these
Thou mayst consider as possibly of size
The least bit less, or larger by a hair
Than they appear—since whatso fires we view
Here in the lands of earth are seen to change
From time to time their size to less or more
Only the least, when more or less away,
So long as still they bicker clear, and still
Their glow's perceived.

Nor need there be for men
Astonishment that yonder sun so small
Can yet send forth so great a light as fills
Oceans and all the lands and sky aflood,
And with its fiery exhalations steeps
The world at large. For it may be, indeed,
That one vast-flowing well-spring of the whole
Wide world from here hath opened and out-gushed,
And shot its light abroad; because thuswise
The elements of fiery exhalations
From all the world around together come,
And thuswise flow into a bulk so big

That from one single fountain-head may stream
This heat and light. And seest thou not, indeed,
How widely one small water-spring may wet
The meadow-lands at times and flood the fields?
'Tis even possible, besides, that heat
From forth the sun's own fire, albeit that fire
Be not a great, may permeate the air
With the fierce hot—if but, perchance, the air
Be of condition and so tempered then
As to be kindled, even when beat upon
Only by little particles of heat—
Just as we sometimes see the standing grain
Or stubble straw in conflagration all
From one lone spark. And possibly the sun,
Agleam on high with rosy lampion,
Possesses about him with invisible heats
A plenteous fire, by no effulgence marked,
So that he maketh, he, the Fraught-with-fire,
Increase to such degree the force of rays.

Nor is there one sure cause revealed to men
How the sun journeys from his summer haunts
On to the mid-most winter turning-points
In Capricorn, the thence reverting veers
Back to solstitial goals of Cancer; nor
How 'tis the moon is seen each month to cross
That very distance which in traversing
The sun consumes the measure of a year.
I say, no one clear reason hath been given
For these affairs. Yet chief in likelihood
Seemeth the doctrine which the holy thought
Of great Democritus lays down: that ever
The nearer the constellations be to earth
The less can they by whirling of the sky
Be borne along, because those skiey powers
Of speed aloft do vanish and decrease
In under-regions, and the sun is thus
Left by degrees behind amongst those signs
That follow after, since the sun he lies
Far down below the starry signs that blaze;
And the moon lags even tardier than the sun:
In just so far as is her course removed
From upper heaven and nigh unto the lands,

In just so far she fails to keep the pace
With starry signs above; for just so far
As feebler is the whirl that bears her on,
(Being, indeed, still lower than the sun),
In just so far do all the starry signs,
Circling around, o'ertake her and o'erpass.
Therefore it happens that the moon appears
More swiftly to return to any sign
Along the Zodiac, than doth the sun,
Because those signs do visit her again
More swiftly than they visit the great sun.
It can be also that two streams of air
Alternately at fixed periods
Blow out from transverse regions of the world,
Of which the one may thrust the sun away
From summer-signs to mid-most winter goals
And rigors of the cold, and the other then
May cast him back from icy shades of chill
Even to the heat-fraught regions and the signs
That blaze along the Zodiac. So, too,
We must suppose the moon and all the stars,
Which through the mighty and sidereal years
Roll round in mighty orbits, may be sped
By streams of air from regions alternate.
Seest thou not also how the clouds be sped
By contrary winds to regions contrary,
The lower clouds diversely from the upper?
Then, why may yonder stars in ether there
Along their mighty orbits not be borne
By currents opposite the one to other?

But night o'erwhelms the lands with vasty murk
Either when sun, after his diurnal course,
Hath walked the ultimate regions of the sky
And wearily hath panted forth his fires,
Shivered by their long journeying and wasted
By traversing the multitudinous air,
Or else because the self-same force that drave
His orb along above the lands compels
Him then to turn his course beneath the lands.
Matuta also at a fixed hour
Spreadeth the roseate morning out along
The coasts of heaven and deploys the light,

Either because the self-same sun, returning
Under the lands, aspires to seize the sky,
Striving to set it blazing with his rays
Ere he himself appear, or else because
Fires then will congregate and many seeds
Of heat are wont, even at a fixed time,
To stream together—gendering evermore
New suns and light. Just so the story goes
That from the Idaean mountain-tops are seen
Dispersed fires upon the break of day
Which thence combine, as 'twere, into one ball
And form an orb. Nor yet in these affairs
Is aught for wonder that these seeds of fire
Can thus together stream at time so fixed
And shape anew the splendour of the sun.
For many facts we see which come to pass
At fixed time in all things: burgeon shrubs
At fixed time, and at a fixed time
They cast their flowers; and Eld commands the teeth,
At time as surely fixed, to drop away,
And Youth commands the growing boy to bloom
With the soft down and let from both his cheeks
The soft beard fall. And lastly, thunder-bolts,
Snow, rains, clouds, winds, at seasons of the year
Nowise unfixed, all do come to pass.
For where, even from their old primordial start
Causes have ever worked in such a way,
And where, even from the world's first origin,
Thuswise have things befallen, so even now
After a fixed order they come round
In sequence also.

Likewise, days may wax
Whilst the nights wane, and daylight minished be
Whilst nights do take their augmentations,
Either because the self-same sun, coursing
Under the lands and over in two arcs,
A longer and a briefer, doth dispart
The coasts of ether and divides in twain
His orbit all unequally, and adds,
As round he's borne, unto the one half there
As much as from the other half he's ta'en,
Until he then arrives that sign of heaven

Where the year's node renders the shades of night
Equal unto the periods of light.
For when the sun is midway on his course
Between the blasts of northwind and of south,
Heaven keeps his two goals parted equally,
By virtue of the fixed position old
Of the whole starry Zodiac, through which
That sun, in winding onward, takes a year,
Illumining the sky and all the lands
With oblique light—as men declare to us
Who by their diagrams have charted well
Those regions of the sky which be adorned
With the arranged signs of Zodiac.
Or else, because in certain parts the air
Under the lands is denser, the tremulous
Bright beams of fire do waver tardily,
Nor easily can penetrate that air
Nor yet emerge unto their rising-place:
For this it is that nights in winter time
Do linger long, ere comes the many-rayed
Round Badge of the day. Or else because, as said,
In alternating seasons of the year
Fires, now more quick, and now more slow, are wont
To stream together,—the fires which make the sun
To rise in some one spot—therefore it is
That those men seem to speak the truth [who hold
A new sun is with each new daybreak born].

The moon she possibly doth shine because
Strook by the rays of sun, and day by day
May turn unto our gaze her light, the more
She doth recede from orb of sun, until,
Facing him opposite across the world,
She hath with full effulgence gleamed abroad,
And, at her rising as she soars above,
Hath there observed his setting; thence likewise
She needs must hide, as 'twere, her light behind
By slow degrees, the nearer now she glides,
Along the circle of the Zodiac,
From her far place toward fires of yonder sun,—
As those men hold who feign the moon to be
Just like a ball and to pursue a course
Betwixt the sun and earth. There is, again,

Some reason to suppose that moon may roll
With light her very own, and thus display
The varied shapes of her resplendence there.
For near her is, percase, another body,
Invisible, because devoid of light,
Borne on and gliding all along with her,
Which in three modes may block and blot her disk.
Again, she may revolve upon herself,
Like to a ball's sphere—if perchance that be—
One half of her dyed o'er with glowing light,
And by the revolution of that sphere
She may beget for us her varying shapes,
Until she turns that fiery part of her
Full to the sight and open eyes of men;
Thence by slow stages round and back she whirls,
Withdrawing thus the luminiferous part
Of her sphered mass and ball, as, verily,
The Babylonian doctrine of Chaldees,
Refuting the art of Greek astrologers,
Labours, in opposition, to prove sure—
As if, forsooth, the thing for which each fights,
Might not alike be true,—or aught there were
Wherefore thou mightest risk embracing one
More than the other notion. Then, again,
Why a new moon might not forevermore
Created be with fixed successions there
Of shapes and with configurations fixed,
And why each day that bright created moon
Might not miscarry and another be,
In its stead and place, engendered anew,
'Tis hard to show by reason, or by words
To prove absurd—since, lo, so many things
Can be create with fixed successions:
Spring-time and Venus come, and Venus' boy,
The winged harbinger, steps on before,
And hard on Zephyr's foot-prints Mother Flora,
Sprinkling the ways before them, filleth all
With colours and with odours excellent;
Whereafter follows arid Heat, and he
Companioned is by Ceres, dusty one,
And by the Etesian Breezes of the north;
Then cometh Autumn on, and with him steps
Lord Bacchus, and then other Seasons too

And other Winds do follow—the high roar
Of great Volturnus, and the Southwind strong
With thunder-bolts. At last earth's Shortest-Day
Bears on to men the snows and brings again
The numbing cold. And Winter follows her,
His teeth with chills a-chatter. Therefore, 'tis
The less a marvel, if at fixed time
A moon is thus begotten and again
At fixed time destroyed, since things so many
Can come to being thus at fixed time.
Likewise, the sun's eclipses and the moon's
Far occultations rightly thou mayst deem

As due to several causes. For, indeed,
Why should the moon be able to shut out
Earth from the light of sun, and on the side
To earthward thrust her high head under sun,
Opposing dark orb to his glowing beams—
And yet, at same time, one suppose the effect
Could not result from some one other body
Which glides devoid of light forevermore?
Again, why could not sun, in weakened state,
At fixed time for-lose his fires, and then,
When he has passed on along the air
Beyond the regions, hostile to his flames,
That quench and kill his fires, why could not he
Renew his light? And why should earth in turn
Have power to rob the moon of light, and there,
Herself on high, keep the sun hid beneath,
Whilst the moon glideth in her monthly course
Athrough the rigid shadows of the cone?—
And yet, at same time, some one other body
Not have the power to under-pass the moon,
Or glide along above the orb of sun,
Breaking his rays and outspread light asunder?
And still, if moon herself refulgent be
With her own sheen, why could she not at times
In some one quarter of the mighty world
Grow weak and weary, whilst she passeth through
Regions unfriendly to the beams her own?

ORIGINS OF VEGETABLE AND ANIMAL LIFE

And now to what remains!—Since I've resolved
By what arrangements all things come to pass
Through the blue regions of the mighty world,—
How we can know what energy and cause
Started the various courses of the sun
And the moon's goings, and by what far means
They can succumb, the while with thwarted light,
And veil with shade the unsuspecting lands,
When, as it were, they blink, and then again
With open eye survey all regions wide,
Resplendent with white radiance—I do now
Return unto the world's primeval age
And tell what first the soft young fields of earth
With earliest parturition had decreed
To raise in air unto the shores of light
And to entrust unto the wayward winds.
In the beginning, earth gave forth, around
The hills and over all the length of plains,
The race of grasses and the shining green;
The flowery meadows sparkled all aglow
With greening colour, and thereafter, lo,
Unto the divers kinds of trees was given
An emulous impulse mightily to shoot,
With a free rein, aloft into the air.
As feathers and hairs and bristles are begot
The first on members of the four-foot breeds
And on the bodies of the strong-y-winged,
Thus then the new Earth first of all put forth
Grasses and shrubs, and afterward begat
The mortal generations, there upsprung—
Innumerable in modes innumerable—
After diverging fashions. For from sky
These breathing-creatures never can have dropped,
Nor the land-dwellers ever have come up
Out of sea-pools of salt. How true remains,
How merited is that adopted name
Of earth—"The Mother!"—since from out the earth
Are all begotten. And even now arise
From out the loams how many living things—
Concreted by the rains and heat of the sun.
Wherefore 'tis less a marvel, if they sprang

In Long Ago more many, and more big,
Matured of those days in the fresh young years
Of earth and ether. First of all, the race
Of the winged ones and parti-coloured birds,
Hatched out in spring-time, left their eggs behind;
As now-a-days in summer tree-crickets
Do leave their shiny husks of own accord,
Seeking their food and living. Then it was
This earth of thine first gave unto the day
The mortal generations; for prevailed
Among the fields abounding hot and wet.
And hence, where any fitting spot was given,
There 'gan to grow womb-cavities, by roots
Affixed to earth. And when in ripened time
The age of the young within (that sought the air
And fled earth's damps) had burst these wombs, O then
Would Nature thither turn the pores of earth
And make her spurt from open veins a juice
Like unto milk; even as a woman now
Is filled, at child-bearing, with the sweet milk,
Because all that swift stream of aliment
Is thither turned unto the mother-breasts.
There earth would furnish to the children food;
Warmth was their swaddling cloth, the grass their bed
Abounding in soft down. Earth's newness then
Would rouse no dour spells of the bitter cold,
Nor extreme heats nor winds of mighty powers—
For all things grow and gather strength through time
In like proportions; and then earth was young.

Wherefore, again, again, how merited
Is that adopted name of Earth—The Mother!—
Since she herself begat the human race,
And at one well-nigh fixed time brought forth
Each breast that ranges raving round about
Upon the mighty mountains and all birds
Aerial with many a varied shape.
But, lo, because her bearing years must end,
She ceased, like to a woman worn by eld.
For lapsing aeons change the nature of
The whole wide world, and all things needs must take
One status after other, nor aught persists
Forever like itself. All things depart;

Nature she changeth all, compelleth all
To transformation. Lo, this moulders down,
A-slack with weary eld, and that, again,
Prospers in glory, issuing from contempt.
In suchwise, then, the lapsing aeons change
The nature of the whole wide world, and earth
Taketh one status after other. And what
She bore of old, she now can bear no longer,
And what she never bore, she can to-day.

In those days also the telluric world
Strove to beget the monsters that upsprung
With their astounding visages and limbs—
The Man-woman—a thing betwixt the twain,
Yet neither, and from either sex remote—
Some gruesome Boggles orphaned of the feet,
Some widowed of the hands, dumb Horrors too
Without a mouth, or blind Ones of no eye,
Or Bulks all shackled by their legs and arms
Cleaving unto the body fore and aft,
Thuswise, that never could they do or go,
Nor shun disaster, nor take the good they would.
And other prodigies and monsters earth
Was then begetting of this sort—in vain,
Since Nature banned with horror their increase,
And powerless were they to reach unto
The coveted flower of fair maturity,
Or to find aliment, or to intertwine
In works of Venus. For we see there must
Concur in life conditions manifold,
If life is ever by begetting life
To forge the generations one by one:
First, foods must be; and, next, a path whereby
The seeds of impregnation in the frame
May ooze, released from the members all;
Last, the possession of those instruments
Whereby the male with female can unite,
The one with other in mutual ravishments.

And in the ages after monsters died,
Perforce there perished many a stock, unable
By propagation to forge a progeny.
For whatsoever creatures thou beholdest

Breathing the breath of life, the same have been
Even from their earliest age preserved alive
By cunning, or by valour, or at least
By speed of foot or wing. And many a stock
Remaineth yet, because of use to man,
And so committed to man's guardianship.
Valour hath saved alive fierce lion-breeds
And many another terrorizing race,
Cunning the foxes, flight the antlered stags.
Light-sleeping dogs with faithful heart in breast,
However, and every kind begot from seed
Of beasts of draft, as, too, the woolly flocks
And horned cattle, all, my Memmius,
Have been committed to guardianship of men.
For anxiously they fled the savage beasts,
And peace they sought and their abundant foods,
Obtained with never labours of their own,
Which we secure to them as fit rewards
For their good service. But those beasts to whom
Nature has granted naught of these same things—
Beasts quite unfit by own free will to thrive
And vain for any service unto us
In thanks for which we should permit their kind
To feed and be in our protection safe—
Those, of a truth, were wont to be exposed,
Enshackled in the gruesome bonds of doom,
As prey and booty for the rest, until
Nature reduced that stock to utter death.

But Centaurs ne'er have been, nor can there be
Creatures of twofold stock and double frame,
Compact of members alien in kind,
Yet formed with equal function, equal force
In every bodily part—a fact thou mayst,
However dull thy wits, well learn from this:
The horse, when his three years have rolled away,
Flowers in his prime of vigour; but the boy
Not so, for oft even then he gropes in sleep
After the milky nipples of the breasts,
An infant still. And later, when at last
The lusty powers of horses and stout limbs,
Now weak through lapsing life, do fail with age,
Lo, only then doth youth with flowering years

Begin for boys, and clothe their ruddy cheeks
With the soft down. So never deem, percase,
That from a man and from the seed of horse,
The beast of draft, can Centaurs be composed
Or e'er exist alive, nor Scyllas be—
The half-fish bodies girdled with mad dogs—
Nor others of this sort, in whom we mark
Members discordant each with each; for ne'er
At one same time they reach their flower of age
Or gain and lose full vigour of their frame,
And never burn with one same lust of love,
And never in their habits they agree,
Nor find the same foods equally delightsome—
Sooth, as one oft may see the bearded goats
Batten upon the hemlock which to man
Is violent poison. Once again, since flame
Is wont to scorch and burn the tawny bulks
Of the great lions as much as other kinds
Of flesh and blood existing in the lands,
How could it be that she, Chimaera lone,
With triple body—fore, a lion she;
And aft, a dragon; and betwixt, a goat—
Might at the mouth from out the body belch
Infuriate flame? Wherefore, the man who feigns
Such beings could have been engendered
When earth was new and the young sky was fresh
(Basing his empty argument on new)
May babble with like reason many whims
Into our ears: he'll say, perhaps, that then
Rivers of gold through every landscape flowed,
That trees were wont with precious stones to flower,
Or that in those far aeons man was born
With such gigantic length and lift of limbs
As to be able, based upon his feet,
Deep oceans to bestride or with his hands
To whirl the firmament around his head.
For though in earth were many seeds of things
In the old time when this telluric world
First poured the breeds of animals abroad,
Still that is nothing of a sign that then
Such hybrid creatures could have been begot
And limbs of all beasts heterogeneous
Have been together knit; because, indeed,

The divers kinds of grasses and the grains
And the delightsome trees—which even now
Spring up abounding from within the earth—
Can still ne'er be begotten with their stems
Begrafted into one; but each sole thing
Proceeds according to its proper wont
And all conserve their own distinctions based
In nature's fixed decree.

ORIGINS AND SAVAGE PERIOD OF MANKIND

But mortal man
Was then far hardier in the old champaign,
As well he should be, since a hardier earth
Had him begotten; builded too was he
Of bigger and more solid bones within,
And knit with stalwart sinews through the flesh,
Nor easily seized by either heat or cold,
Or alien food or any ail or irk.
And whilst so many lustrums of the sun
Rolled on across the sky, men led a life
After the roving habit of wild beasts.
Not then were sturdy guiders of curved ploughs,
And none knew then to work the fields with iron,
Or plant young shoots in holes of delved loam,
Or lop with hooked knives from off high trees
The boughs of yester-year. What sun and rains
To them had given, what earth of own accord
Created then, was boon enough to glad
Their simple hearts. Mid acorn-laden oaks
Would they refresh their bodies for the nonce;
And the wild berries of the arbute-tree,
Which now thou seest to ripen purple-red
In winter time, the old telluric soil
Would bear then more abundant and more big.
And many coarse foods, too, in long ago
The blooming freshness of the rank young world
Produced, enough for those poor wretches there.
And rivers and springs would summon them of old
To slake the thirst, as now from the great hills
The water's down-rush calls aloud and far
The thirsty generations of the wild.

So, too, they sought the grottos of the Nymphs—
The woodland haunts discovered as they ranged—
From forth of which they knew that gliding rills
With gush and splash abounding laved the rocks,
The dripping rocks, and trickled from above
Over the verdant moss; and here and there
Welled up and burst across the open flats.
As yet they knew not to enkindle fire
Against the cold, nor hairy pelts to use
And clothe their bodies with the spoils of beasts;
But huddled in groves, and mountain-caves, and woods,
And 'mongst the thickets hid their squalid backs,
When driven to flee the lashings of the winds
And the big rains. Nor could they then regard
The general good, nor did they know to use
In common any customs, any laws:
Whatever of booty fortune unto each
Had proffered, each alone would bear away,
By instinct trained for self to thrive and live.
And Venus in the forests then would link
The lovers' bodies; for the woman yielded
Either from mutual flame, or from the man's
Impetuous fury and insatiate lust,
Or from a bribe—as acorn-nuts, choice pears,
Or the wild berries of the arbute-tree.
And trusting wondrous strength of hands and legs,
They'd chase the forest-wanderers, the beasts;
And many they'd conquer, but some few they fled,
A-skulk into their hiding-places...
With the flung stones and with the ponderous heft
Of gnarled branch. And by the time of night
O'ertaken, they would throw, like bristly boars,
Their wildman's limbs naked upon the earth,
Rolling themselves in leaves and fronded boughs.
Nor would they call with lamentations loud
Around the fields for daylight and the sun,
Quaking and wand'ring in shadows of the night;
But, silent and buried in a sleep, they'd wait
Until the sun with rosy flambeau brought
The glory to the sky. From childhood wont
Ever to see the dark and day begot
In times alternate, never might they be
Wildered by wild misgiving, lest a night

Eternal should possess the lands, with light
Of sun withdrawn forever. But their care
Was rather that the clans of savage beasts
Would often make their sleep-time horrible
For those poor wretches; and, from home y-driven,
They'd flee their rocky shelters at approach
Of boar, the spumy-lipped, or lion strong,
And in the midnight yield with terror up
To those fierce guests their beds of out-spread leaves.
And yet in those days not much more than now
Would generations of mortality
Leave the sweet light of fading life behind.
Indeed, in those days here and there a man,
More oftener snatched upon, and gulped by fangs,
Afforded the beasts a food that roared alive,
Echoing through groves and hills and forest-trees,
Even as he viewed his living flesh entombed
Within a living grave; whilst those whom flight
Had saved, with bone and body bitten, shrieked,
Pressing their quivering palms to loathsome sores,
With horrible voices for eternal death—
Until, forlorn of help, and witless what
Might medicine their wounds, the writhing pangs
Took them from life. But not in those far times
Would one lone day give over unto doom
A soldiery in thousands marching on
Beneath the battle-banners, nor would then
The ramping breakers of the main seas dash
Whole argosies and crews upon the rocks.
But ocean uprisen would often rave in vain,
Without all end or outcome, and give up
Its empty menacings as lightly too;
Nor soft seductions of a serene sea
Could lure by laughing billows any man
Out to disaster: for the science bold
Of ship-sailing lay dark in those far times.
Again, 'twas then that lack of food gave o'er
Men's fainting limbs to dissolution: now
'Tis plenty overwhelms. Unwary, they
Oft for themselves themselves would then outpour
The poison; now, with nicer art, themselves
They give the drafts to others.

BEGINNINGS OF CIVILIZATION

Afterwards,
When huts they had procured and pelts and fire,
And when the woman, joined unto the man,
Withdrew with him into one dwelling place,
Were known; and when they saw an offspring born
From out themselves, then first the human race
Began to soften. For 'twas now that fire
Rendered their shivering frames less staunch to bear,
Under the canopy of the sky, the cold;
And Love reduced their shaggy hardiness;
And children, with the prattle and the kiss,
Soon broke the parents' haughty temper down.
Then, too, did neighbours 'gin to league as friends,
Eager to wrong no more or suffer wrong,
And urged for children and the womankind
Mercy, of fathers, whilst with cries and gestures
They stammered hints how meet it was that all
Should have compassion on the weak. And still,
Though concord not in every wise could then
Begotten be, a good, a goodly part
Kept faith inviolate—or else mankind
Long since had been unutterably cut off,
And propagation never could have brought
The species down the ages.

Lest, perchance,
Concerning these affairs thou ponderest
In silent meditation, let me say
'Twas lightning brought primevally to earth
The fire for mortals, and from thence hath spread
O'er all the lands the flames of heat. For thus
Even now we see so many objects, touched
By the celestial flames, to flash aglow,
When thunderbolt has dowered them with heat.
Yet also when a many-branched tree,
Beaten by winds, writhes swaying to and fro,
Pressing 'gainst branches of a neighbour tree,
There by the power of mighty rub and rub
Is fire engendered; and at times out-flares
The scorching heat of flame, when boughs do chafe

Against the trunks. And of these causes, either
May well have given to mortal men the fire.
Next, food to cook and soften in the flame
The sun instructed, since so oft they saw
How objects mellowed, when subdued by warmth
And by the raining blows of fiery beams,
Through all the fields.

And more and more each day
Would men more strong in sense, more wise in heart,
Teach them to change their earlier mode and life
By fire and new devices. Kings began
Cities to found and citadels to set,
As strongholds and asylums for themselves,
And flocks and fields to portion for each man
After the beauty, strength, and sense of each—
For beauty then imported much, and strength
Had its own rights supreme. Thereafter, wealth
Discovered was, and gold was brought to light,
Which soon of honour stripped both strong and fair;
For men, however beautiful in form
Or valorous, will follow in the main
The rich man's party. Yet were man to steer
His life by sounder reasoning, he'd own
Abounding riches, if with mind content
He lived by thrift; for never, as I guess,
Is there a lack of little in the world.
But men wished glory for themselves and power
Even that their fortunes on foundations firm
Might rest forever, and that they themselves,
The opulent, might pass a quiet life—
In vain, in vain; since, in the strife to climb
On to the heights of honour, men do make
Their pathway terrible; and even when once
They reach them, envy like the thunderbolt
At times will smite, O hurling headlong down
To murkiest Tartarus, in scorn; for, lo,
All summits, all regions loftier than the rest,
Smoke, blasted as by envy's thunderbolts;
So better far in quiet to obey,
Than to desire chief mastery of affairs
And ownership of empires. Be it so;
And let the weary sweat their life-blood out

All to no end, battling in hate along
The narrow path of man's ambition;
Since all their wisdom is from others' lips,
And all they seek is known from what they've heard
And less from what they've thought. Nor is this folly
Greater to-day, nor greater soon to be,
Than' twas of old.

And therefore kings were slain,
And pristine majesty of golden thrones
And haughty sceptres lay o'erturned in dust;
And crowns, so splendid on the sovereign heads,
Soon bloody under the proletarian feet,
Groaned for their glories gone—for erst o'er-much
Dreaded, thereafter with more greedy zest
Trampled beneath the rabble heel. Thus things
Down to the vilest lees of brawling mobs
Succumbed, whilst each man sought unto himself
Dominion and supremacy. So next
Some wiser heads instructed men to found
The magisterial office, and did frame
Codes that they might consent to follow laws.
For humankind, o'er wearied with a life
Fostered by force, was ailing from its feuds;
And so the sooner of its own free will
Yielded to laws and strictest codes. For since
Each hand made ready in its wrath to take
A vengeance fiercer than by man's fair laws
Is now conceded, men on this account
Loathed the old life fostered by force. 'Tis thence
That fear of punishments defiles each prize
Of wicked days; for force and fraud ensnare
Each man around, and in the main recoil
On him from whence they sprung. Not easy 'tis
For one who violates by ugly deeds
The bonds of common peace to pass a life
Composed and tranquil. For albeit he 'scape
The race of gods and men, he yet must dread
'Twill not be hid forever—since, indeed,
So many, oft babbling on amid their dreams
Or raving in sickness, have betrayed themselves
(As stories tell) and published at last
Old secrets and the sins.

But nature 'twas
Urged men to utter various sounds of tongue
And need and use did mould the names of things,
About in same wise as the lack-speech years
Compel young children unto gesturings,
Making them point with finger here and there
At what's before them. For each creature feels
By instinct to what use to put his powers.
Ere yet the bull-calf's scarce begotten horns
Project above his brows, with them he 'gins
Enraged to butt and savagely to thrust.
But whelps of panthers and the lion's cubs
With claws and paws and bites are at the fray
Already, when their teeth and claws be scarce
As yet engendered. So again, we see
All breeds of winged creatures trust to wings
And from their fledgling pinions seek to get
A fluttering assistance. Thus, to think
That in those days some man apportioned round
To things their names, and that from him men learned
Their first nomenclature, is foolery.
For why could he mark everything by words
And utter the various sounds of tongue, what time
The rest may be supposed powerless
To do the same? And, if the rest had not
Already one with other used words,
Whence was implanted in the teacher, then,
Fore-knowledge of their use, and whence was given
To him alone primordial faculty
To know and see in mind what 'twas he willed?
Besides, one only man could scarce subdue
An overmastered multitude to choose
To get by heart his names of things. A task
Not easy 'tis in any wise to teach
And to persuade the deaf concerning what
'Tis needful for to do. For ne'er would they
Allow, nor ne'er in anywise endure
Perpetual vain dingdong in their ears
Of spoken sounds unheard before. And what,
At last, in this affair so wondrous is,
That human race (in whom a voice and tongue
Were now in vigour) should by divers words

Denote its objects, as each divers sense
Might prompt?—since even the speechless herds, aye, since
The very generations of wild beasts
Are wont dissimilar and divers sounds
To rouse from in them, when there's fear or pain,
And when they burst with joys. And this, forsooth,
'Tis thine to know from plainest facts: when first
Huge flabby jowls of mad Molossian hounds,
Baring their hard white teeth, begin to snarl,
They threaten, with infuriate lips peeled back,
In sounds far other than with which they bark
And fill with voices all the regions round.
And when with fondling tongue they start to lick
Their puppies, or do toss them round with paws,
Feigning with gentle bites to gape and snap,
They fawn with yelps of voice far other then
Than when, alone within the house, they bay,
Or whimpering slink with cringing sides from blows.
Again the neighing of the horse, is that
Not seen to differ likewise, when the stud
In buoyant flower of his young years raves,
Goaded by winged Love, amongst the mares,
And when with widening nostrils out he snorts
The call to battle, and when haply he
Whinnies at times with terror-quaking limbs?
Lastly, the flying race, the dappled birds,
Hawks, ospreys, sea-gulls, searching food and life
Amid the ocean billows in the brine,
Utter at other times far other cries
Than when they fight for food, or with their prey
Struggle and strain. And birds there are which change
With changing weather their own raucous songs—
As long-lived generations of the crows
Or flocks of rooks, when they be said to cry
For rain and water and to call at times
For winds and gales. Ergo, if divers moods
Compel the brutes, though speechless evermore,
To send forth divers sounds, O truly then
How much more likely 'twere that mortal men
In those days could with many a different sound
Denote each separate thing.
And now what cause
Hath spread divinities of gods abroad

Through mighty nations, and filled the cities full
Of the high altars, and led to practices
Of solemn rites in season—rites which still
Flourish in midst of great affairs of state
And midst great centres of man's civic life,
The rites whence still a poor mortality
Is grafted that quaking awe which rears aloft
Still the new temples of gods from land to land
And drives mankind to visit them in throngs
On holy days—'tis not so hard to give
Reason thereof in speech. Because, in sooth,
Even in those days would the race of man
Be seeing excelling visages of gods
With mind awake; and in his sleeps, yet more—
Bodies of wondrous growth. And, thus, to these
Would men attribute sense, because they seemed
To move their limbs and speak pronouncements high,
Befitting glorious visage and vast powers.
And men would give them an eternal life,
Because their visages forevermore
Were there before them, and their shapes remained,
And chiefly, however, because men would not think
Beings augmented with such mighty powers
Could well by any force o'ermastered be.
And men would think them in their happiness
Excelling far, because the fear of death
Vexed no one of them at all, and since
At same time in men's sleeps men saw them do
So many wonders, and yet feel therefrom
Themselves no weariness. Besides, men marked
How in a fixed order rolled around
The systems of the sky, and changed times
Of annual seasons, nor were able then
To know thereof the causes. Therefore 'twas
Men would take refuge in consigning all
Unto divinities, and in feigning all
Was guided by their nod. And in the sky
They set the seats and vaults of gods, because
Across the sky night and the moon are seen
To roll along—moon, day, and night, and night's
Old awesome constellations evermore,
And the night-wandering fireballs of the sky,
And flying flames, clouds, and the sun, the rains,

Snow and the winds, the lightnings, and the hail,
And the swift rumblings, and the hollow roar
Of mighty menacings forevermore.
O humankind unhappy!—when it ascribed
Unto divinities such awesome deeds,
And coupled thereto rigours of fierce wrath!
What groans did men on that sad day beget
Even for themselves, and O what wounds for us,
What tears for our children's children! Nor, O man,
Is thy true piety in this: with head
Under the veil, still to be seen to turn
Fronting a stone, and ever to approach
Unto all altars; nor so prone on earth
Forward to fall, to spread upturned palms
Before the shrines of gods, nor yet to dew
Altars with profuse blood of four-foot beasts,
Nor vows with vows to link. But rather this:
To look on all things with a master eye
And mind at peace. For when we gaze aloft
Upon the skiey vaults of yon great world
And ether, fixed high o'er twinkling stars,
And into our thought there come the journeyings
Of sun and moon, O then into our breasts,
O'erburdened already with their other ills,
Begins forthwith to rear its sudden head
One more misgiving: lest o'er us, percase,
It be the gods' immeasurable power
That rolls, with varied motion, round and round
The far white constellations. For the lack
Of aught of reasons tries the puzzled mind:
Whether was ever a birth-time of the world,
And whether, likewise, any end shall be
How far the ramparts of the world can still
Outstand this strain of ever-roused motion,
Or whether, divinely with eternal weal
Endowed, they can through endless tracts of age
Glide on, defying the o'er-mighty powers
Of the immeasurable ages. Lo,
What man is there whose mind with dread of gods
Cringes not close, whose limbs with terror-spell
Crouch not together, when the parched earth
Quakes with the horrible thunderbolt amain,
And across the mighty sky the rumblings run?

Do not the peoples and the nations shake,
And haughty kings do they not hug their limbs,
Strook through with fear of the divinities,
Lest for aught foully done or madly said
The heavy time be now at hand to pay?
When, too, fierce force of fury-winds at sea
Sweepeth a navy's admiral down the main
With his stout legions and his elephants,
Doth he not seek the peace of gods with vows,
And beg in prayer, a-tremble, lulled winds
And friendly gales?—in vain, since, often up-caught
In fury-cyclones, is he borne along,
For all his mouthings, to the shoals of doom.
Ah, so irrevocably some hidden power
Betramples forevermore affairs of men,
And visibly grindeth with its heel in mire
The lictors' glorious rods and axes dire,
Having them in derision! Again, when earth
From end to end is rocking under foot,
And shaken cities ruin down, or threaten
Upon the verge, what wonder is it then
That mortal generations abase themselves,
And unto gods in all affairs of earth
Assign as last resort almighty powers
And wondrous energies to govern all?

Now for the rest: copper and gold and iron
Discovered were, and with them silver's weight
And power of lead, when with prodigious heat
The conflagrations burned the forest trees
Among the mighty mountains, by a bolt
Of lightning from the sky, or else because
Men, warring in the woodlands, on their foes
Had hurled fire to frighten and dismay,
Or yet because, by goodness of the soil
Invited, men desired to clear rich fields
And turn the countryside to pasture-lands,
Or slay the wild and thrive upon the spoils.
(For hunting by pit-fall and by fire arose
Before the art of hedging the covert round
With net or stirring it with dogs of chase.)
Howso the fact, and from what cause soever
The flamy heat with awful crack and roar

Had there devoured to their deepest roots
The forest trees and baked the earth with fire,
Then from the boiling veins began to ooze
O rivulets of silver and of gold,
Of lead and copper too, collecting soon
Into the hollow places of the ground.
And when men saw the cooled lumps anon
To shine with splendour-sheen upon the ground,
Much taken with that lustrous smooth delight,
They 'gan to pry them out, and saw how each
Had got a shape like to its earthy mould.
Then would it enter their heads how these same lumps,
If melted by heat, could into any form
Or figure of things be run, and how, again,
If hammered out, they could be nicely drawn
To sharpest points or finest edge, and thus
Yield to the forgers tools and give them power
To chop the forest down, to hew the logs,
To shave the beams and planks, besides to bore
And punch and drill. And men began such work
At first as much with tools of silver and gold
As with the impetuous strength of the stout copper;
But vainly—since their over-mastered power
Would soon give way, unable to endure,
Like copper, such hard labour. In those days
Copper it was that was the thing of price;
And gold lay useless, blunted with dull edge.
Now lies the copper low, and gold hath come
Unto the loftiest honours. Thus it is
That rolling ages change the times of things:
What erst was of a price, becomes at last
A discard of no honour; whilst another
Succeeds to glory, issuing from contempt,
And day by day is sought for more and more,
And, when 'tis found, doth flower in men's praise,
Objects of wondrous honour.

Now, Memmius,
How nature of iron discovered was, thou mayst
Of thine own self divine. Man's ancient arms
Were hands, and nails and teeth, stones too and boughs—
Breakage of forest trees—and flame and fire,
As soon as known. Thereafter force of iron

287

And copper discovered was; and copper's use
Was known ere iron's, since more tractable
Its nature is and its abundance more.
With copper men to work the soil began,
With copper to rouse the hurly waves of war,
To straw the monstrous wounds, and seize away
Another's flocks and fields. For unto them,
Thus armed, all things naked of defence
Readily yielded. Then by slow degrees
The sword of iron succeeded, and the shape
Of brazen sickle into scorn was turned:
With iron to cleave the soil of earth they 'gan,
And the contentions of uncertain war
Were rendered equal.

And, lo, man was wont
Armed to mount upon the ribs of horse
And guide him with the rein, and play about
With right hand free, oft times before he tried
Perils of war in yoked chariot;
And yoked pairs abreast came earlier
Than yokes of four, or scythed chariots
Whereinto clomb the men-at-arms. And next
The Punic folk did train the elephants—
Those curst Lucanian oxen, hideous,
The serpent-handed, with turrets on their bulks—
To dure the wounds of war and panic-strike
The mighty troops of Mars. Thus Discord sad
Begat the one Thing after other, to be
The terror of the nations under arms,
And day by day to horrors of old war
She added an increase.

Bulls, too, they tried
In war's grim business; and essayed to send
Outrageous boars against the foes. And some
Sent on before their ranks puissant lions
With armed trainers and with masters fierce
To guide and hold in chains—and yet in vain,
Since fleshed with pell-mell slaughter, fierce they flew,
And blindly through the squadrons havoc wrought,
Shaking the frightful crests upon their heads,
Now here, now there. Nor could the horsemen calm

Their horses, panic-breasted at the roar,
And rein them round to front the foe. With spring
The infuriate she-lions would up-leap
Now here, now there; and whoso came apace
Against them, these they'd rend across the face;
And others unwitting from behind they'd tear
Down from their mounts, and twining round them, bring
Tumbling to earth, o'ermastered by the wound,
And with those powerful fangs and hooked claws
Fasten upon them. Bulls would toss their friends,
And trample under foot, and from beneath
Rip flanks and bellies of horses with their horns,
And with a threat'ning forehead jam the sod;
And boars would gore with stout tusks their allies,
Splashing in fury their own blood on spears
Splintered in their own bodies, and would fell
In rout and ruin infantry and horse.
For there the beasts-of-saddle tried to scape
The savage thrusts of tusk by shying off,
Or rearing up with hoofs a-paw in air.
In vain—since there thou mightest see them sink,
Their sinews severed, and with heavy fall
Bestrew the ground. And such of these as men
Supposed well-trained long ago at home,
Were in the thick of action seen to foam
In fury, from the wounds, the shrieks, the flight,
The panic, and the tumult; nor could men
Aught of their numbers rally. For each breed
And various of the wild beasts fled apart
Hither or thither, as often in wars to-day
Flee those Lucanian oxen, by the steel
Grievously mangled, after they have wrought
Upon their friends so many a dreadful doom.
(If 'twas, indeed, that thus they did at all:
But scarcely I'll believe that men could not
With mind foreknow and see, as sure to come,
Such foul and general disaster.—This
We, then, may hold as true in the great All,
In divers worlds on divers plan create,—
Somewhere afar more likely than upon
One certain earth.) But men chose this to do
Less in the hope of conquering than to give
Their enemies a goodly cause of woe,

Even though thereby they perished themselves,
Since weak in numbers and since wanting arms.

Now, clothes of roughly inter-plaited strands
Were earlier than loom-wove coverings;
The loom-wove later than man's iron is,
Since iron is needful in the weaving art,
Nor by no other means can there be wrought
Such polished tools—the treadles, spindles, shuttles,
And sounding yarn-beams. And nature forced the men,
Before the woman kind, to work the wool:
For all the male kind far excels in skill,
And cleverer is by much—until at last
The rugged farmer folk jeered at such tasks,
And so were eager soon to give them o'er
To women's hands, and in more hardy toil
To harden arms and hands.

But nature herself,
Mother of things, was the first seed-sower
And primal grafter; since the berries and acorns,
Dropping from off the trees, would there beneath
Put forth in season swarms of little shoots;
Hence too men's fondness for ingrafting slips
Upon the boughs and setting out in holes
The young shrubs o'er the fields. Then would they try
Ever new modes of tilling their loved crofts,
And mark they would how earth improved the taste
Of the wild fruits by fond and fostering care.
And day by day they'd force the woods to move
Still higher up the mountain, and to yield
The place below for tilth, that there they might,
On plains and uplands, have their meadow-plats,
Cisterns and runnels, crops of standing grain,
And happy vineyards, and that all along
O'er hillocks, intervales, and plains might run
The silvery-green belt of olive-trees,
Marking the plotted landscape; even as now
Thou seest so marked with varied loveliness
All the terrain which men adorn and plant
With rows of goodly fruit-trees and hedge round
With thriving shrubberies sown.

But by the mouth
To imitate the liquid notes of birds
Was earlier far 'mongst men than power to make,
By measured song, melodious verse and give
Delight to ears. And whistlings of the wind
Athrough the hollows of the reeds first taught
The peasantry to blow into the stalks
Of hollow hemlock-herb. Then bit by bit
They learned sweet plainings, such as pipe out-pours,
Beaten by finger-tips of singing men,
When heard through unpathed groves and forest deeps
And woodsy meadows, through the untrod haunts
Of shepherd folk and spots divinely still.
Thus time draws forward each and everything
Little by little unto the midst of men,
And reason uplifts it to the shores of light.
These tunes would soothe and glad the minds of mortals
When sated with food,—for songs are welcome then.
And often, lounging with friends in the soft grass
Beside a river of water, underneath
A big tree's branches, merrily they'd refresh
Their frames, with no vast outlay—most of all
If the weather were smiling and the times of the year
Were painting the green of the grass around with flowers.
Then jokes, then talk, then peals of jollity
Would circle round; for then the rustic muse
Was in her glory; then would antic Mirth
Prompt them to garland head and shoulders about
With chaplets of intertwined flowers and leaves,
And to dance onward, out of tune, with limbs
Clownishly swaying, and with clownish foot
To beat our mother earth—from whence arose
Laughter and peals of jollity, for, lo,
Such frolic acts were in their glory then,
Being more new and strange. And wakeful men
Found solaces for their unsleeping hours
In drawing forth variety of notes,
In modulating melodies, in running
With puckered lips along the tuned reeds,
Whence, even in our day do the watchmen guard
These old traditions, and have learned well
To keep true measure. And yet they no whit
Do get a larger fruit of gladsomeness

Than got the woodland aborigines
In olden times. For what we have at hand—
If theretofore naught sweeter we have known—
That chiefly pleases and seems best of all;
But then some later, likely better, find
Destroys its worth and changes our desires
Regarding good of yesterday.

And thus
Began the loathing of the acorn; thus
Abandoned were those beds with grasses strewn
And with the leaves beladen. Thus, again,
Fell into new contempt the pelts of beasts—
Erstwhile a robe of honour, which, I guess,
Aroused in those days envy so malign
That the first wearer went to woeful death
By ambuscades,—and yet that hairy prize,
Rent into rags by greedy foemen there
And splashed by blood, was ruined utterly
Beyond all use or vantage. Thus of old
'Twas pelts, and of to-day 'tis purple and gold
That cark men's lives with cares and weary with war.
Wherefore, methinks, resides the greater blame
With us vain men to-day: for cold would rack,
Without their pelts, the naked sons of earth;
But us it nothing hurts to do without
The purple vestment, broidered with gold
And with imposing figures, if we still
Make shift with some mean garment of the Plebs.
So man in vain futilities toils on
Forever and wastes in idle cares his years—
Because, of very truth, he hath not learnt
What the true end of getting is, nor yet
At all how far true pleasure may increase.
And 'tis desire for better and for more
Hath carried by degrees mortality
Out onward to the deep, and roused up
From the far bottom mighty waves of war.

But sun and moon, those watchmen of the world,
With their own lanterns traversing around
The mighty, the revolving vault, have taught
Unto mankind that seasons of the years

Return again, and that the Thing takes place
After a fixed plan and order fixed.

Already would they pass their life, hedged round
By the strong towers; and cultivate an earth
All portioned out and boundaried; already
Would the sea flower and sail-winged ships;
Already men had, under treaty pacts,
Confederates and allies, when poets began
To hand heroic actions down in verse;
Nor long ere this had letters been devised—
Hence is our age unable to look back
On what has gone before, except where reason
Shows us a footprint.

Sailings on the seas,
Tillings of fields, walls, laws, and arms, and roads,
Dress and the like, all prizes, all delights
Of finer life, poems, pictures, chiselled shapes
Of polished sculptures—all these arts were learned
By practice and the mind's experience,
As men walked forward step by eager step.
Thus time draws forward each and everything
Little by little into the midst of men,
And reason uplifts it to the shores of light.
For one thing after other did men see
Grow clear by intellect, till with their arts
They've now achieved the supreme pinnacle.

BOOK VI

PROEM

'Twas Athens first, the glorious in name,
That whilom gave to hapless sons of men
The sheaves of harvest, and re-ordered life,
And decreed laws; and she the first that gave
Life its sweet solaces, when she begat
A man of heart so wise, who whilom poured
All wisdom forth from his truth-speaking mouth;
The glory of whom, though dead, is yet to-day,
Because of those discoveries divine
Renowned of old, exalted to the sky.
For when saw he that well-nigh everything
Which needs of man most urgently require
Was ready to hand for mortals, and that life,
As far as might be, was established safe,
That men were lords in riches, honour, praise,
And eminent in goodly fame of sons,
And that they yet, O yet, within the home,
Still had the anxious heart which vexed life
Unpausingly with torments of the mind,
And raved perforce with angry plaints, then he,
Then he, the master, did perceive that 'twas
The vessel itself which worked the bane, and all,
However wholesome, which from here or there
Was gathered into it, was by that bane
Spoilt from within,—in part, because he saw
The vessel so cracked and leaky that nowise
'T could ever be filled to brim; in part because
He marked how it polluted with foul taste
Whate'er it got within itself. So he,
The master, then by his truth-speaking words,
Purged the breasts of men, and set the bounds
Of lust and terror, and exhibited
The supreme good whither we all endeavour,
And showed the path whereby we might arrive
Thereunto by a little cross-cut straight,
And what of ills in all affairs of mortals

Upsprang and flitted deviously about
(Whether by chance or force), since nature thus
Had destined; and from out what gates a man
Should sally to each combat. And he proved
That mostly vainly doth the human race
Roll in its bosom the grim waves of care.
For just as children tremble and fear all
In the viewless dark, so even we at times
Dread in the light so many things that be
No whit more fearsome than what children feign,
Shuddering, will be upon them in the dark.
This terror then, this darkness of the mind,
Not sunrise with its flaring spokes of light,
Nor glittering arrows of morning can disperse,
But only nature's aspect and her law.
Wherefore the more will I go on to weave
In verses this my undertaken task.

And since I've taught thee that the world's great vaults
Are mortal and that sky is fashioned
Of frame e'en born in time, and whatsoe'er
Therein go on and must perforce go on
The most I have unravelled; what remains
Do thou take in, besides; since once for all
To climb into that chariot' renowned
Of winds arise; and they appeased are
So that all things again...

Which were, are changed now, with fury stilled;
All other movements through the earth and sky
Which mortals gaze upon (O anxious oft
In quaking thoughts!), and which abase their minds
With dread of deities and press them crushed
Down to the earth, because their ignorance
Of cosmic causes forces them to yield
All things unto the empery of gods
And to concede the kingly rule to them.
For even those men who have learned full well
That godheads lead a long life free of care,
If yet meanwhile they wonder by what plan
Things can go on (and chiefly yon high things
Observed o'erhead on the ethereal coasts),
Again are hurried back unto the fears

Of old religion and adopt again
Harsh masters, deemed almighty,—wretched men,
Unwitting what can be and what cannot,
And by what law to each its scope prescribed,
Its boundary stone that clings so deep in Time.
Wherefore the more are they borne wandering on
By blindfold reason. And, Memmius, unless
From out thy mind thou spuest all of this
And casteth far from thee all thoughts which be
Unworthy gods and alien to their peace,
Then often will the holy majesties
Of the high gods be harmful unto thee,
As by thy thought degraded,—not, indeed,
That essence supreme of gods could be by this
So outraged as in wrath to thirst to seek
Revenges keen; but even because thyself
Thou plaguest with the notion that the gods,
Even they, the Calm Ones in serene repose,
Do roll the mighty waves of wrath on wrath;
Nor wilt thou enter with a serene breast
Shrines of the gods; nor wilt thou able be
In tranquil peace of mind to take and know
Those images which from their holy bodies
Are carried into intellects of men,
As the announcers of their form divine.
What sort of life will follow after this
'Tis thine to see. But that afar from us
Veriest reason may drive such life away,
Much yet remains to be embellished yet
In polished verses, albeit hath issued forth
So much from me already; lo, there is
The law and aspect of the sky to be
By reason grasped; there are the tempest times
And the bright lightnings to be hymned now—
Even what they do and from what cause soe'er
They're borne along—that thou mayst tremble not,
Marking off regions of prophetic skies
For auguries, O foolishly distraught
Even as to whence the flying flame hath come,
Or to which half of heaven it turns, or how
Through walled places it hath wound its way,
Or, after proving its dominion there,
How it hath speeded forth from thence amain—

Whereof nowise the causes do men know,
And think divinities are working there.
Do thou, Calliope, ingenious Muse,
Solace of mortals and delight of gods,
Point out the course before me, as I race
On to the white line of the utmost goal,
That I may get with signal praise the crown,
With thee my guide!

GREAT METEOROLOGICAL PHENOMENA, ETC.

And so in first place, then,
With thunder are shaken the blue deeps of heaven,
Because the ethereal clouds, scudding aloft,
Together clash, what time 'gainst one another
The winds are battling. For never a sound there comes
From out the serene regions of the sky;
But wheresoever in a host more dense
The clouds foregather, thence more often comes
A crash with mighty rumbling. And, again,
Clouds cannot be of so condensed a frame
As stones and timbers, nor again so fine
As mists and flying smoke; for then perforce
They'd either fall, borne down by their brute weight,
Like stones, or, like the smoke, they'd powerless be
To keep their mass, or to retain within
Frore snows and storms of hail. And they give forth
O'er skiey levels of the spreading world
A sound on high, as linen-awning, stretched
O'er mighty theatres, gives forth at times
A cracking roar, when much 'tis beaten about
Betwixt the poles and cross-beams. Sometimes, too,
Asunder rent by wanton gusts, it raves
And imitates the tearing sound of sheets
Of paper—even this kind of noise thou mayst
In thunder hear—or sound as when winds whirl
With lashings and do buffet about in air
A hanging cloth and flying paper-sheets.
For sometimes, too, it chances that the clouds
Cannot together crash head-on, but rather
Move side-wise and with motions contrary
Graze each the other's body without speed,

It becomes hot of own velocity:
Just as thou seest how motion will o'erheat
And set ablaze all objects,—verily
A leaden ball, hurtling through length of space,
Even melts. Therefore, when this same wind a-fire
Hath split black cloud, it scatters the fire-seeds,
Which, so to say, have been pressed out by force
Of sudden from the cloud;—and these do make
The pulsing flashes of flame; thence followeth
The detonation which attacks our ears
More tardily than aught which comes along
Unto the sight of eyeballs. This takes place—
As know thou mayst—at times when clouds are dense
And one upon the other piled aloft
With wonderful upheavings—nor be thou
Deceived because we see how broad their base
From underneath, and not how high they tower.
For make thine observations at a time
When winds shall bear athwart the horizon's blue
Clouds like to mountain-ranges moving on,
Or when about the sides of mighty peaks
Thou seest them one upon the other massed
And burdening downward, anchored in high repose,
With the winds sepulchred on all sides round:
Then canst thou know their mighty masses, then
Canst view their caverns, as if builded there
Of beetling crags; which, when the hurricanes
In gathered storm have filled utterly,
Then, prisoned in clouds, they rave around
With mighty roarings, and within those dens
Bluster like savage beasts, and now from here,
And now from there, send growlings through the clouds,
And seeking an outlet, whirl themselves about,
And roll from 'mid the clouds the seeds of fire,
And heap them multitudinously there,
And in the hollow furnaces within
Wheel flame around, until from bursted cloud
In forky flashes they have gleamed forth.

Again, from following cause it comes to pass
That yon swift golden hue of liquid fire
Darts downward to the earth: because the clouds
Themselves must hold abundant seeds of fire;

For, when they be without all moisture, then
They be for most part of a flamy hue
And a resplendent. And, indeed, they must
Even from the light of sun unto themselves
Take multitudinous seeds, and so perforce
Redden and pour their bright fires all abroad.
And therefore, when the wind hath driven and thrust,
Hath forced and squeezed into one spot these clouds,
They pour abroad the seeds of fire pressed out,
Which make to flash these colours of the flame.
Likewise, it lightens also when the clouds
Grow rare and thin along the sky; for, when
The wind with gentle touch unravels them
And breaketh asunder as they move, those seeds
Which make the lightnings must by nature fall;
At such an hour the horizon lightens round
Without the hideous terror of dread noise
And skiey uproar.

To proceed apace,
What sort of nature thunderbolts possess
Is by their strokes made manifest and by
The brand-marks of their searing heat on things,
And by the scorched scars exhaling round
The heavy fumes of sulphur. For all these
Are marks, O not of wind or rain, but fire.
Again, they often enkindle even the roofs
Of houses and inside the very rooms
With swift flame hold a fierce dominion.
Know thou that nature fashioned this fire
Subtler than fires all other, with minute
And dartling bodies,—a fire 'gainst which there's naught
Can in the least hold out: the thunderbolt,
The mighty, passes through the hedging walls
Of houses, like to voices or a shout,—
Through stones, through bronze it passes, and it melts
Upon the instant bronze and gold; and makes,
Likewise, the wines sudden to vanish forth,
The wine-jars intact,—because, ye see,
Its heat arriving renders loose and porous
Readily all the wine—jar's earthen sides,
And winding its way within, it scattereth
The elements primordial of the wine

With speedy dissolution—process which
Even in an age the fiery steam of sun
Could not accomplish, however puissant he
With his hot coruscations: so much more
Agile and overpowering is this force.
Now in what manner engendered are these things,
How fashioned of such impetuous strength
As to cleave towers asunder, and houses all
To overtopple, and to wrench apart
Timbers and beams, and heroes' monuments
To pile in ruins and upheave amain,
And to take breath forever out of men,
And to o'erthrow the cattle everywhere,—
Yes, by what force the lightnings do all this,
All this and more, I will unfold to thee,
Nor longer keep thee in mere promises.

The bolts of thunder, then, must be conceived
As all begotten in those crasser clouds
Up-piled aloft; for, from the sky serene
And from the clouds of lighter density,
None are sent forth forever. That 'tis so
Beyond a doubt, fact plain to sense declares:
To wit, at such a time the densed clouds
So mass themselves through all the upper air
That we might think that round about all murk
Had parted forth from Acheron and filled
The mighty vaults of sky—so grievously,
As gathers thus the storm-clouds' gruesome might,
Do faces of black horror hang on high—
When tempest begins its thunderbolts to forge.
Besides, full often also out at sea
A blackest thunderhead, like cataract
Of pitch hurled down from heaven, and far away
Bulging with murkiness, down on the waves
Falls with vast uproar, and draws on amain
The darkling tempests big with thunderbolts
And hurricanes, itself the while so crammed
Tremendously with fires and winds, that even
Back on the lands the people shudder round
And seek for cover. Therefore, as I said,
The storm must be conceived as o'er our head
Towering most high; for never would the clouds

O'erwhelm the lands with such a massy dark,
Unless up-builded heap on lofty heap,
To shut the round sun off. Nor could the clouds,
As on they come, engulf with rain so vast
As thus to make the rivers overflow
And fields to float, if ether were not thus
Furnished with lofty-piled clouds. Lo, then,
Here be all things fulfilled with winds and fires—
Hence the long lightnings and the thunders loud.
For, verily, I've taught thee even now
How cavernous clouds hold seeds innumerable
Of fiery exhalations, and they must
From off the sunbeams and the heat of these
Take many still. And so, when that same wind
(Which, haply, into one region of the sky
Collects those clouds) hath pressed from out the same
The many fiery seeds, and with that fire
Hath at the same time inter-mixed itself,
O then and there that wind, a whirlwind now,
Deep in the belly of the cloud spins round
In narrow confines, and sharpens there inside
In glowing furnaces the thunderbolt.
For in a two-fold manner is that wind
Enkindled all: it trembles into heat
Both by its own velocity and by
Repeated touch of fire. Thereafter, when
The energy of wind is heated through
And the fierce impulse of the fire hath sped
Deeply within, O then the thunderbolt,
Now ripened, so to say, doth suddenly
Splinter the cloud, and the aroused flash
Leaps onward, lumining with forky light
All places round. And followeth anon
A clap so heavy that the skiey vaults,
As if asunder burst, seem from on high
To engulf the earth. Then fearfully a quake
Pervades the lands, and 'long the lofty skies
Run the far rumblings. For at such a time
Nigh the whole tempest quakes, shook through and through,
And roused are the roarings,—from which shock
Comes such resounding and abounding rain,
That all the murky ether seems to turn
Now into rain, and, as it tumbles down,

To summon the fields back to primeval floods:
So big the rains that be sent down on men
By burst of cloud and by the hurricane,
What time the thunder-clap, from burning bolt
That cracks the cloud, flies forth along. At times
The force of wind, excited from without,
Smiteth into a cloud already hot
With a ripe thunderbolt. And when that wind
Hath splintered that cloud, then down there cleaves forthwith
Yon fiery coil of flame which still we call,
Even with our fathers' word, a thunderbolt.
The same thing haps toward every other side
Whither that force hath swept. It happens, too,
That sometimes force of wind, though hurtled forth
Without all fire, yet in its voyage through space
Igniteth, whilst it comes along, along,—
Losing some larger bodies which cannot
Pass, like the others, through the bulks of air,—
And, scraping together out of air itself
Some smaller bodies, carries them along,
And these, commingling, by their flight make fire:
Much in the manner as oft a leaden ball
Grows hot upon its aery course, the while
It loseth many bodies of stark cold
And taketh into itself along the air
New particles of fire. It happens, too,
That force of blow itself arouses fire,
When force of wind, a-cold and hurtled forth
Without all fire, hath strook somewhere amain—
No marvel, because, when with terrific stroke
'Thas smitten, the elements of fiery-stuff
Can stream together from out the very wind
And, simultaneously, from out that thing
Which then and there receives the stroke: as flies
The fire when with the steel we hack the stone;
Nor yet, because the force of steel's a-cold,
Rush the less speedily together there
Under the stroke its seeds of radiance hot.
And therefore, thuswise must an object too
Be kindled by a thunderbolt, if haply
'Thas been adapt and suited to the flames.
Yet force of wind must not be rashly deemed
As altogether and entirely cold—

That force which is discharged from on high
With such stupendous power; but if 'tis not
Upon its course already kindled with fire,
It yet arriveth warmed and mixed with heat.

And, now, the speed and stroke of thunderbolt
Is so tremendous, and with glide so swift
Those thunderbolts rush on and down, because
Their roused force itself collects itself
First always in the clouds, and then prepares
For the huge effort of their going-forth;
Next, when the cloud no longer can retain
The increment of their fierce impetus,
Their force is pressed out, and therefore flies
With impetus so wondrous, like to shots
Hurled from the powerful Roman catapults.
Note, too, this force consists of elements
Both small and smooth, nor is there aught that can
With ease resist such nature. For it darts
Between and enters through the pores of things;
And so it never falters in delay
Despite innumerable collisions, but
Flies shooting onward with a swift elan.
Next, since by nature always every weight
Bears downward, doubled is the swiftness then
And that elan is still more wild and dread,
When, verily, to weight are added blows,
So that more madly and more fiercely then
The thunderbolt shakes into shivers all
That blocks its path, following on its way.
Then, too, because it comes along, along
With one continuing elan, it must
Take on velocity anew, anew,
Which still increases as it goes, and ever
Augments the bolt's vast powers and to the blow
Gives larger vigour; for it forces all,
All of the thunder's seeds of fire, to sweep
In a straight line unto one place, as 'twere,—
Casting them one by other, as they roll,
Into that onward course. Again, perchance,
In coming along, it pulls from out the air
Some certain bodies, which by their own blows
Enkindle its velocity. And, lo,

It comes through objects leaving them unharmed,
It goes through many things and leaves them whole,
Because the liquid fire flieth along
Athrough their pores. And much it does transfix,
When these primordial atoms of the bolt
Have fallen upon the atoms of these things
Precisely where the intertwined atoms
Are held together. And, further, easily
Brass it unbinds and quickly fuseth gold,
Because its force is so minutely made
Of tiny parts and elements so smooth
That easily they wind their way within,
And, when once in, quickly unbind all knots
And loosen all the bonds of union there.

And most in autumn is shaken the house of heaven,
The house so studded with the glittering stars,
And the whole earth around—most too in spring
When flowery times unfold themselves: for, lo,
In the cold season is there lack of fire,
And winds are scanty in the hot, and clouds
Have not so dense a bulk. But when, indeed,
The seasons of heaven are betwixt these twain,
The divers causes of the thunderbolt
Then all concur; for then both cold and heat
Are mixed in the cross-seas of the year,
So that a discord rises among things
And air in vast tumultuosity
Billows, infuriate with the fires and winds—
Of which the both are needed by the cloud
For fabrication of the thunderbolt.
For the first part of heat and last of cold
Is the time of spring; wherefore must things unlike
Do battle one with other, and, when mixed,
Tumultuously rage. And when rolls round
The latest heat mixed with the earliest chill—
The time which bears the name of autumn—then
Likewise fierce cold-spells wrestle with fierce heats.
On this account these seasons of the year
Are nominated "cross-seas."—And no marvel
If in those times the thunderbolts prevail
And storms are roused turbulent in heaven,
Since then both sides in dubious warfare rage

Tumultuously, the one with flames, the other
With winds and with waters mixed with winds.

This, this it is, O Memmius, to see through
The very nature of fire-fraught thunderbolt;
O this it is to mark by what blind force
It maketh each effect, and not, O not
To unwind Etrurian scrolls oracular,
Inquiring tokens of occult will of gods,
Even as to whence the flying flame hath come,
Or to which half of heaven it turns, or how
Through walled places it hath wound its way,
Or, after proving its dominion there,
How it hath speeded forth from thence amain,
Or what the thunderstroke portends of ill
From out high heaven. But if Jupiter
And other gods shake those refulgent vaults
With dread reverberations and hurl fire
Whither it pleases each, why smite they not
Mortals of reckless and revolting crimes,
That such may pant from a transpierced breast
Forth flames of the red levin—unto men
A drastic lesson?—why is rather he—
O he self-conscious of no foul offence—
Involved in flames, though innocent, and clasped
Up-caught in skiey whirlwind and in fire?
Nay, why, then, aim they at eternal wastes,
And spend themselves in vain?—perchance, even so
To exercise their arms and strengthen shoulders?
Why suffer they the Father's javelin
To be so blunted on the earth? And why
Doth he himself allow it, nor spare the same
Even for his enemies? O why most oft
Aims he at lofty places? Why behold we
Marks of his lightnings most on mountain tops?
Then for what reason shoots he at the sea?—
What sacrilege have waves and bulk of brine
And floating fields of foam been guilty of?
Besides, if 'tis his will that we beware
Against the lightning-stroke, why feareth he
To grant us power for to behold the shot?
And, contrariwise, if wills he to o'erwhelm us,
Quite off our guard, with fire, why thunders he

Off in yon quarter, so that we may shun?
Why rouseth he beforehand darkling air
And the far din and rumblings? And O how
Canst thou believe he shoots at one same time
Into diverse directions? Or darest thou
Contend that never hath it come to pass
That divers strokes have happened at one time?
But oft and often hath it come to pass,
And often still it must, that, even as showers
And rains o'er many regions fall, so too
Dart many thunderbolts at one same time.
Again, why never hurtles Jupiter
A bolt upon the lands nor pours abroad
Clap upon clap, when skies are cloudless all?
Or, say, doth he, so soon as ever the clouds
Have come thereunder, then into the same
Descend in person, that from thence he may
Near-by decide upon the stroke of shaft?
And, lastly, why, with devastating bolt
Shakes he asunder holy shrines of gods
And his own thrones of splendour, and to-breaks
The well-wrought idols of divinities,
And robs of glory his own images
By wound of violence?

But to return apace,
Easy it is from these same facts to know
In just what wise those things (which from their sort
The Greeks have named "bellows") do come down,
Discharged from on high, upon the seas.
For it haps that sometimes from the sky descends
Upon the seas a column, as if pushed,
Round which the surges seethe, tremendously
Aroused by puffing gusts; and whatso'er
Of ships are caught within that tumult then
Come into extreme peril, dashed along.
This haps when sometimes wind's aroused force
Can't burst the cloud it tries to, but down-weighs
That cloud, until 'tis like a column from sky
Upon the seas pushed downward—gradually,
As if a Somewhat from on high were shoved
By fist and nether thrust of arm, and lengthened
Far to the waves. And when the force of wind

Hath rived this cloud, from out the cloud it rushes
Down on the seas, and starts among the waves
A wondrous seething, for the eddying whirl
Descends and downward draws along with it
That cloud of ductile body. And soon as ever
'Thas shoved unto the levels of the main
That laden cloud, the whirl suddenly then
Plunges its whole self into the waters there
And rouses all the sea with monstrous roar,
Constraining it to seethe. It happens too
That very vortex of the wind involves
Itself in clouds, scraping from out the air
The seeds of cloud, and counterfeits, as 'twere,
The "bellows" pushed from heaven. And when this shape
Hath dropped upon the lands and burst apart,
It belches forth immeasurable might
Of whirlwind and of blast. Yet since 'tis formed
At most but rarely, and on land the hills
Must block its way, 'tis seen more oft out there
On the broad prospect of the level main
Along the free horizons.

INTO BEING

The clouds condense, when in this upper space
Of the high heaven have gathered suddenly,
As round they flew, unnumbered particles—
World's rougher ones, which can, though interlinked
With scanty couplings, yet be fastened firm,
The one on other caught. These particles
First cause small clouds to form; and, thereupon,
These catch the one on other and swarm in a flock
And grow by their conjoining, and by winds
Are borne along, along, until collects
The tempest fury. Happens, too, the nearer
The mountain summits neighbour to the sky,
The more unceasingly their far crags smoke
With the thick darkness of swart cloud, because
When first the mists do form, ere ever the eyes
Can there behold them (tenuous as they be),
The carrier-winds will drive them up and on
Unto the topmost summits of the mountain;

And then at last it happens, when they be
In vaster throng upgathered, that they can
By this very condensation lie revealed,
And that at same time they are seen to surge
From very vertex of the mountain up
Into far ether. For very fact and feeling,
As we up-climb high mountains, proveth clear
That windy are those upward regions free.
Besides, the clothes hung-out along the shore,
When in they take the clinging moisture, prove
That nature lifts from over all the sea
Unnumbered particles. Whereby the more
'Tis manifest that many particles
Even from the salt upheavings of the main
Can rise together to augment the bulk
Of massed clouds. For moistures in these twain
Are near akin. Besides, from out all rivers,
As well as from the land itself, we see
Up-rising mists and steam, which like a breath
Are forced out from them and borne aloft,
To curtain heaven with their murk, and make,
By slow foregathering, the skiey clouds.
For, in addition, lo, the heat on high
Of constellated ether burdens down
Upon them, and by sort of condensation
Weaveth beneath the azure firmament
The reek of darkling cloud. It happens, too,
That hither to the skies from the Beyond
Do come those particles which make the clouds
And flying thunderheads. For I have taught
That this their number is innumerable
And infinite the sum of the Abyss,
And I have shown with what stupendous speed
Those bodies fly and how they're wont to pass
Amain through incommunicable space.
Therefore, 'tis not exceeding strange, if oft
In little time tempest and darkness cover
With bulking thunderheads hanging on high
The oceans and the lands, since everywhere
Through all the narrow tubes of yonder ether,
Yea, so to speak, through all the breathing-holes
Of the great upper-world encompassing,
There be for the primordial elements

Exits and entrances.

Now come, and how
The rainy moisture thickens into being
In the lofty clouds, and how upon the lands
'Tis then discharged in down-pour of large showers,
I will unfold. And first triumphantly
Will I persuade thee that up-rise together,
With clouds themselves, full many seeds of water
From out all things, and that they both increase—
Both clouds and water which is in the clouds—
In like proportion, as our frames increase
In like proportion with our blood, as well
As sweat or any moisture in our members.
Besides, the clouds take in from time to time
Much moisture risen from the broad marine,—
Whilst the winds bear them o'er the mighty sea,
Like hanging fleeces of white wool. Thuswise,
Even from all rivers is there lifted up
Moisture into the clouds. And when therein
The seeds of water so many in many ways
Have come together, augmented from all sides,
The close-jammed clouds then struggle to discharge
Their rain-storms for a two-fold reason: lo,
The wind's force crowds them, and the very excess
Of storm-clouds (massed in a vaster throng)
Giveth an urge and pressure from above
And makes the rains out-pour. Besides when, too,
The clouds are winnowed by the winds, or scattered
Smitten on top by heat of sun, they send
Their rainy moisture, and distil their drops,
Even as the wax, by fiery warmth on top,
Wasteth and liquefies abundantly.
But comes the violence of the bigger rains
When violently the clouds are weighted down
Both by their cumulated mass and by
The onset of the wind. And rains are wont
To endure awhile and to abide for long,
When many seeds of waters are aroused,
And clouds on clouds and racks on racks outstream
In piled layers and are borne along
From every quarter, and when all the earth
Smoking exhales her moisture. At such a time

When sun with beams amid the tempest-murk
Hath shone against the showers of black rains,
Then in the swart clouds there emerges bright
The radiance of the bow.

And as to things
Not mentioned here which of themselves do grow
Or of themselves are gendered, and all things
Which in the clouds condense to being—all,
Snow and the winds, hail and the hoar-frosts chill,
And freezing, mighty force—of lakes and pools
The mighty hardener, and mighty check
Which in the winter curbeth everywhere
The rivers as they go—'tis easy still,
Soon to discover and with mind to see
How they all happen, whereby gendered,
When once thou well hast understood just what
Functions have been vouchsafed from of old
Unto the procreant atoms of the world.
Now come, and what the law of earthquakes is
Hearken, and first of all take care to know
That the under-earth, like to the earth around us,
Is full of windy caverns all about;
And many a pool and many a grim abyss
She bears within her bosom, ay, and cliffs
And jagged scarps; and many a river, hid
Beneath her chine, rolls rapidly along
Its billows and plunging boulders. For clear fact
Requires that earth must be in every part
Alike in constitution. Therefore, earth,
With these things underneath affixed and set,
Trembleth above, jarred by big down-tumblings,
When time hath undermined the huge caves,
The subterranean. Yea, whole mountains fall,
And instantly from spot of that big jar
There quiver the tremors far and wide abroad.
And with good reason: since houses on the street
Begin to quake throughout, when jarred by a cart
Of no large weight; and, too, the furniture
Within the house up-bounds, when a paving-block
Gives either iron rim of the wheels a jolt.
It happens, too, when some prodigious bulk
Of age-worn soil is rolled from mountain slopes

Into tremendous pools of water dark,
That the reeling land itself is rocked about
By the water's undulations; as a basin
Sometimes won't come to rest until the fluid
Within it ceases to be rocked about
In random undulations.

And besides,
When subterranean winds, up-gathered there
In the hollow deeps, bulk forward from one spot,
And press with the big urge of mighty powers
Against the lofty grottos, then the earth
Bulks to that quarter whither push amain
The headlong winds. Then all the builded houses
Above ground—and the more, the higher up-reared
Unto the sky—lean ominously, careening
Into the same direction; and the beams,
Wrenched forward, over-hang, ready to go.
Yet dread men to believe that there awaits
The nature of the mighty world a time
Of doom and cataclysm, albeit they see
So great a bulk of lands to bulge and break!
And lest the winds blew back again, no force
Could rein things in nor hold from sure career
On to disaster. But now because those winds
Blow back and forth in alternation strong,
And, so to say, rallying charge again,
And then repulsed retreat, on this account
Earth oftener threatens than she brings to pass
Collapses dire. For to one side she leans,
Then back she sways; and after tottering
Forward, recovers then her seats of poise.
Thus, this is why whole houses rock, the roofs
More than the middle stories, middle more
Than lowest, and the lowest least of all.

Arises, too, this same great earth-quaking,
When wind and some prodigious force of air,
Collected from without or down within
The old telluric deeps, have hurled themselves
Amain into those caverns sub-terrene,
And there at first tumultuously chafe
Among the vasty grottos, borne about

In mad rotations, till their lashed force
Aroused out-bursts abroad, and then and there,
Riving the deep earth, makes a mighty chasm—
What once in Syrian Sidon did befall,
And once in Peloponnesian Aegium,
Twain cities which such out-break of wild air
And earth's convulsion, following hard upon,
O'erthrew of old. And many a walled town,
Besides, hath fall'n by such omnipotent
Convulsions on the land, and in the sea
Engulfed hath sunken many a city down
With all its populace. But if, indeed,
They burst not forth, yet is the very rush
Of the wild air and fury-force of wind
Then dissipated, like an ague-fit,
Through the innumerable pores of earth,
To set her all a-shake—even as a chill,
When it hath gone into our marrow-bones,
Sets us convulsively, despite ourselves,
A-shivering and a-shaking. Therefore, men
With two-fold terror bustle in alarm
Through cities to and fro: they fear the roofs
Above the head; and underfoot they dread
The caverns, lest the nature of the earth
Suddenly rend them open, and she gape,
Herself asunder, with tremendous maw,
And, all confounded, seek to chock it full
With her own ruins. Let men, then, go on
Feigning at will that heaven and earth shall be
Inviolable, entrusted evermore
To an eternal weal: and yet at times
The very force of danger here at hand
Prods them on some side with this goad of fear—
This among others—that the earth, withdrawn
Abruptly from under their feet, be hurried down,
Down into the abyss, and the Sum-of-Things
Be following after, utterly fordone,
Till be but wrack and wreckage of a world.

EXTRAORDINARY AND PARADOXICAL TELLURIC PHENOMENA

In chief, men marvel nature renders not
Bigger and bigger the bulk of ocean, since
So vast the down-rush of the waters be,
And every river out of every realm
Cometh thereto; and add the random rains
And flying tempests, which spatter every sea
And every land bedew; add their own springs:
Yet all of these unto the ocean's sum
Shall be but as the increase of a drop.
Wherefore 'tis less a marvel that the sea,
The mighty ocean, increaseth not. Besides,
Sun with his heat draws off a mighty part:
Yea, we behold that sun with burning beams
To dry our garments dripping all with wet;
And many a sea, and far out-spread beneath,
Do we behold. Therefore, however slight
The portion of wet that sun on any spot
Culls from the level main, he still will take
From off the waves in such a wide expanse
Abundantly. Then, further, also winds,
Sweeping the level waters, can bear off
A mighty part of wet, since we behold
Oft in a single night the highways dried
By winds, and soft mud crusted o'er at dawn.
Again, I've taught thee that the clouds bear off
Much moisture too, up-taken from the reaches
Of the mighty main, and sprinkle it about
O'er all the zones, when rain is on the lands
And winds convey the aery racks of vapour.
Lastly, since earth is porous through her frame,
And neighbours on the seas, girdling their shores,
The water's wet must seep into the lands
From briny ocean, as from lands it comes
Into the seas. For brine is filtered off,
And then the liquid stuff seeps back again
And all re-poureth at the river-heads,
Whence in fresh-water currents it returns
Over the lands, adown the channels which
Were cleft erstwhile and erstwhile bore along

The liquid-footed floods.

And now the cause
Whereby athrough the throat of Aetna's Mount
Such vast tornado-fires out-breathe at times,
I will unfold: for with no middling might
Of devastation the flamy tempest rose
And held dominion in Sicilian fields:
Drawing upon itself the upturned faces
Of neighbouring clans, what time they saw afar
The skiey vaults a-fume and sparkling all,
And filled their bosoms with dread anxiety
Of what new thing nature were travailing at.

In these affairs it much behooveth thee
To look both wide and deep, and far abroad
To peer to every quarter, that thou mayst
Remember how boundless is the Sum-of-Things,
And mark how infinitely small a part
Of the whole Sum is this one sky of ours—
O not so large a part as is one man
Of the whole earth. And plainly if thou viewest
This cosmic fact, placing it square in front,
And plainly understandest, thou wilt leave
Wondering at many things. For who of us
Wondereth if some one gets into his joints
A fever, gathering head with fiery heat,
Or any other dolorous disease
Along his members? For anon the foot
Grows blue and bulbous; often the sharp twinge
Seizes the teeth, attacks the very eyes;
Out-breaks the sacred fire, and, crawling on
Over the body, burneth every part
It seizeth on, and works its hideous way
Along the frame. No marvel this, since, lo,
Of things innumerable be seeds enough,
And this our earth and sky do bring to us
Enough of bane from whence can grow the strength
Of maladies uncounted. Thuswise, then,
We must suppose to all the sky and earth
Are ever supplied from out the infinite
All things, O all in stores enough whereby
The shaken earth can of a sudden move,

And fierce typhoons can over sea and lands
Go tearing on, and Aetna's fires o'erflow,
And heaven become a flame-burst. For that, too,
Happens at times, and the celestial vaults
Glow into fire, and rainy tempests rise
In heavier congregation, when, percase,
The seeds of water have foregathered thus
From out the infinite. "Aye, but passing huge
The fiery turmoil of that conflagration!"
So sayst thou; well, huge many a river seems
To him that erstwhile ne'er a larger saw;
Thus, huge seems tree or man; and everything
Which mortal sees the biggest of each class,
That he imagines to be "huge"; though yet
All these, with sky and land and sea to boot,
Are all as nothing to the sum entire
Of the all-Sum.

But now I will unfold
At last how yonder suddenly angered flame
Out-blows abroad from vasty furnaces
Aetnaean. First, the mountain's nature is
All under-hollow, propped about, about
With caverns of basaltic piers. And, lo,
In all its grottos be there wind and air—
For wind is made when air hath been uproused
By violent agitation. When this air
Is heated through and through, and, raging round,
Hath made the earth and all the rocks it touches
Horribly hot, and hath struck off from them
Fierce fire of swiftest flame, it lifts itself
And hurtles thus straight upwards through its throat
Into high heav'n, and thus bears on afar
Its burning blasts and scattereth afar
Its ashes, and rolls a smoke of pitchy murk
And heaveth the while boulders of wondrous weight—
Leaving no doubt in thee that 'tis the air's
Tumultuous power. Besides, in mighty part,
The sea there at the roots of that same mount
Breaks its old billows and sucks back its surf.
And grottos from the sea pass in below
Even to the bottom of the mountain's throat.
Herethrough thou must admit there go...

And the conditions force [the water and air]
Deeply to penetrate from the open sea,
And to out-blow abroad, and to up-bear
Thereby the flame, and to up-cast from deeps
The boulders, and to rear the clouds of sand.
For at the top be "bowls," as people there
Are wont to name what we at Rome do call
The throats and mouths.

There be, besides, some thing
Of which 'tis not enough one only cause
To state—but rather several, whereof one
Will be the true: lo, if thou shouldst espy
Lying afar some fellow's lifeless corse,
'Twere meet to name all causes of a death,
That cause of his death might thereby be named:
For prove thou mayst he perished not by steel,
By cold, nor even by poison nor disease,
Yet somewhat of this sort hath come to him
We know—And thus we have to say the same
In divers cases.

Toward the summer, Nile
Waxeth and overfloweth the champaign,
Unique in all the landscape, river sole
Of the Aegyptians. In mid-season heats
Often and oft he waters Aegypt o'er,
Either because in summer against his mouths
Come those northwinds which at that time of year
Men name the Etesian blasts, and, blowing thus
Upstream, retard, and, forcing back his waves,
Fill him o'erfull and force his flow to stop.
For out of doubt these blasts which driven be
From icy constellations of the pole
Are borne straight up the river. Comes that river
From forth the sultry places down the south,
Rising far up in midmost realm of day,
Among black generations of strong men
With sun-baked skins. 'Tis possible, besides,
That a big bulk of piled sand may bar
His mouths against his onward waves, when sea,
Wild in the winds, tumbles the sand to inland;
Whereby the river's outlet were less free,

Likewise less headlong his descending floods.
It may be, too, that in this season rains
Are more abundant at its fountain head,
Because the Etesian blasts of those northwinds
Then urge all clouds into those inland parts.
And, soothly, when they're thus foregathered there,
Urged yonder into midmost realm of day,
Then, crowded against the lofty mountain sides,
They're massed and powerfully pressed. Again,
Perchance, his waters wax, O far away,
Among the Aethiopians' lofty mountains,
When the all-beholding sun with thawing beams
Drives the white snows to flow into the vales.

Now come; and unto thee I will unfold,
As to the Birdless spots and Birdless tarns,
What sort of nature they are furnished with.
First, as to name of "birdless,"—that derives
From very fact, because they noxious be
Unto all birds. For when above those spots
In horizontal flight the birds have come,
Forgetting to oar with wings, they furl their sails,
And, with down-drooping of their delicate necks,
Fall headlong into earth, if haply such
The nature of the spots, or into water,
If haply spreads thereunder Birdless tarn.
Such spot's at Cumae, where the mountains smoke,
Charged with the pungent sulphur, and increased
With steaming springs. And such a spot there is
Within the walls of Athens, even there
On summit of Acropolis, beside
Fane of Tritonian Pallas bountiful,
Where never cawing crows can wing their course,
Not even when smoke the altars with good gifts,—
But evermore they flee—yet not from wrath
Of Pallas, grieved at that espial old,
As poets of the Greeks have sung the tale;
But very nature of the place compels.
In Syria also—as men say—a spot
Is to be seen, where also four-foot kinds,
As soon as ever they've set their steps within,
Collapse, o'ercome by its essential power,
As if there slaughtered to the under-gods.

Lo, all these wonders work by natural law,
And from what causes they are brought to pass
The origin is manifest; so, haply,
Let none believe that in these regions stands
The gate of Orcus, nor us then suppose,
Haply, that thence the under-gods draw down
Souls to dark shores of Acheron—as stags,
The wing-footed, are thought to draw to light,
By sniffing nostrils, from their dusky lairs
The wriggling generations of wild snakes.
How far removed from true reason is this,
Perceive thou straight; for now I'll try to say
Somewhat about the very fact.

And, first,
This do I say, as oft I've said before:
In earth are atoms of things of every sort;
And know, these all thus rise from out the earth—
Many life-giving which be good for food,
And many which can generate disease
And hasten death, O many primal seeds
Of many things in many modes—since earth
Contains them mingled and gives forth discrete.
And we have shown before that certain things
Be unto certain creatures suited more
For ends of life, by virtue of a nature,
A texture, and primordial shapes, unlike
For kinds alike. Then too 'tis thine to see
How many things oppressive be and foul
To man, and to sensation most malign:
Many meander miserably through ears;
Many in-wind athrough the nostrils too,
Malign and harsh when mortal draws a breath;
Of not a few must one avoid the touch;
Of not a few must one escape the sight;
And some there be all loathsome to the taste;
And many, besides, relax the languid limbs
Along the frame, and undermine the soul
In its abodes within. To certain trees
There hath been given so dolorous a shade
That often they gender achings of the head,
If one but be beneath, outstretched on the sward.
There is, again, on Helicon's high hills

A tree that's wont to kill a man outright
By fetid odour of its very flower.
And when the pungent stench of the night-lamp,
Extinguished but a moment since, assails
The nostrils, then and there it puts to sleep
A man afflicted with the falling sickness
And foamings at the mouth. A woman, too,
At the heavy castor drowses back in chair,
And from her delicate fingers slips away
Her gaudy handiwork, if haply she
Hath got the whiff at menstruation-time.
Once more, if thou delayest in hot baths,
When thou art over-full, how readily
From stool in middle of the steaming water
Thou tumblest in a fit! How readily
The heavy fumes of charcoal wind their way
Into the brain, unless beforehand we
Of water 've drunk. But when a burning fever,
O'ermastering man, hath seized upon his limbs,
Then odour of wine is like a hammer-blow.
And seest thou not how in the very earth
Sulphur is gendered and bitumen thickens
With noisome stench?—What direful stenches, too,
Scaptensula out-breathes from down below,
When men pursue the veins of silver and gold,
With pick-axe probing round the hidden realms
Deep in the earth?—Or what of deadly bane
The mines of gold exhale? O what a look,
And what a ghastly hue they give to men!
And seest thou not, or hearest, how they're wont
In little time to perish, and how fail
The life-stores in those folk whom mighty power
Of grim necessity confineth there
In such a task? Thus, this telluric earth
Out-streams with all these dread effluvia
And breathes them out into the open world
And into the visible regions under heaven.

Thus, too, those Birdless places must up-send
An essence bearing death to winged things,
Which from the earth rises into the breezes
To poison part of skiey space, and when
Thither the winged is on pennons borne,

There, seized by the unseen poison, 'tis ensnared,
And from the horizontal of its flight
Drops to the spot whence sprang the effluvium.
And when 'thas there collapsed, then the same power
Of that effluvium takes from all its limbs
The relics of its life. That power first strikes
The creatures with a wildering dizziness,
And then thereafter, when they're once down-fallen
Into the poison's very fountains, then
Life, too, they vomit out perforce, because
So thick the stores of bane around them fume.

Again, at times it happens that this power,
This exhalation of the Birdless places,
Dispels the air betwixt the ground and birds,
Leaving well-nigh a void. And thither when
In horizontal flight the birds have come,
Forthwith their buoyancy of pennons limps,
All useless, and each effort of both wings
Falls out in vain. Here, when without all power
To buoy themselves and on their wings to lean,
Lo, nature constrains them by their weight to slip
Down to the earth, and lying prostrate there
Along the well-nigh empty void, they spend
Their souls through all the openings of their frame.

Further, the water of wells is colder then
At summer time, because the earth by heat
Is rarefied, and sends abroad in air
Whatever seeds it peradventure have
Of its own fiery exhalations.
The more, then, the telluric ground is drained
Of heat, the colder grows the water hid
Within the earth. Further, when all the earth
Is by the cold compressed, and thus contracts
And, so to say, concretes, it happens, lo,
That by contracting it expresses then
Into the wells what heat it bears itself.

'Tis said at Hammon's fane a fountain is,
In daylight cold and hot in time of night.
This fountain men be-wonder over-much,
And think that suddenly it seethes in heat

By intense sun, the subterranean, when
Night with her terrible murk hath cloaked the lands—
What's not true reasoning by a long remove:
I' faith when sun o'erhead, touching with beams
An open body of water, had no power
To render it hot upon its upper side,
Though his high light possess such burning glare,
How, then, can he, when under the gross earth,
Make water boil and glut with fiery heat?—
And, specially, since scarcely potent he
Through hedging walls of houses to inject
His exhalations hot, with ardent rays.
What, then's, the principle? Why, this, indeed:
The earth about that spring is porous more
Than elsewhere the telluric ground, and be
Many the seeds of fire hard by the water;
On this account, when night with dew-fraught shades
Hath whelmed the earth, anon the earth deep down
Grows chill, contracts; and thuswise squeezes out
Into the spring what seeds she holds of fire
(As one might squeeze with fist), which render hot
The touch and steam of the fluid. Next, when sun,
Up-risen, with his rays has split the soil
And rarefied the earth with waxing heat,
Again into their ancient abodes return
The seeds of fire, and all the Hot of water
Into the earth retires; and this is why
The fountain in the daylight gets so cold.
Besides, the water's wet is beat upon
By rays of sun, and, with the dawn, becomes
Rarer in texture under his pulsing blaze;
And, therefore, whatso seeds it holds of fire
It renders up, even as it renders oft
The frost that it contains within itself
And thaws its ice and looseneth the knots.
There is, moreover, a fountain cold in kind
That makes a bit of tow (above it held)
Take fire forthwith and shoot a flame; so, too,
A pitch-pine torch will kindle and flare round
Along its waves, wherever 'tis impelled
Afloat before the breeze. No marvel, this:
Because full many seeds of heat there be
Within the water; and, from earth itself

Out of the deeps must particles of fire
Athrough the entire fountain surge aloft,
And speed in exhalations into air
Forth and abroad (yet not in numbers enow
As to make hot the fountain). And, moreo'er,
Some force constrains them, scattered through the water,
Forthwith to burst abroad, and to combine
In flame above. Even as a fountain far
There is at Aradus amid the sea,
Which bubbles out sweet water and disparts
From round itself the salt waves; and, behold,
In many another region the broad main
Yields to the thirsty mariners timely help,
Belching sweet waters forth amid salt waves.
Just so, then, can those seeds of fire burst forth
Athrough that other fount, and bubble out
Abroad against the bit of tow; and when
They there collect or cleave unto the torch,
Forthwith they readily flash aflame, because
The tow and torches, also, in themselves
Have many seeds of latent fire. Indeed,
And seest thou not, when near the nightly lamps
Thou bringest a flaxen wick, extinguished
A moment since, it catches fire before
'Thas touched the flame, and in same wise a torch?
And many another object flashes aflame
When at a distance, touched by heat alone,
Before 'tis steeped in veritable fire.
This, then, we must suppose to come to pass
In that spring also.

Now to other things!
And I'll begin to treat by what decree
Of nature it came to pass that iron can be
By that stone drawn which Greeks the magnet call
After the country's name (its origin
Being in country of Magnesian folk).
This stone men marvel at; and sure it oft
Maketh a chain of rings, depending, lo,
From off itself! Nay, thou mayest see at times
Five or yet more in order dangling down
And swaying in the delicate winds, whilst one
Depends from other, cleaving to under-side,

And ilk one feels the stone's own power and bonds—
So over-masteringly its power flows down.

In things of this sort, much must be made sure
Ere thou account of the thing itself canst give,
And the approaches roundabout must be;
Wherefore the more do I exact of thee
A mind and ears attent.

First, from all things
We see soever, evermore must flow,
Must be discharged and strewn about, about,
Bodies that strike the eyes, awaking sight.
From certain things flow odours evermore,
As cold from rivers, heat from sun, and spray
From waves of ocean, eater-out of walls
Along the coasts. Nor ever cease to seep
The varied echoings athrough the air.
Then, too, there comes into the mouth at times
The wet of a salt taste, when by the sea
We roam about; and so, whene'er we watch
The wormwood being mixed, its bitter stings.
To such degree from all things is each thing
Borne streamingly along, and sent about
To every region round; and nature grants
Nor rest nor respite of the onward flow,
Since 'tis incessantly we feeling have,
And all the time are suffered to descry
And smell all things at hand, and hear them sound.

Now will I seek again to bring to mind
How porous a body all things have—a fact
Made manifest in my first canto, too.
For, truly, though to know this doth import
For many things, yet for this very thing
On which straightway I'm going to discourse,
'Tis needful most of all to make it sure
That naught's at hand but body mixed with void.
A first ensample: in grottos, rocks o'erhead
Sweat moisture and distil the oozy drops;
Likewise, from all our body seeps the sweat;
There grows the beard, and along our members all
And along our frame the hairs. Through all our veins

Disseminates the foods, and gives increase
And aliment down to the extreme parts,
Even to the tiniest finger-nails. Likewise,
Through solid bronze the cold and fiery heat
We feel to pass; likewise, we feel them pass
Through gold, through silver, when we clasp in hand
The brimming goblets. And, again, there flit
Voices through houses' hedging walls of stone;
Odour seeps through, and cold, and heat of fire
That's wont to penetrate even strength of iron.
Again, where corselet of the sky girds round
And at same time, some Influence of bane,
When from Beyond 'thas stolen into [our world].
And tempests, gathering from the earth and sky,
Back to the sky and earth absorbed retire—
With reason, since there's naught that's fashioned not
With body porous.

Furthermore, not all
The particles which be from things thrown off
Are furnished with same qualities for sense,
Nor be for all things equally adapt.
A first ensample: the sun doth bake and parch
The earth; but ice he thaws, and with his beams
Compels the lofty snows, up-reared white
Upon the lofty hills, to waste away;
Then, wax, if set beneath the heat of him,
Melts to a liquid. And the fire, likewise,
Will melt the copper and will fuse the gold,
But hides and flesh it shrivels up and shrinks.
The water hardens the iron just off the fire,
But hides and flesh (made hard by heat) it softens.
The oleaster-tree as much delights
The bearded she-goats, verily as though
'Twere nectar-steeped and shed ambrosia;
Than which is naught that burgeons into leaf
More bitter food for man. A hog draws back
For marjoram oil, and every unguent fears
Fierce poison these unto the bristled hogs,
Yet unto us from time to time they seem,
As 'twere, to give new life. But, contrariwise,
Though unto us the mire be filth most foul,
To hogs that mire doth so delightsome seem

That they with wallowing from belly to back
Are never cloyed.

A point remains, besides,
Which best it seems to tell of, ere I go
To telling of the fact at hand itself.
Since to the varied things assigned be
The many pores, those pores must be diverse
In nature one from other, and each have
Its very shape, its own direction fixed.
And so, indeed, in breathing creatures be
The several senses, of which each takes in
Unto itself, in its own fashion ever,
Its own peculiar object. For we mark
How sounds do into one place penetrate,
Into another flavours of all juice,
And savour of smell into a third. Moreover,
One sort through rocks we see to seep, and, lo,
One sort to pass through wood, another still
Through gold, and others to go out and off
Through silver and through glass. For we do see
Through some pores form-and-look of things to flow,
Through others heat to go, and some things still
To speedier pass than others through same pores.
Of verity, the nature of these same paths,
Varying in many modes (as aforesaid)
Because of unlike nature and warp and woof
Of cosmic things, constrains it so to be.

Wherefore, since all these matters now have been
Established and settled well for us
As premises prepared, for what remains
'Twill not be hard to render clear account
By means of these, and the whole cause reveal
Whereby the magnet lures the strength of iron.
First, stream there must from off the lode-stone seeds
Innumerable, a very tide, which smites
By blows that air asunder lying betwixt
The stone and iron. And when is emptied out
This space, and a large place between the two
Is made a void, forthwith the primal germs
Of iron, headlong slipping, fall conjoined
Into the vacuum, and the ring itself

By reason thereof doth follow after and go
Thuswise with all its body. And naught there is
That of its own primordial elements
More thoroughly knit or tighter linked coheres
Than nature and cold roughness of stout iron.
Wherefore, 'tis less a marvel what I said,
That from such elements no bodies can
From out the iron collect in larger throng
And be into the vacuum borne along,
Without the ring itself do follow after.
And this it does, and followeth on until
'Thath reached the stone itself and cleaved to it
By links invisible. Moreover, likewise,
The motion's assisted by a thing of aid
(Whereby the process easier becomes),—
Namely, by this: as soon as rarer grows
That air in front of the ring, and space between
Is emptied more and made a void, forthwith
It happens all the air that lies behind
Conveys it onward, pushing from the rear.
For ever doth the circumambient air
Drub things unmoved, but here it pushes forth
The iron, because upon one side the space
Lies void and thus receives the iron in.
This air, whereof I am reminding thee,
Winding athrough the iron's abundant pores
So subtly into the tiny parts thereof,
Shoves it and pushes, as wind the ship and sails.
The same doth happen in all directions forth:
From whatso side a space is made a void,
Whether from crosswise or above, forthwith
The neighbour particles are borne along
Into the vacuum; for of verity,
They're set a-going by poundings from elsewhere,
Nor by themselves of own accord can they
Rise upwards into the air. Again, all things
Must in their framework hold some air, because
They are of framework porous, and the air
Encompasses and borders on all things.
Thus, then, this air in iron so deeply stored
Is tossed evermore in vexed motion,
And therefore drubs upon the ring sans doubt
And shakes it up inside....

In sooth, that ring is thither borne along
To where 'thas once plunged headlong—thither, lo,
Unto the void whereto it took its start.

It happens, too, at times that nature of iron
Shrinks from this stone away, accustomed
By turns to flee and follow. Yea, I've seen
Those Samothracian iron rings leap up,
And iron filings in the brazen bowls
Seethe furiously, when underneath was set
The magnet stone. So strongly iron seems
To crave to flee that rock. Such discord great
Is gendered by the interposed brass,
Because, forsooth, when first the tide of brass
Hath seized upon and held possession of
The iron's open passage-ways, thereafter
Cometh the tide of the stone, and in that iron
Findeth all spaces full, nor now hath holes
To swim through, as before. 'Tis thus constrained
With its own current 'gainst the iron's fabric
To dash and beat; by means whereof it spues
Forth from itself—and through the brass stirs up—
The things which otherwise without the brass
It sucks into itself. In these affairs
Marvel thou not that from this stone the tide
Prevails not likewise other things to move
With its own blows: for some stand firm by weight,
As gold; and some cannot be moved forever,
Because so porous in their framework they
That there the tide streams through without a break,
Of which sort stuff of wood is seen to be.
Therefore, when iron (which lies between the two)
Hath taken in some atoms of the brass,
Then do the streams of that Magnesian rock
Move iron by their smitings.

Yet these things
Are not so alien from others, that I
Of this same sort am ill prepared to name
Ensamples still of things exclusively
To one another adapt. Thou seest, first,
How lime alone cementeth stones: how wood
Only by glue-of-bull with wood is joined—

So firmly too that oftener the boards
Crack open along the weakness of the grain
Ere ever those taurine bonds will lax their hold.
The vine-born juices with the water-springs
Are bold to mix, though not the heavy pitch
With the light oil-of-olive. And purple dye
Of shell-fish so uniteth with the wool's
Body alone that it cannot be ta'en
Away forever—nay, though thou gavest toil
To restore the same with the Neptunian flood,
Nay, though all ocean willed to wash it out
With all its waves. Again, gold unto gold
Doth not one substance bind, and only one?
And is not brass by tin joined unto brass?
And other ensamples how many might one find!
What then? Nor is there unto thee a need
Of such long ways and roundabout, nor boots it
For me much toil on this to spend. More fit
It is in few words briefly to embrace
Things many: things whose textures fall together
So mutually adapt, that cavities
To solids correspond, these cavities
Of this thing to the solid parts of that,
And those of that to solid parts of this—
Such joinings are the best. Again, some things
Can be the one with other coupled and held,
Linked by hooks and eyes, as 'twere; and this
Seems more the fact with iron and this stone.
Now, of diseases what the law, and whence
The Influence of bane upgathering can
Upon the race of man and herds of cattle
Kindle a devastation fraught with death,
I will unfold. And, first, I've taught above
That seeds there be of many things to us
Life-giving, and that, contrariwise, there must
Fly many round bringing disease and death.
When these have, haply, chanced to collect
And to derange the atmosphere of earth,
The air becometh baneful. And, lo, all
That Influence of bane, that pestilence,
Or from Beyond down through our atmosphere,
Like clouds and mists, descends, or else collects
From earth herself and rises, when, a-soak

And beat by rains unseasonable and suns,
Our earth hath then contracted stench and rot.
Seest thou not, also, that whoso arrive
In region far from fatherland and home
Are by the strangeness of the clime and waters
Distempered?—since conditions vary much.
For in what else may we suppose the clime
Among the Britons to differ from Aegypt's own
(Where totters awry the axis of the world),
Or in what else to differ Pontic clime
From Gades' and from climes adown the south,
On to black generations of strong men
With sun-baked skins? Even as we thus do see
Four climes diverse under the four main-winds
And under the four main-regions of the sky,
So, too, are seen the colour and face of men
Vastly to disagree, and fixed diseases
To seize the generations, kind by kind:
There is the elephant-disease which down
In midmost Aegypt, hard by streams of Nile,
Engendered is—and never otherwise.
In Attica the feet are oft attacked,
And in Achaean lands the eyes. And so
The divers spots to divers parts and limbs
Are noxious; 'tis a variable air
That causes this. Thus when an atmosphere,
Alien by chance to us, begins to heave,
And noxious airs begin to crawl along,
They creep and wind like unto mist and cloud,
Slowly, and everything upon their way
They disarrange and force to change its state.
It happens, too, that when they've come at last
Into this atmosphere of ours, they taint
And make it like themselves and alien.
Therefore, asudden this devastation strange,
This pestilence, upon the waters falls,
Or settles on the very crops of grain
Or other meat of men and feed of flocks.
Or it remains a subtle force, suspense
In the atmosphere itself; and when therefrom
We draw our inhalations of mixed air,
Into our body equally its bane
Also we must suck in. In manner like,

Oft comes the pestilence upon the kine,
And sickness, too, upon the sluggish sheep.
Nor aught it matters whether journey we
To regions adverse to ourselves and change
The atmospheric cloak, or whether nature
Herself import a tainted atmosphere
To us or something strange to our own use
Which can attack us soon as ever it come.

THE PLAGUE ATHENS

'Twas such a manner of disease, 'twas such
Mortal miasma in Cecropian lands
Whilom reduced the plains to dead men's bones,
Unpeopled the highways, drained of citizens
The Athenian town. For coming from afar,
Rising in lands of Aegypt, traversing
Reaches of air and floating fields of foam,
At last on all Pandion's folk it swooped;
Whereat by troops unto disease and death
Were they o'er-given. At first, they'd bear about
A skull on fire with heat, and eyeballs twain
Red with suffusion of blank glare. Their throats,
Black on the inside, sweated oozy blood;
And the walled pathway of the voice of man
Was clogged with ulcers; and the very tongue,
The mind's interpreter, would trickle gore,
Weakened by torments, tardy, rough to touch.
Next when that Influence of bane had chocked,
Down through the throat, the breast, and streamed had
E'en into sullen heart of those sick folk,
Then, verily, all the fences of man's life
Began to topple. From the mouth the breath
Would roll a noisome stink, as stink to heaven
Rotting cadavers flung unburied out.
And, lo, thereafter, all the body's strength
And every power of mind would languish, now
In very doorway of destruction.
And anxious anguish and ululation (mixed
With many a groan) companioned alway
The intolerable torments. Night and day,
Recurrent spasms of vomiting would rack

Alway their thews and members, breaking down
With sheer exhaustion men already spent.
And yet on no one's body couldst thou mark
The skin with o'er-much heat to burn aglow,
But rather the body unto touch of hands
Would offer a warmish feeling, and thereby
Show red all over, with ulcers, so to say,
Inbranded, like the "sacred fires" o'erspread
Along the members. The inward parts of men,
In truth, would blaze unto the very bones;
A flame, like flame in furnaces, would blaze
Within the stomach. Nor couldst aught apply
Unto their members light enough and thin
For shift of aid—but coolness and a breeze
Ever and ever. Some would plunge those limbs
On fire with bane into the icy streams,
Hurling the body naked into the waves;
Many would headlong fling them deeply down
The water-pits, tumbling with eager mouth
Already agape. The insatiable thirst
That whelmed their parched bodies, lo, would make
A goodly shower seem like to scanty drops.
Respite of torment was there none. Their frames
Forspent lay prone. With silent lips of fear
Would Medicine mumble low, the while she saw
So many a time men roll their eyeballs round,
Staring wide-open, unvisited of sleep,
The heralds of old death. And in those months
Was given many another sign of death:
The intellect of mind by sorrow and dread
Deranged, the sad brow, the countenance
Fierce and delirious, the tormented ears
Beset with ringings, the breath quick and short
Or huge and intermittent, soaking sweat
A-glisten on neck, the spittle in fine gouts
Tainted with colour of crocus and so salt,
The cough scarce wheezing through the rattling throat.
Aye, and the sinews in the fingered hands
Were sure to contract, and sure the jointed frame
To shiver, and up from feet the cold to mount
Inch after inch: and toward the supreme hour
At last the pinched nostrils, nose's tip
A very point, eyes sunken, temples hollow,

Skin cold and hard, the shuddering grimace,
The pulled and puffy flesh above the brows!—
O not long after would their frames lie prone
In rigid death. And by about the eighth
Resplendent light of sun, or at the most
On the ninth flaming of his flambeau, they
Would render up the life. If any then
Had 'scaped the doom of that destruction, yet
Him there awaited in the after days
A wasting and a death from ulcers vile
And black discharges of the belly, or else
Through the clogged nostrils would there ooze along
Much fouled blood, oft with an aching head:
Hither would stream a man's whole strength and flesh.
And whoso had survived that virulent flow
Of the vile blood, yet into thews of him
And into his joints and very genitals
Would pass the old disease. And some there were,
Dreading the doorways of destruction
So much, lived on, deprived by the knife
Of the male member; not a few, though lopped
Of hands and feet, would yet persist in life,
And some there were who lost their eyeballs: O
So fierce a fear of death had fallen on them!
And some, besides, were by oblivion
Of all things seized, that even themselves they knew
No longer. And though corpse on corpse lay piled
Unburied on ground, the race of birds and beasts
Would or spring back, scurrying to escape
The virulent stench, or, if they'd tasted there,
Would languish in approaching death. But yet
Hardly at all during those many suns
Appeared a fowl, nor from the woods went forth
The sullen generations of wild beasts—
They languished with disease and died and died.
In chief, the faithful dogs, in all the streets
Outstretched, would yield their breath distressfully
For so that Influence of bane would twist
Life from their members. Nor was found one sure
And universal principle of cure:
For what to one had given the power to take
The vital winds of air into his mouth,
And to gaze upward at the vaults of sky,

The same to others was their death and doom.

In those affairs, O awfullest of all,
O pitiable most was this, was this:
Whoso once saw himself in that disease
Entangled, ay, as damned unto death,
Would lie in wanhope, with a sullen heart,
Would, in fore-vision of his funeral,
Give up the ghost, O then and there. For, lo,
At no time did they cease one from another
To catch contagion of the greedy plague,—
As though but woolly flocks and horned herds;
And this in chief would heap the dead on dead:
For who forbore to look to their own sick,
O these (too eager of life, of death afeard)
Would then, soon after, slaughtering Neglect
Visit with vengeance of evil death and base—
Themselves deserted and forlorn of help.
But who had stayed at hand would perish there
By that contagion and the toil which then
A sense of honour and the pleading voice
Of weary watchers, mixed with voice of wail
Of dying folk, forced them to undergo.
This kind of death each nobler soul would meet.
The funerals, uncompanioned, forsaken,
Like rivals contended to be hurried through.

And men contending to ensepulchre
Pile upon pile the throng of their own dead:
And weary with woe and weeping wandered home;
And then the most would take to bed from grief.
Nor could be found not one, whom nor disease
Nor death, nor woe had not in those dread times
Attacked.

By now the shepherds and neatherds all,
Yea, even the sturdy guiders of curved ploughs,
Began to sicken, and their bodies would lie
Huddled within back-corners of their huts,
Delivered by squalor and disease to death.
O often and often couldst thou then have seen
On lifeless children lifeless parents prone,
Or offspring on their fathers', mothers' corpse

Yielding the life. And into the city poured
O not in least part from the countryside
That tribulation, which the peasantry
Sick, sick, brought thither, thronging from every quarter,
Plague-stricken mob. All places would they crowd,
All buildings too; whereby the more would death
Up-pile a-heap the folk so crammed in town.
Ah, many a body thirst had dragged and rolled
Along the highways there was lying strewn
Besides Silenus-headed water-fountains,—
The life-breath choked from that too dear desire
Of pleasant waters. Ah, everywhere along
The open places of the populace,
And along the highways, O thou mightest see
Of many a half-dead body the sagged limbs,
Rough with squalor, wrapped around with rags,
Perish from very nastiness, with naught
But skin upon the bones, well-nigh already
Buried—in ulcers vile and obscene filth.
All holy temples, too, of deities
Had Death becrammed with the carcasses;
And stood each fane of the Celestial Ones
Laden with stark cadavers everywhere—
Places which warders of the shrines had crowded
With many a guest. For now no longer men
Did mightily esteem the old Divine,
The worship of the gods: the woe at hand
Did over-master. Nor in the city then
Remained those rites of sepulture, with which
That pious folk had evermore been wont
To buried be. For it was wildered all
In wild alarms, and each and every one
With sullen sorrow would bury his own dead,
As present shift allowed. And sudden stress
And poverty to many an awful act
Impelled; and with a monstrous screaming they
Would, on the frames of alien funeral pyres,
Place their own kin, and thrust the torch beneath
Oft brawling with much bloodshed round about
Rather than quit dead bodies loved in life.

THE END

Printed in Poland
by Amazon Fulfillment
Poland Sp. z o.o., Wrocław